Understandir
Security
Electronics

Written by: John E. Cunningham

Revised by: Joseph J. Carr

HOWARD W. SAMS & COMPANY

A Division of Macmillan, Inc.

4300 West 62nd Street

Indianapolis, Indiana 46268 USA

©1987 by Howard W. Sams & Co.

Special thanks to Bonnie Cohen of LSI Computer Systems, Inc.;
Sheila Colleen Armstrong of the U.S. Department of Justice; Steve Eldard
of SRS Systems; Debby Taylor of Antenna Specialists Co.; Don Campbell
of Meldrum and Campbell; Mary Lou Parker; and Grace Slavik.

FIRST EDITION
THIRD PRINTING—1989

International Standard Book Number: 0-672-27069-2
Library of Congress Catalog Card Number: 86-82256

Acquisitions Editor: Greg Michael
Editor: Don MacLaren
Designer: Plunk Design
Illustrator: T. R. Emrick
Cover Art: Diebold Glascock Advertising, Inc.
Photography: Cassell Productions, Inc.
Components Courtesy of: Honeywell Protection Services
Compositor: Shepard Poorman Communications Corp.

Printed in the United States of America

KLAXON® is a registered trademark of General Motors Company.

Table of Contents

Preface

In a world that is terribly short of utopian, the necessity exists to protect one's belongings and, indeed, life itself. Electronics made a tremendous impact on the world of security systems, and computers made these systems both simpler and more sophisticated. One goal of this book is to make you aware of the extent of the security problem and to define security needs.

Electronic security systems include output devices such as bells, telephone dialers, and so forth, as well as a wide assortment of sensor devices. We will examine each of these devices, the circuits they are used in, and their respective advantages and limitations. By the end of the book, you should understand security needs and be able to help design a system.

This book is arranged somewhat like a textbook. Each chapter starts by saying what it covers, ends by saying what it has covered, and provides a short multiple-choice quiz of the chapter contents. Like other books in the series, this book builds understanding step-by-step. Try to master each chapter before going on to the next one.

If your objective is to obtain general information about this subject, you can bypass the more detailed portions of the text. This will allow you to absorb the information more easily and, I hope, enjoy the style of presentation.

JC

HOWARD W. SAMS & COMPANY
HAYDEN BOOKS

Related Titles

Electronics Versus Crime

ABOUT THIS BOOK

To understand electronic security systems you must understand the types of security threats that exist, the various sensors that are used to detect intrusion, and the output devices that are used to elicit a response.

This book is intended to explain how electronic security systems and their various hardware components and sensors work. It is not intended to tell you how to build equipment, nor will it tell you how to design security systems professionally. This book does provide a basis for understanding electronic security systems in general and some tips for selecting or setting up your own system.

Readers who seek a deeper understanding of the subject are encouraged to obtain texts on the specific subject areas covered in the various chapters.

ABOUT THIS CHAPTER

Before we can understand electronic security systems we must understand the scope of the security problem. In this chapter, we have an overview of crime and criminals...and some idea of how electronics can help defeat their efforts.

BACKGROUND

There is no question that crime in the United States is increasing. In a report, Arthur J. Bilek, chairman of a Task Force on private security, referred to the situation as a "crime epidemic." Much of the increase in crime has come about as a result of changes in our society. As society becomes more complex, the opportunities for crime increase. For example, the widespread proliferation of the computer has opened up an entire new field for criminal activity.

The use of electricity and electronics in the fight against crime is not new. In 1858, Edwin Holmes began the first central office burglar alarm system. This later evolved into Holmes Protection, Inc. The American District Telegraph Company (ADT) was formed in 1874. By 1889, wired electric protection systems were well established in New York City.

The application of electronic methods tends to lag behind the spread of crime; partially from naiveté, but also partially because of costs.

Unfortunately, the application of electronic techniques and principles to increasing security has tended to lag somewhat behind the spread of crime into new areas. This is partly due to a sort of naiveté that seems to accompany new developments. Another factor is the initial cost of development of new security systems. Although it may be known that a particular situation contains a security problem, few want to fund the development of a protective system until crime begins to proliferate.

There also seems to be a tendency to underestimate the ingenuity of the criminal. Nowhere is this more evident than in what is called computer crime. Early computer systems were developed and installed with only a modicum of security. These systems had the potential for easy manipulation by anyone with criminal tendencies. Those who were responsible for purchasing such systems had little or no technical talent of their own, and found it difficult to realize that others not only could, but would, use such systems to their own advantage. The result was a virtual wave of various types of computer crime. Many incidents were detected quite by chance; there is no way of knowing just how much undetected computer crime has taken place.

The type of crime that proliferates most rapidly is one in which the criminal believes it possible to escape apprehension. The result is that when an opportunity for crime develops before protective measures are taken, the crime will spread rapidly.

Between 1968 and 1972 there were nearly 34 times as many airliner hijackings as in the previous four-year period. In a ten-month period, more than 1600 handguns, 22,000 rounds of ammunition, and 37,000 knives were confiscated at airline terminals.

Between 1963 and 1967 there were exactly four attempts at skyjacking of commercial aircraft. In the next five-year period, between 1968 and 1972, there were 134 attempts at skyjacking, 82 of which were successful. It was during this period that the surveillance and object detection systems were rapidly developed. When these devices were widely deployed in the first ten months of 1979, they were used to screen 165 million passengers and 125 million nonpassengers at airports. Of these, 9766 were spotted carrying forbidden objects and 2092 people were arrested. The FBI report for this ten-month period showed that the following items were detected: 1600 handguns, 37,000 knives, 156 explosive devices, 22,700 rounds of ammunition, and 2485 assorted items such as starting pistols, rifles, and tear gas devices.

Similar stories can be told about many different types of crimes. For some reason the crime gets started and proliferates rapidly. Then the countermeasures are put in place and the crime diminishes.

THE AMATEUR CRIMINAL

Most burglaries and thefts are committed by amateurs—opportunists who think that they can get away with their crimes.

Most crimes of burglary and theft are committed by what law enforcement agencies call amateurs. These are people who usually hold regular jobs and do not depend on crime for their livelihood. They are, however, opportunists. If they see a situation in which they can steal something with little chance of getting caught, they will steal it. Criminals of this type account for much burglary, shoplifting, and internal theft. Usually, the value of what these criminals take isn't extremely great, but there are so many of them and their crimes occur so frequently that the total amount of loss is staggering.

The best protection against this type of criminal is to make the crime difficult to achieve and to increase the probability of apprehension.

THE PROFESSIONAL CRIMINAL

Although there are not as many professional criminals as there are amateurs, the professional criminal is an expert at the trade. The professional knows such things as how to quietly force open doors and windows, how to defeat simple intrusion alarms, and how to crack safes. A specialized version of professional crime involves people who are computer experts.

The number of professional criminals is increasing. Not only are brilliant people turning to crime, but amateurs who are incarcerated receive a liberal education while in prison. One prison had a reasonably well organized safe-cracking school operating within its walls.

Amateurish protection methods, such as phony window decals and dummy TV cameras, are typically effective only against amateur thieves. Professionals are rarely fooled by such measures.

Because of the fact that the majority of crimes such as burglaries are committed by amateurs, many people resort to very amateurish methods of protection. These simple measures are often effective in discouraging the amateur, but to the professional they are an invitation to steal something with impunity.

A typical measure of this type is the window decal that announces that the premises are protected electronically. In fact, there is no protection other than the decal. The amateur might be fooled by this, but to the professional it is an invitation to break into the place.

Another amateurish method is the use of dummy cameras to defeat shoplifting. Again the amateur might be fooled, but the professional can spot these dummy cameras immediately.

THE BATTLE OF WITS

While some criminals act for the thrill of the crime, others are motivated by the technical challenge of overcoming a security system. Engineers often decode pay-TV signals for the sense of accomplishment, as do computer "hackers" who break into high-security systems.

Many people who are not really criminals at all cannot seem to resist the challenge of defeating some sort of protective system. To these people, the challenge of defeating some sort of security system is so great that they can't seem to resist it. A typical problem of this type involves encoded pay-TV signals. To many people, the very presence of an encoded signal is a challenge to decode it. It is almost like trying to solve a puzzle. There are many electronics engineers who have developed rather ingenious decoders for these signals without ever bothering to use them. Once the signal has been decoded, the challenge is gone. Often, such people spend a great deal of time and money in their decoding efforts. It would have been to their economic advantage to simply subscribe to the service, but, of course, there would have been no challenge.

Much computer crime is originally started through a battle of wits. A mediocre security measure is implemented and a computer programmer thinks that it is so so simple that it can be defeated. There is a challenge to try. Occasionally, defeating the security system is so easy that the programmer uses the system to his or her own advantage.

There are few really secure computer systems. Corporate computers, school computers, personal computers, law enforcement computers, and even a top-secret nuclear weapons system computer have been cracked by amateur hackers who operate small computers. Devices called modems (modulator/demodulators) enable the computer to communicate with other systems by telephone lines.

Telephone companies have suffered a great amount of lost revenue in the battle of wits. Many technicians have found that the telephone system is controlled by a series of tones. There is a challenge to decode the tones so that one can make long distance calls at no charge. Many people have broken the rather simple codes and have built circuits that will defeat the system. Many of the people who have managed to do this have used their new-found knowledge to make long-distance calls that they never would have made otherwise. The code wasn't broken for financial gain.

Once circuits were developed that would defeat the telephone security system, opportunists built and sold them for a profit. A few years ago, there were many "black boxes" and "blue boxes" available on the underground market. *Figure 1-1* is a sketch of a blue box that generates three tones that a coin telephone system would interpret as the signals generated when coins are deposited.

A second type of blue box is a multi-key touch-tone keyboard. Certain 16-button keyboards are able to generate telephone company internal control codes that disable the billing computer. Although intended to allow the telephone company to make "free" calls along its own network, they are also used by telephone thieves to steal long-distance service.

**Figure 1-1.
Blue Box**

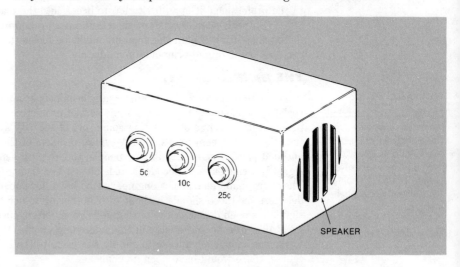

Whenever a security system is installed to protect something that the public has access to, such as a TV signal or a telephone system, there will be a challenge to many people to defeat the system. It is difficult to spot the tinkerers because they are not professional criminals.

FIGHTING "THE ESTABLISHMENT"

There is another type of crime that was popular in recent years. This includes crimes by people who justify their acts as fighting some sort of evil force, which is usually called "the establishment." Many businesses and institutions found themselves the enemy of various radical causes. During the Viet Nam war many people, who were opposed in principle to the war, felt that certain government institutions and businesses were their enemies. Acts performed against these enemies seemed just to the radicals, even though the acts themselves might be clearly illegal.

The lack of potential financial gain for the criminal is no guarantee against crime. Political extremists and irrational criminals might attack a facility for reasons of their own—or for no reason at all.

No business, institution, or home is safe from burglary and violence from one or another anti-establishment cause. The practical implication of this is that a facility isn't safe from criminal acts even though there is no way that anyone can gain financially from the acts. Many businesses with facilities in urban areas have been subject to vandalism, even though there was nothing of immediate value in the facility. Schools have been subject to this sort of thing and, in fact, most school security is aimed at protection against vandalism.

TERRORISTS

A new security threat has been recognized in recent years. The new and frightening beast that has stuck its toes under our door is international terrorism. More and more radical groups are turning to guns, grenades, and bombs to redress real or imagined grievances. More often than not, the targets of these terrorists are neither military nor economic, but civilians. It is not always the nationals or ethnics who believe themselves grieved, but often international cooperating terrorist groups, who commit the acts. In addition to military, economic, and governmental facilities, terrorists also target airlines, industrial plants, religious meetings, and sporting events.

THE IRRATIONAL CRIMINAL

A criminal may act for potential financial gain or to harm an enemy. Regardless of the motive, the main attraction for most criminals is that there appears to be little chance of apprehension.

By far, most crimes are committed in the interest of the criminal, who usually believes that something can be gained from the crime with little chance of being apprehended. The gain is usually financial but it might be the satisfaction of harming an enemy. In recent years, another type of crime has appeared. In this type, the criminal takes a great risk to commit a crime where there is clearly little opportunity to gain anything and a great chance of being caught.

Irrational crime is hard to anticipate and protect against. Some such crime is drug related. A person addicted to drugs may feel the need for them so strongly that rational thought is nearly impossible.

Many crimes of violence, such as assaults and rapes, are committed by the irrational criminal. Although the irrational criminal is by definition not rational, there seems to be some relationship to opportunity. Not an opportunity to commit a crime with impunity, but at least to be able to complete the crime before help can arrive.

ELECTRONIC SECURITY MEASURES

History shows that once any type of crime becomes widespread, electronic systems can be developed that can combat it. These systems aid not only in criminals being apprehended, but also act as deterrents. Unfortunately, the development of security systems usually lags behind crime. Of course, this is to be expected; most people are honest and do not think in terms of crimes that might possibly be committed. No one protects against an inconceivable threat.

Many normal electronic developments have security features. The old-fashioned cash register at the left in *Figure 1-2* was used for many years in all types of retail establishments. If money was missing, it was usually taken by ringing up a "no sale." The bell on the register was the only protection.

**Figure 1-2.
Old and Modern Cash
Registers**

Microprocessor controllers allow ordinary household and business appliances to be used also as part of a security system.

The modern cash register at the right in the figure was developed to simplify business procedures, not as a security device. Nevertheless, being microprocessor controlled, it can be used to provide a great deal of protection. It can sound an alarm if used in an unauthorized manner or by an unauthorized person. It can record the types of sales, so that if a particular person rings up an unreasonable number of certain types of sales, the fact can be noticed quickly. The modern cash register can also control inventory, thus providing a correlation between the recorded sales and the actual inventory.

Some electronic systems that were developed for completely different purposes can be used to enhance security and should not be overlooked. These devices can be used to support systems specifically designed for security.

Electronic systems usually detect some event associated with intrusion, rather than intrusion itself. For example, they can detect motion or sounds where there should be none.

Electronic systems are usually not capable of detecting an actual crime. They detect something that a criminal does in connection with the crime. For example, a microwave intrusion alarm does not detect the actual presence of an intruder. It detects motion in a protected area where there shouldn't be any motion. The selection of an electronic system to protect against any type of crime should be based on the circumstances that accompany the crime.

Inasmuch as burglary is by far the most common type of crime today, intrusion alarms account for the majority of electronic security systems. More sophisticated systems are used to combat more sophisticated types of crimes. For example, data encoders can be used to protect against theft of computer data by wiretapping.

MEASURE AND COUNTERMEASURE

As time passes, criminals will find ways to defeat any new type of intrusion alarm system, so continuing development of new systems is required.

As a system becomes widely developed, more and more people will understand how it works. This means that as time passes if there is a way of defeating a security system, more people will become familiar with the foiling techniques. It is necessary, therefore, that development of new systems be continued.

When the ultrasonic intrusion alarm was first introduced it was considered nearly impossible to defeat. Before long, it became generally known that the system used the Doppler principle and thus responded not to the presence nor the motion of an intruder, but to the velocity of the motion. It was also realized that in order to prevent false alarms from air currents, there was a lower limit to the velocity to which the system would respond. It was also realized that the system responded to reflections of ultrasonic energy. Once this information became widespread, criminals began to defeat ultrasonic systems by wearing absorbent clothing and moving very slowly. Of course, the requirement that the burglar move very slowly increased the time required for a crime to be committed and thus acted as a deterrent.

The important aspect of this discussion is that there is no safety in the fact that a system is hard to defeat. The relentless process of measure and countermeasure will continue. The professional criminal will continue to develop methods of defeating security systems.

WARNING *It is emotionally tempting to create an alarm system that harms the intruder. Typical of this idea are traps involving high-voltage electrical shocks, physical injury, poisonous snakes, or "set guns." All forms of trap are illegal in all states. Laws governing these "alarms" are called "Set Gun Laws," and violating them can set you up for either criminal charges or a civil lawsuit. In one case, a farmer set a shotgun to blast the legs of a barn burglar with birdshot. The burglar tripped the gun trigger when he entered the barn and received disabling wounds to his lower legs. The burglar was sentenced to thirty days in prison, which was suspended, and promptly sued the farmer for $50,000— and won.*

WHAT HAVE WE LEARNED?

1. Electrical/electronic security alarm systems have been available for more than 100 years.
2. Amateur criminals tends to be opportunists; professional criminals tend to be experts at their trade; irrational criminals tend to be unpredictable.
3. All security systems can eventually be defeated by clever crooks. Thus new development and constant change is required to keep the crooks off balance.
4. Alarms don't actually detect intrusion, but rather, something associated with intrusion (for example, motion where there should be none).

Quiz for Chapter 1

1. Edwin Holmes opened the first central office burglar alarm system in:
   a. 1858.
   b. 1877.
   c. 1898.
   d. 1921.

2. Application of known electronic techniques tend to lead the spread of crime. True or false?

3. The type of crime that proliferates is that in which criminals believe:
   a. they can escape apprehension.
   b. the police are on strike.
   c. the victims are at home.
   d. that there is an element of risk present.

4. Between 19____ and 1972 there was a tremendous jump in the number of airliner hijackings.
   a. 1940
   b. 1962
   c. 1968
   d. 1970

5. Amateur criminals tend to be:
   a. opportunists.
   b. unemployed.
   c. drug addicts.
   d. poverty stricken.

6. The best defense against amateur criminals is to:
   a. increase the difficulty of committing the crime.
   b. decrease the value of the crime.
   c. increase the probability of apprehension.
   d. a and c above.

7. The professional criminal is:
   a. alcoholic.
   b. expert.
   c. rarely apprehended.
   d. easily thwarted.

8. Dummy TV cameras and bogus "Electronic Security System in Use" decals are effective deterrents against burglars. True or false?

9. Two types of "blue box" are used. One generates telephone control codes, and the other:
   a. simulates coin-denomination signals on pay phones.
   b. turns off the billing computer.
   c. turns off the operator alert.
   d. gives billing computer a bogus credit card number.

10. Criminals commit their acts for:
    a. financial gain.
    b. thrills.
    c. harm to enemies.
    d. all of the above.

11. Modern appliances, such as cash registers, can do double duty as part of a security system because of:
    a. solid-state circuitry.
    b. clever mechanical design.
    c. microprocessors.
    d. analog circuits.

12. The most common crime today is:
    a. murder.
    b. burglary.
    c. mugging.
    d. holdup.

HOWARD W. SAMS & COMPANY

Bookmark

DEAR VALUED CUSTOMER:

Howard W. Sams & Company is dedicated to bringing you timely and authoritative books for your personal and professional library. Our goal is to provide you with excellent technical books written by the most qualified authors. You can assist us in this endeavor by checking the box next to your particular areas of interest.

We appreciate your comments and will use the information to provide you with a more comprehensive selection of titles.

Thank you,

Vice President, Book Publishing
Howard W. Sams & Company

COMPUTER TITLES:

Hardware
- ☐ Apple 140   ☐ Macintosh 101
- ☐ Commodore 110
- ☐ IBM & Compatibles 114

Business Applications
- ☐ Word Processing J01
- ☐ Data Base J04
- ☐ Spreadsheets J02

Operating Systems
- ☐ MS-DOS K05   ☐ OS/2 K10
- ☐ CP/M K01   ☐ UNIX K03

Programming Languages
- ☐ C L03   ☐ Pascal L05
- ☐ Prolog L12   ☐ Assembly L01
- ☐ BASIC L02   ☐ HyperTalk L14

Troubleshooting & Repair
- ☐ Computers S05
- ☐ Peripherals S10

Other
- ☐ Communications/Networking M03
- ☐ AI/Expert Systems T18

ELECTRONICS TITLES:

- ☐ Amateur Radio T01
- ☐ Audio T03
- ☐ Basic Electronics T20
- ☐ Basic Electricity T21
- ☐ Electronics Design T12
- ☐ Electronics Projects T04
- ☐ Satellites T09

- ☐ Instrumentation T05
- ☐ Digital Electronics T11

Troubleshooting & Repair
- ☐ Audio S11   ☐ Television S04
- ☐ VCR S01   ☐ Compact Disc S02
- ☐ Automotive S06
- ☐ Microwave Oven S03

Other interests or comments: _____
_____
_____

Name_____
Title _____
Company _____
Address _____
City _____
State/Zip _____
Daytime Telephone No. _____

A Division of Macmillan, Inc.

4300 West 62nd Street   Indianapolis, Indiana 46268

27069

Bookmark

BUSINESS REPLY CARD

FIRST CLASS   PERMIT NO. 1076   INDIANAPOLIS, IND.

POSTAGE WILL BE PAID BY ADDRESSEE

HOWARD W. SAMS & CO.
ATTN: Public Relations Department
P.O. BOX 7092
Indianapolis, IN 46209-9921

HOWARD W. SAMS
& COMPANY

General Security Measures

ABOUT THIS CHAPTER

Even the best, most sophisticated electronic security system cannot protect the utterly careless homeowner or business executive. If you do not take certain precautions, you increase the risk of loss. In this chapter, we will discuss commonsense general security measures that ought to be taken whether or not an alarm system is installed.

COMMONSENSE RULES

When considering an electronic security system of any kind, there is a tendency to neglect what we might call commonsense security measures. In fact, one of the most common reasons for the ineffectiveness of electronic security devices is that no attention was paid to general security measures. For example, even the most sophisticated electronic intrusion alarm system is of little value if a burglar can trip the alarm when entering the premises, make the theft, and leave before anyone has time to respond to the alarm. Even audible alarms won't scare away a bold thief who believes that no one will respond.

The first general rule of security is to make a crime difficult, time-consuming, and attention-getting. This rule applies not only to burglary and robbery, but to crime in general. Much computer crime and white collar crime could be prevented if it were made more difficult. Many situations where crimes occur are almost invitations to the criminal to visit with impunity.

The practiced criminal considers the risk...and tries to choose a situation where the risk of apprehension is minimal.

The experienced criminal always evaluates the risk involved in any crime. No one wants to be apprehended. One who has given a lot of thought to crime will always try to choose a situation where the risk of being caught is minimal.

Many crimes are committed by opportunists who do not depend on crime for their livelihood, but are not above committing a crime if it appears perfectly safe to do so. In 1974, over two-thirds of the criminals who were incarcerated in state correctional facilities had held regular jobs before they were arrested.

Oftentimes, burglars enter through an unlocked door or window, use a key hidden in a "secret place" near a door, or enter with minimal force through poorly secured doors or windows.

The U.S. Department of Justice conducted a survey of crime in the United States over a period of several years in an attempt to detect patterns and statistics that would be useful in crime prevention. This survey showed that during the reporting period Americans lost more than one billion dollars from nine million household burglaries where no force at all was required on the part of the burglar to gain entry. In most of these burglaries, the burglar entered a home or garage either through an unlocked door or window or by using a key. These statistics do not include the many cases where some force was required to gain entry, but the amount of force was minimal. Entry and escape could be accomplished quickly.

Similar statistics could be gathered about almost any kind of crime. The point is that the crimes that are actually committed are the ones that seem to be the easiest to commit with the least chance of being caught.

There seems to be a general belief that a sophisticated electronic system can prevent much more crime than it was designed to do. Although the presence of an electronic security system might act as a deterrent, it cannot prevent a crime if commonsense security measures have been neglected.

PROTECTING THE HOUSEHOLD

The survey conducted by the U.S. Department of Justice mentioned previously provided a great deal of information on household crime. *Figure 2-1*, which is based on this survey, shows the distribution of household burglaries according to the race of the head of the house, family income, and location. Surprisingly, household burglaries are almost as likely to occur in the suburbs as in urban areas.

As might be expected high income households are more likely to be burglarized than low income homes, but the difference is not as great as might be expected.

**Figure 2-1.
Characteristics of
Households Touched by
Crime**

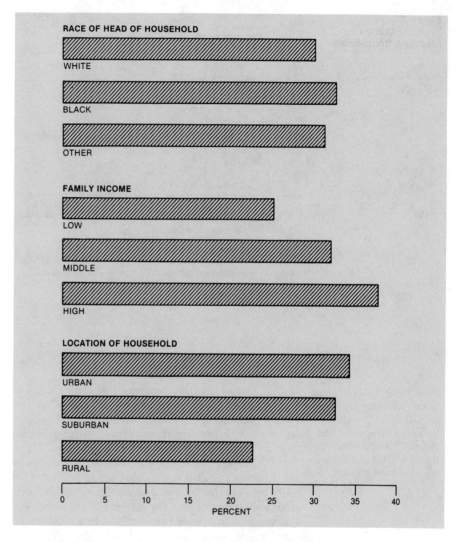

RACE OF HEAD OF HOUSEHOLD

WHITE

BLACK

OTHER

FAMILY INCOME

LOW

MIDDLE

HIGH

LOCATION OF HOUSEHOLD

URBAN

SUBURBAN

RURAL

0   5   10   15   20   25   30   35   40

PERCENT

In addition to the loss that is suffered in a burglary, there is always the danger of personal injury. *Figure 2-2* shows that a substantial number of household crimes involved personal injury and that many involved both personal injury and theft.

**Figure 2-2.
Types of Crimes
Affecting Households**

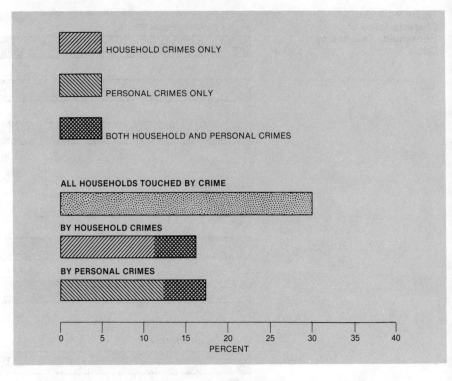

Burglars are quick to notice (a) habitually unlocked doors or windows, or (b) the homeowner who leaves a note directing that deliveries be placed inside an unlocked door.

One of the first measures that can be taken to protect a home is to make it appear to be secure. Careless habits of not locking doors and windows are quickly noticed. Such extreme mistakes as leaving notes for delivery people advising them to leave merchandise inside the unlocked door are practically an invitation for a burglary.

Perhaps the most serious aspect of careless habits of leaving doors and windows unlocked is that they are indicative of the fact that a person really believes that "it can't happen here." Such a person is not in a very good position to evaluate the security of the home. It is indeed difficult for a person who has never been exposed to a burglary to realize that he or she is a potential victim. Nevertheless, the fact is that no home is completely safe but that the risk of a burglary can be minimized by taking the proper precautions.

A secure home is one that is difficult to enter illegally. This means having good doors and windows. In many localities, building codes are written to ensure that the doors and windows of homes are burglar resistant.

Door Locks and Hinges

Another important feature is very good door locks. A homeowner without criminal tendencies usually has no idea of how easy it is for an experienced burglar to pick many of the commonly used door locks.

A security expert retired from a government intelligence unit gave a lecture on physical security to a class of newly employed nurses in a hospital. In front of him on a table were two boxes: one empty and one filled with cheap padlocks (both combination and key). While delivering his lecture the expert didn't say one word about padlocks, but, one at a time, he took every lock out of the box, opened it with a simple tool (or no tool, in some cases), and then dropped the newly opened lock into the other box. He gave no word of warning about cheap locks, but the nurses got the point nonetheless. Good locks that are nearly pick-proof are available. Of course, they cost more, but the added protection is worth the additional expense.

Figure 2-3 shows a deadbolt latch which is a part of some door locks. The latch has a small bar that lies along the side of the main bolt. When the door is closed, the small bar fits into the mechanism of the lock and prevents the main bolt from being pushed back. Without this feature, many door locks can be opened by forcing a piece of celluloid or plastic into the space between the door and the door jamb. This process is sometimes called "loiding."

**Figure 2-3.
Deadbolt Latch**

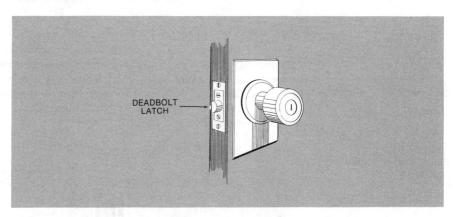

DEADBOLT
LATCH

A good deadbolt lock requires a key to unlock it on both outside and inside and will have a bolt that extends at least 1 inch outside the lock frame.

External door hinges are used on some garage or shed doors. These can be defeated by tapping out the hinge pins.

A deadbolt lock is one where a bolt slips into the door jamb and is locked and unlocked with a key from both the inside and the outside. When this type of lock is used, the bolt should extend out of the lock at least an inch. Many such locks have a very short bolt and the door can be forced open by jimmying—i.e., bending the strike plate slightly so that the bolt will slip out.

Another weak point in most homes is the hinges on the doors. Often a door between a shed or a garage and the house will have the pins of the hinges on the outside. Such a door can be removed by tapping out the hinge pins. This can be prevented with the arrangement shown in *Figure 2-4*. Here, two of the hinge screws, opposite each other, have been removed. A concrete nail is installed in place of one of the screws so that it protrudes about a half inch. The hole on the opposite side is drilled so that the head of the nail will fit into it when the door is closed. When this is done to both the top and bottom hinge of a door, the hinge pins can be removed and the door will still remain securely closed.

**Figure 2-4.
Modification of Door
Hinge**

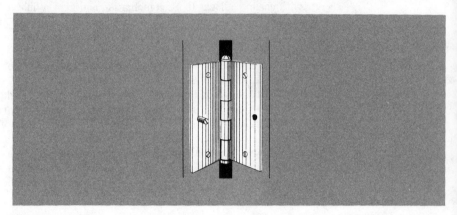

Windows

Windows are also a possible avenue of entry for a burglar. Although any window can be broken, this makes noise and a burglar would prefer a quieter mode of entry. The jalousie type of window consisting of louvres of glass is particularly vulnerable because the individual glass panes can often be slid out noiselessly. They are better replaced by the type of window shown in *Figure 2-5*.

**Figure 2-5.
Reasonably Secure
Window**

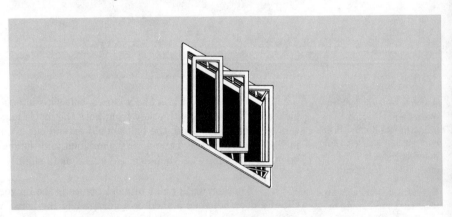

Basement windows often provide a relatively easy means of entry. They are usually casement windows that are hinged at the top and open inwards. Often, the original latch can be opened easily after cutting a small hole in the glass. The use of two simple inexpensive barrel bolts of the type shown in *Figure 2-6* at each side of the window will make it more secure. Of course, they can be opened readily, but it will take time for the burglar to locate them.

**Figure 2-6.
Barrel Bolt**

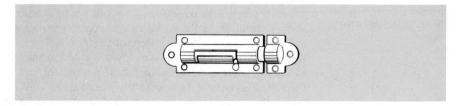

Household Items

According to police files, when household items are missing, the most common thief is one who has access to the home. This includes household help, repair people, and cleaning people. Often such people have had access to a home for a long period of time and are usually trusted. The homeowner then becomes careless and fails to take commonsense measures to reduce risks. This, of course, should not be a temptation to an inherently honest person, but many people are opportunists who will take advantage of such a situation.

People working regularly in a home are much more apt to be honest if they are bonded. Sometimes even making such a person fill out an application for bonding will accomplish the result. It at least creates the impression that the householder is security conscious.

Probably, the best way for the average homeowner to check the security of the home is to consult the local police department. The police are very familiar with the various methods of entry used by burglars and can spot high security risks quickly. Usually, the police department will be very cooperative because it wants to prevent burglaries as much as the homeowner does.

PROTECTING THE BUSINESS ESTABLISHMENT

What we said earlier about crimes of opportunity applies particularly to crimes against business. If any crime against business is easy to commit, the chances are that it will be committed.

Crime costs American business more than $25 billion annually. In one city, 72% of businesses were victimized. One insurer claims that nearly one-third of all business failures are attributable to crime.

The amount of crime against business is staggering. Every year, crime costs businesses over $25 billion. In one year, over 72% of the retail stores in one major city were burglarized. According to one insurance company estimate, 30% of all business failures are primarily attributable to theft.

Of course, the risk of crime applies equally to small and large businesses, but small businesses seem to suffer more. This is because there are many more small businesses, they tend to be more accessible to criminals, and small business executives tend to be less security conscious.

Crimes against businesses include robbery, burglary, shoplifting, internal (employee) theft, theft of proprietary information and business secrets, and sabotage.

Crimes against small business can be grouped into four categories: robbery, burglary, shoplifting, and internal theft. Larger businesses also suffer from theft of proprietary information, business secrets, and forms of sabotage.

Along with businesses for profit we must also consider religious and not-for-profit facilities. There was recently the case of a church that lost its silver communion service set to thieves. The embarrassed priest showed the police detective who investigated the theft how the key to the sacristy (storage room for altar fixtures) was kept under the seat cushion of the bishop's chair, right next to the locked door. The thief walked in undetected during office hours, robbed the church of a $2000 communion chalice (solid sterling) and a $1500 communion bread holder. This church (or their insurer) was lucky; a diligent detective who routinely makes the rounds of the pawnshops in that city found the chalice and recovered it. He threatened the pawnbroker with arrest for receiving stolen property, and the chalice was surrendered immediately. When asked whether he could have made a case for the "stolen property" charge, he replied: "I think so. After all, it's a reasonably good bet that he knew that a shabbily dressed thief bringing a sterling silver chalice engraved 'St. Anthony's Church (and a suburban address)' into a ghetto hock shop was a thief."

There are electronic devices that will help in combatting all of these crimes, but before electronic devices are even considered, other measures must be taken to minimize the risks.

Robbery

Of all of the crimes against business, robbery is the most violent and frightening. One who has not been the victim of a robbery cannot begin to imagine the feeling of terror that accompanies looking into the barrel of a gun in the hand of someone who might not hesitate to use it. There are over 100,000 commercial robberies each year—one every five minutes!

Ideal robbery targets are lonely establishments operated at night by a single employee, with the day's receipts still on the premises. Examples are convenience stores, gas stations, liquor stores, and drive-in restaurants.

According to the U.S. Department of Justice, most robbers plan their work carefully. They generally want easy money quickly and they look for targets that appear to offer little resistance and enough money to make the risk worthwhile. In selecting an establishment to rob, a criminal looks for places that are isolated from their neighbors, that are easy to enter and leave, and that permit the robber to overcome the resistance of a cashier with the least effort. Ideal robbery targets include a lone convenience store, a gas station, a drive-through, or liquor store located on or near a major thoroughfare. Preferred targets are staffed by one person and operate late at night with the receipts of the day still on the premises.

Burglary

Burglary is also a common crime against business, but it usually doesn't involve violence unless the burglar surprises someone who is working late or a guard who is on duty. As with any other form of burglary, the burglar who victimizes a business is looking for an opportunity to gain something with minimal risk. Very frequently burglars will "case" a business before actually breaking in. This casing is to evaluate both the anticipated gain and the risk. For this reason, if a business looks secure, it is not as apt to be burglarized.

Burglars can be grouped into three major categories: amateur (70%), semiprofessional, and professional. The amateur is most often an opportunist looking for the least secure premises to rob.

Burglars can be roughly divided into three categories. The rank amateur is the most common. Some 70% of the burglars who have been apprehended fall into this category. The rank amateur is always looking for the most insecure business establishments.

The semiprofessional burglar has considerably more skill and usually can do a better job of gaining entry to a facility without detection.

The final class of burglar is the professional. The professional is indeed an artisan, skilled at lock picking, defeating intrusion alarms, and safe cracking, who frequently is not apprehended. Fortunately only about 2% of all burglars fall into this classification.

Thus, the first line of defense for any business is against the rank amateur because they are most common. The amateur always wants to enter and leave a facility as quickly as possible. Many burglaries do not take more than two to four minutes from the time entry is started. Quite frequently whatever is stolen is disposed of through a "fence" within an hour of the time that it is taken.

Professional burglars may take an hour or more to accomplish their deeds. Usually what they are after has considerable value and the extra time and risk seem to be justified.

Burglars usually prefer to avoid violence and will not resort to it unless they come upon someone unexpectedly. Thus, the first thing that a burglar looks for in selecting a target is an unoccupied location, such as a home during the day or a business at night.

Burglars will first seek a means of entry where they will be unobserved, but failing that will select a point of least resistance. Some professionals have little difficulty picking locks that foil amateurs.

All burglars seem to look for a point of entry such as an unlocked door, window, or skylight that will be unobserved. Failing to find a point that guarantees that entry will not be observed, the burglar looks for a point of entry that offers the least resistance and is least likely to attract attention. Of course, the amount of resistance that a given point of entry will offer depends on the skill of the burglar. A professional might find very little trouble picking a lock that would effectively deter an amateur.

Failing to find a desirable point of entry, the burglar will have to use a certain amount of physical force to gain entry. A great deal of protection can be gained by making any means of entry as noisy as possible. Burglars are uneasy when they are making a lot of noise because it increases the probability that they will be caught.

Some of the things that can be done to make a business establishment less attractive to burglars are shown in *Figure 2-7.*

**Figure 2-7.
Good Security
Measures**

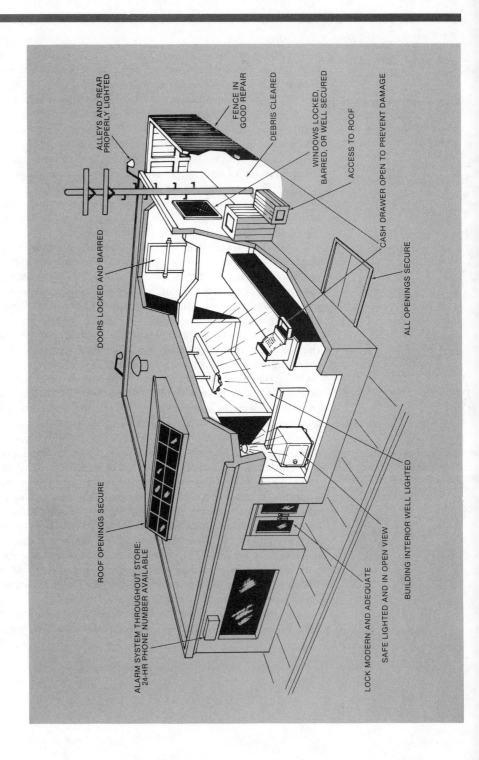

ALLEYS AND REAR PROPERLY LIGHTED

FENCE IN GOOD REPAIR

DEBRIS CLEARED

WINDOWS LOCKED, BARRED, OR WELL SECURED

ACCESS TO ROOF

CASH DRAWER OPEN TO PREVENT DAMAGE

ALL OPENINGS SECURE

DOORS LOCKED AND BARRED

ROOF OPENINGS SECURE

ALARM SYSTEM THROUGHOUT STORE: 24-HR PHONE NUMBER AVAILABLE

LOCK MODERN AND ADEQUATE

SAFE LIGHTED AND IN OPEN VIEW

BUILDING INTERIOR WELL LIGHTED

Shoplifting

Another security risk faced by retail businesses is shoplifting. Shoplifting is very common and is very difficult to detect. It is estimated that losses from shoplifting amount to between one and two billion dollars each year. There are two categories of shoplifting. One is where an item of comparatively high value is stolen. The other is where the value of the items taken is small, but the quantity is large. The Department of Justice has estimated that the average shoplifter's take is in the vicinity of $4–$6.

High-value items are often stolen by professional or semiprofessional shoplifters who intend to fence the items almost immediately. Neither age nor apparent economic status are reliable indicators of the professional shoplifter. One reasonably reliable giveaway, however, is that some of these thieves wear large overcoats with oversized pockets, even when the outside temperature would suggest a lighter weight coat (or no coat). Many amateur shoplifters seem to be either teenagers or housewives from "good homes" in middle- to upper middle-class neighborhoods. Presumably, they commit their crimes either for thrills or out of rebelliousness because they often have credit cards or adequate cash to pay for the merchandise when they are caught.

The retailer faces a problem in trying to protect against shoplifting. If security is too lax, the crime will increase. If security is too stringent, customers will feel uneasy in the establishment and business will suffer. Another problem facing the retailer is whether to prosecute when a shoplifter is discovered. Often the dollar value of the theft is so low that it seems cruel to prosecute.

Vigorous prosecution of shoplifters—even those who steal tiny amounts—can significantly reduce losses. One department store decided on a "100% prosecution" policy for shoplifters and employee thieves. Their losses for the following year were half those of the previous year. Either the universe experienced an unusual burst of righteousness, or word got out and shoplifters stayed away from the "dangerous" store—there were still plenty of stores that did not prosecute petty thieves.

There are a few steps that can be taken that will minimize shoplifting. The first thing that can be done without offending most customers is to secure the more expensive merchandise, such as jewelry and furs, so that they cannot be taken without physical force. This reduces the store's risk of loss to smaller items that cannot be secured without offending customers or hurting business.

Protecting Small Items

There are several ways to protect small items. One is training employees in the habits of shoplifters. Another is to be sure that all store locations are under the supervision of a particular person. Phones that might be used by employees should be located so that while on the phone the employee can still see the part of the establishment for which he or she is responsible.

A code system, such as a chime or coded announcement that alerts all employees to the fact that a suspicious person is in the establishment, is a great deterrent. Any employee should be able to initiate this alarm without drawing any attention to the act. Thus, when someone who displays the habits of a shoplifter enters any part of the establishment, everyone will be on guard.

Internal Theft

The final source of great loss to businesses of all types is internal theft—the theft of company property by an employee. The employee may be someone working at an hourly wage or it may be someone at the executive level.

There have been various estimates of the annual loss to business from internal theft, but the simple fact is that it amounts to much more than any of the estimates. Just describing what is meant by internal theft isn't easy. The fact is that every item of property that belongs to a company has some value even though it might be very small. In many cases the value is so small as to seem trivial. An employee can hardly be expected to take the company pen that he has been using all day out of his pocket before he leaves for the day. Nevertheless small items add up. One company estimated that in the course of a year it had purchased over 150 pencils for each employee of the firm.

The insidious part of internal theft is that each theft tends to be small, but when all such thefts are added up, the losses are staggering. As with shoplifting, there is a problem in taking adequate security measures to protect company property. If security is too lax, the losses will be great. If security is too tight, employees will feel uncomfortable and productivity will drop.

Sometimes very tight security is taken by employees as a challenge. They do not bother to think of whether or not a particular action is honest or not, they are simply challenged to outwit one or more security measures. Many employees delight in taking something of little value that they probably have no need for just for the thrill of "beating the system."

One of the best steps that can be taken to minimize internal theft is to have a very clear company policy that is known by all employees. Another step is complete fairness in the administration of this policy. If a supervisor is allowed to appropriate company property with impunity, it is nearly certain that other employees will seek ways to do the same things.

One good policy is that no company property can be taken out of the premises without some kind of accountability. This includes things, such as books and tools, that an employee may need in connection with his or her work. If an employee is made accountable for property, he or she will usually accept the responsibility. If there is no system of accountability, there is no incentive to return the items promptly.

WHAT HAVE WE LEARNED?

1. An effective alarm system will bring a response before the thief has a chance to escape.
2. The first general rule of security is to make the crime difficult, time-consuming, noisy, and attention-getting.
3. Home security depends upon properly locked doors and windows, plus such commonsense precautions as not allowing unsupervised access to the premises by delivery people and workers.
4. "It *can* happen here" is the only safe attitude.
5. Crimes against small businesses include robbery, burglary, shoplifting, internal theft, and vandalism.
6. Large businesses are afflicted with the same crimes as small businesses, but they are also susceptible to theft of proprietary information and business secrets and sabotage.
7. Burglars can be divided into three main categories: amateur, semiprofessional, and professional.
8. A well-publicized, strictly enforced policy of prosecuting thieves will deter many people who might be tempted to try.

Quiz for Chapter 2

1. Even a sophisticated security system is useless:
   a. unless it traps the criminal.
   b. unless it calls the police.
   c. if it does not deter the criminal.
   d. unless it has an audible alarm.

2. The first general rule of security is to make a crime difficult, time-consuming, and:
   a. physically dangerous.
   b. attention-getting.
   c. less lucrative.
   d. more lucrative.

3. Professional criminals will always try to choose a situation where:
   a. there is little light.
   b. there is only one employee.
   c. the risk of getting caught is minimal.
   d. there are no firearms.

4. Burglars rarely enter a premises where at least minimal force is required. True or false?

5. Low-income homes are all but immune from burglary. True or false?

6. "It can't happen here!" True or false?

7. Household crimes rarely involve personal injury even when the occupants are at home when the crime occurs. True or false?

8. Door locks are nearly pick proof. True or false?

9. _____windows are particularly vulnerable because the glass panels easily slide out.
   a. Sash
   b. Casement
   c. Jalousie
   d. Slider

10. _____windows are relatively easy to enter because they are hinged at the top and open inward.
    a. Casement
    b. Basement
    c. Jalousie
    d. Kitchen

11. _____ burglars make up about 70% of those who are apprehended.
    a. Professional
    b. Nighttime
    c. Amateur
    d. Semiprofessional

Electronic Intrusion Alarms

ABOUT THIS CHAPTER

Electrical and electronic alarm systems have been around for quite a while and have taken on many forms. In this chapter, we will discuss the principles of alarm systems and look at the different types of alarm systems available today.

ELECTRONICS IN SECURITY

In the past, the word "electronics" had an almost magic connotation. The mere fact that a business was protected by an "electronic" system was enough to discourage all but the most intrepid burglar. Many small businesses took advantage of this fact and, without bothering to invest in the actual system, merely displayed signs or window decals that indicated that an electronic intrusion alarm was in use. Dummy systems such as imitation closed-circuit TV cameras, complete with lenses and flashing lights, are still to be found in some establishments. These devices are just empty boxes. They might frighten away an amateur, but to the skilled burglar of today they are nothing but an invitation to break in with impunity.

Many people incorrectly assume that criminals are stupid people. Many of them, however, are skilled craftspeople or well-educated technicians. Thus, alarm systems have to work properly when skilled technicians are trying their best to defeat them.

There is a tendency for the law-abiding citizen to think of a burglar as a rather stupid person. This simply is not true of professional burglars. That burglar is a skilled craftsperson, equipped with up-to-the-minute tools for the trade. A professional's stock-in-trade often includes a detailed knowledge of the principles of intrusion alarms and techniques that can be used to foil them. This has lead to a striking difference between electronic intrusion alarms and other types of electronic equipment. Whereas most commercial electronic equipment must work as reliably as possible with the help of skilled electronic technicians, an intrusion alarm must operate reliably, even with a technician trying to keep it from working.

TYPES OF ALARM SYSTEMS

The ultimate goal of the alarm system is to prevent crime by sounding the alarm early and bringing a quick response.

Many different types of intrusion alarms, using different operating principles, are available. Each type has its own advantages and limitations. The selection of an alarm for a particular installation is based on the following considerations:

1. If possible, burglaries, holdups, and acts of vandalism should be prevented from happening. The presence of an effective alarm system is definitely a deterrent to potential burglars and vandals. No one wants to break into a home or establishment where all previous intruders have been caught and sent to jail.
2. The presence of an intruder must be detected as early as possible. There is a saying in the security field that, given enough time, a burglar can open any safe or vault.
3. The alarm must bring a quick response. An alarm is useless unless action is taken.

Intrusion alarm systems are usually classified in one of three general categories:

1. Proprietary alarm systems
2. Central station alarm systems
3. Local alarm systems.

The principal features of each type of system are described in the following paragraphs.

Proprietary Alarm Systems

A proprietary alarm system is one in which an on-site central location is used to monitor building-wide or plant-wide alarms. Security guards can then be dispatched to the scene of an intrusion.

A proprietary system is one in which the presence of an intruder in any protected area of a facility is indicated at some on-site central location, such as the headquarters of the security guard. This type of installation is widely used in industries and in institutions such as schools and manufacturing plants that have their own security police forces. The facility may include many different buildings that require different degrees of protection. Each area is equipped with the type of alarm system best suited to the application. The signal outputs from the individual areas are then connected by wires to a control panel at the central location. A typical central station console is shown in *Figure 3-1.*

With a properly designed installation of this type, one guard can monitor the security status of an entire industrial plant. When an intruder enters any of the protected areas, a signal is flashed to the central console. One or more security guards can be immediately dispatched to the scene.

Proprietary alarm systems are often used for much more than intrusion alarms. The central console is arranged to provide an indication (and often a printed record) of such things as the operation of fire sensors and guard patrol stations. As a guard patrols a facility, a record of the time that he or she checks in at each patrol station along the route is recorded. If the guard encounters trouble and takes more than the scheduled amount of time in patrolling, an alarm will be sounded so that another guard may be dispatched to help. This type of proprietary alarm system is often called a supervisory alarm system.

In many plants, the supervisory system will maintain a printed record of each time that a gate is opened or closed. Thus, any unauthorized entry can be pinned down.

**Figure 3-1.
Centralized Protection
Control Console**

Many proprietary systems are very complex and utilize computer control. The principles of protection are the same as in other systems, but the computer enables the system to be tailored to a particular application rather easily and provides a great deal of flexibility. The details of computer control are covered in Chapter 14.

Central Station Alarm Systems

A central station alarm system is much like a proprietary system, except that the alarms are tied to an off-site central station by radio, leased wires, or telephone lines, where they are monitored by security company personnel.

The central station alarm system differs from the proprietary alarm system in that the central alarm point is operated by an off-site security company rather than employees of the protected facility; otherwise, they may be quite similar. Again, each of the protected areas has its own intrusion detector. The outputs of the detectors are connected to the headquarters of the security company.

The connection to the remote location may be provided by a radio link, leased wires, or regular telephone lines.

When an alarm is received at the security company, a guard is dispatched to the scene; usually the police are called as well. Many central station alarm systems have audio monitors so that when an alarm is received, the guard at headquarters can actually listen to what is happening in the protected premises. In this way, an unnecessary call to the police department can be avoided if there is no aural evidence of an intrusion. For example, the alarm may be triggered by a thunderstorm. The person monitoring the system can hear the thunder. When there is no evidence of footsteps or breaking into safes or cabinets, the police need not be called.

Figure 3-2 shows the console of a system which can be used in either a proprietary or a central station. This system is computer controlled and can provide a wide variety of security functions.

**Figure 3-2.
Computer-controlled
Security System**
(Courtesy Kidde, Inc.)

Local Alarm Systems

Local alarm systems, as the names implies, sound a bell or siren on the premises whenever an intruder trips the alarm. These systems are usually employed where the other systems are not practical. For example, a local alarm would be used in a remote facility where the time required for the police or representatives of a security service to arrive would be so long that they would invariably reach the scene after the burglar had gone.

One disadvantage of the local alarm is that burglars know when their presence has been detected. They know they can stay only a minute or two. Consequently, many local alarms bring a response only after the intruder has gone.

A disadvantage of a local alarm system is that the intruder knows of the detection and can escape.

In spite of this limitation, the local alarm has its applications. For example, a homeowner may not be willing to pay for a large system that will bring the police. Being alert to the presence of an intruder may enable the homeowner to defend family and possessions adequately. A well-designed local alarm will detect an intruder at entry and will alert the resident. In many neighborhoods, people have a great enough sense of responsibility that they will call the police if they hear a burglar alarm in the area.

The Psychological Effect

One factor that should not be ignored when considering the local alarm is its ability to produce a strong psychological effect. For example, an intrusion alarm arranged to activate an ear-splitting siren will unnerve most intruders. In addition to the disturbance, the siren will make it impossible for the intruder to hear the approach of a police cruiser. This alone might force a burglar to leave prematurely. The psychological effect can be enhanced considerably by adding flashing, blinding lights to the audible alarm.

A local alarm system may be used with a remote signaling device, such as an automatic telephone dialer, arranged to call the police in the event of an intrusion. This gives the system many of the advantages of a central station system without the cost.

Many police departments have had unfortunate experiences with telephone dialers because of a large number of false alarms. For this reason, many communities have ordinances regulating their use. Any such installation must be carefully coordinated with the local police department.

TYPES OF PROTECTION

Most of the chapters of this book describe the detailed principles of operation of different types of intrusion alarms. The type of alarm that is best suited to a particular installation depends to a great extent on the exact type of protection that is required and the extent of protection that is economically feasible. The action taken by a prospective intruder usually depends on the expected reward. If the prize is great enough, a crook will resort to any plan, no matter how elaborate, that seems to have a chance of success, making every attempt to frustrate any detection system and taking risks. On the other hand, if the maximum possible return from breaking into a home or business is probably small, not worth great risks, a comparatively simple system might be an adequate deterrent.

Three general categories of protection are available.

1. Perimeter, or point-of-entry, protection
2. Specific-area protection
3. Spot protection.

One or more types should be considered for every installation.

Point-of-Entry Protection

Where practical, it is usually advisable to detect an intruder as early as possible. This is usually accomplished by installing detectors on doors, windows, gates, and fences. The system is designed to initiate an alarm as early as possible, before the intruder has a chance to accomplish anything. Stores and other places of business that are closed during the night usually require this type of protection.

The principal limitation of this arrangement is that it is rarely practical to provide complete protection. Even if all the doors, windows, and even walls of an area are protected, it is still possible, and not at all uncommon, for burglars to enter an area by cutting through the floor or ceiling.

There are also facilities where perimeter protection is not practical. It might not be desirable, for example, for an alarm to sound every time an intruder passes through a freight yard. Similarly, a facility that is open for business twenty-four hours a day has no use for perimeter protection.

Perimeter alarms are a first line of defense, but can be thwarted by cutting through walls, roofs, and so forth.

Another limitation of perimeter protection is that it is useless against the "stay-behind." The "stay-behind" is a burglar who enters a place of business during normal business hours, finds a hiding place, and remains hidden until after the place is closed and all employees have gone. When it seems safe, the burglar comes out of hiding, takes the merchandise, and breaks out of the store, tripping the perimeter alarm on the way out. By the time the police or security guard arrives, the burglar is gone.

When using point-of-entry protection, consideration should be given to all points through which a burglar might enter. *Figure 3-3* shows many such points in a business establishment. Similar considerations apply to a home. The skillful burglar will consider all possible points of entry before actually breaking into a building. For example, if it is probable that all doors and windows might be protected by an alarm system, the burglar might enter through some sort of air vent. Of course, the burglar can leave through a door or window, tripping the alarm when doing so. The burglar can usually get away before anyone responds to the alarm.

**Figure 3-3.
Areas of Concern in
Point-of-Entry
Protection**

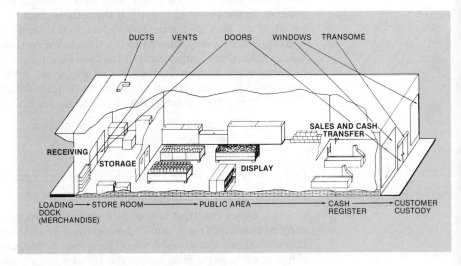

Specific-Area Protection

Specific area protection can be used either as a second line of defense or to protect certain limited areas in a facility that are in use during odd hours.

Specific-area protection uses systems that detect the presence or movement of an intruder in an area. This type of protection is an excellent addition to a perimeter system. It will pick up the stay-behind who decides that all is clear and starts to move around.

Specific-area protection systems frequently used where a particularly sensitive area needs extra protection and where perimeter systems are not practical. For example, part of a factory may operate twenty-four hours a day while other parts are only open during the daytime. A perimeter system should be useless because it would be tripped whenever a legitimate worker entered the plant. In such a case, the areas that are not normally occupied at night can be equipped with a specific-area protection system. Thus, if anyone attempts to enter a closed area such as an office or stockroom, an alarm will be actuated.

Spot Protection

A spot protection system is usually associated with one or more specific objects, such as a safe or a jewelry case. It trips an alarm whenever anyone touches, or in some cases even comes near, the protected object. This type of system is used to back up other systems to provide maximum protection for highly sensitive objects. File cabinets containing secret data, safes, and cases containing valuables are often protected in this manner.

Spot protection systems are often used as annunciator systems during normal business hours. For example, the proprietor of a store may be happy for customers to browse through the store, but would want to know if they attempted to open a shadowcase containing valuables. A system that is connected to a regular system during the night can be connected to a small bell or buzzer during the day. In this way, there would be a warning whenever anyone tried to open the protected case. Similar systems can be used to protect file cabinets containing government or business secrets. *Figure 3-4* shows typical applications of spot or point protection in a business establishment.

Spot protection alarm systems are used to protect certain small spaces, such as display cases or secret data files.

**Figure 3-4.
Areas of Concern in
Spot Protection**

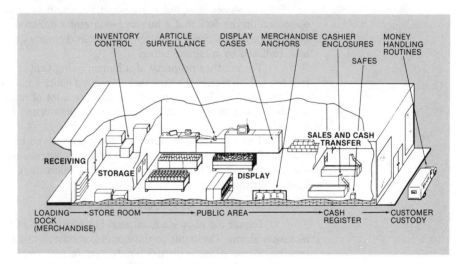

Intrusion Detection

Every electronic intrusion alarm must have some means of detecting the presence of a human being in the protected area. The part of the system that accomplishes this is called a detector or sensor.

A properly designed alarm system will not create false alarms, or fail to operate, because of normal ranges of temperature, humidity, wind, sound level, or vibration.

The ideal intrusion detector responds only to the presence of a human being and not to the presence of such animals as dogs and cats, or even mice or rats. It should not respond to any normal changes in ambient conditions such as temperature, humidity, wind, rain, sound level, or vibration. Unfortunately, most devices that will respond to the presence of a human being may also respond to one or another of these extraneous influences. The art of selecting and installing an effective intrusion alarm is to tailor the system to the application so that it will not respond to anything other than an intrusion and, at the same time, will respond to every intrusion.

There are several properties of human intruders that can be used as the basis of an intrusion alarm system. Probably the most obvious is that intruders must remove barriers before they can enter a premises. They must open a door or window, or cut a hole in the walls, floor, or roof. Switches can be arranged so that they will be actuated by any attempt at entry.

Photoelectric Detectors

Another property of a human being that can be used as the basis of an intrusion alarm is the fact that a human is opaque to light and infrared emission. A photoelectric system can be arranged to detect the passage of an intruder.

A less obvious, but quite effective, alarm system depends for its operation on the fact that a human being emits infrared energy due to normal body heat. Such a system has infrared sensors that will detect the heat radiated by a human being.

Yet another property of a human being that is taken advantage of in intrusion alarms is the fact that in many facilities an intruder cannot steal anything or do damage without making a lot of noise. An audio alarm will detect any sounds that are louder than the normal sounds in the protected facility.

Two very popular alarm systems operate on the principle that motion of a human being will disturb either an ultrasonic or an electromagnetic field. Ultrasonic alarms and microwave intrusion detectors operate on this principle.

PRINCIPLES OF INTRUSION ALARMS

Figure 3-5 shows a functional block diagram of an electronic intrusion alarm. The input to the system, shown at the left of the figure, consists of one or more intrusion detectors or sensors. The detector is the device that initiates the action of the alarm. It either responds directly to the presence of an intruder, or, more commonly, responds to something that the intruder does, such as walking, breaking a window, or making noise.

Figure 3-5.
Intrusion Alarm
Functional Diagram

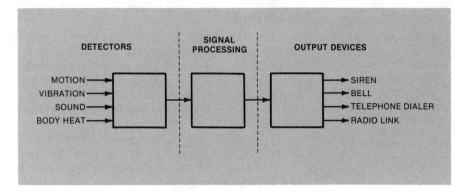

Many different types of intrusion detectors with differing operating principles are available. Each has its own advantages and limitations. Much of the effectiveness of an alarm system depends on the proper selection and installation of detectors that will provide adequate protection in any given application. Sensors often include protection against tampering or attempts to defeat the system.

At the right-hand side of *Figure 3-5* we have the output devices. These are what actually bring a response in the event of an intrusion. Most commonly, the output device is some kind of alarm, such as a siren, horn, or bell, that will sound when the alarm is tripped. Other output devices include automatic telephone dialers, monitor speakers, or TV screens.

The middle of *Figure 3-5* shows signal conditioning equipment, access control, and timing devices. These circuits adapt particular sensors to the appropriate alarm device and provide control over the entire system.

Tailoring the System

Inasmuch as very few homes or business establishments are identical, very few intrusion alarms are identical. In order to provide optimal protection, it is usually necessary to tailor the alarm system to the particular facility in which it is used. In fact, this tailoring often makes the difference between a very good alarm system and a useless one.

Usually an intrusion detector responds to something that an intruder does while trying to gain entry. This means that it might respond to something else that provides the same effect. Thus, an audio detector that is supposed to respond to the sounds made by an intruder may also respond to other sounds in the protected area. Similarly, an ultrasonic detector may respond to ultrasonic radiation from a steam valve. In an effective alarm system, the detectors are chosen so that there is a minimal chance of their reacting to extraneous influences.

FALSE ALARMS

A false alarm is an alarm from a system that is not caused by an intruder. It may be caused by component failure, or by some external influence. It is impossible to over stress the importance of false alarms. At the best, they can be very annoying, especially when they occur at an inconvenient hour. At worst, they can cause police or security guards to speed to the scene needlessly, thus jeopardizing their safety and the safety of others.

In some instances, store managers have been called out of bed so often by false alarms that they no longer use the alarm system at all.

It is quite common for a burglar as a part of a casing operation to find that an intrusion alarm is in service. If the burglar doesn't know how to defeat it, he or she may want to find out just how much time elapses between the tripping of the alarm and when someone responds to it. If the response time is long enough it might not be a very risky burglary.

One way to measure the response time is for the burglar to do something inconspicuous that will trip the alarm and then wait nearby to see just how much time is available before someone responds.

"Boy Who Cried 'Wolf'"

Another trick that has been used by burglars is to trip the intrusion alarm and then leave immediately. The police or security guards arrive on the scene only to find no trouble. After this has happened a few times, no one will take the alarm seriously. This situation is called the "boy who cried 'wolf'" syndrome. The burglar can then execute a quick burglary before anyone will respond to the alarm.

For these reasons, the cause of every false alarm should be found. If the alarm is caused by equipment failure, the situation should be corrected. If absolutely no cause can be found, there is a possibility that the alarm was caused by a prospective burglar.

WHAT HAVE WE LEARNED?

1. The goal of the alarm system is to prevent crime by ensuring that all perpetrators are caught.
2. Alarm systems are classified as (a) proprietary, (b) central station, and (c) local alarms.
3. Three types of protection are available: (a) point-of-entry, (b) area, and (c) spot. A properly designed system may employ any or all of these, depending upon the situation.
4. Alarm systems consist of (a) detectors, (b) signal processors, and (c) output devices.
5. False alarms must be kept to a minimum to avoid the "boy who cried 'wolf'" syndrome.

Quiz for Chapter 3

1. There is a tendency for law-abiding people to regard criminals as _____ people.
   a. violent
   b. misunderstood
   c. poverty stricken
   d. stupid

2. An effective alarm must bring:
   a. quick response.
   b. the police.
   c. the proprietor.
   d. rapid incapacitation.

3. An alarm system that sounds a warning at an on-site central location is called a(n) _____ alarm system.
   a. local
   b. proprietary
   c. monitored
   d. area protection

4. The "supervisory alarm" function is most often associated with _____ alarm systems.
   a. local
   b. central station
   c. proprietary
   d. burglar

5. The _____ alarm system also often operates with fire detectors.
   a. local
   b. proprietary
   c. central
   d. perimeter

6. A _____ alarm system is similar to the proprietary system, except that it is operated by the employees at an off-site security office.
   a. perimeter
   b. fire
   c. radio
   d. central station

7. Some _____ alarm systems have an audio monitor function to allow security personnel to listen to what is happening on the protected premises.
   a. computerized
   b. local
   c. area protection
   d. central

8. A _____ alarm system sounds a siren or bell to indicate intrusion.
   a. local
   b. premises
   c. central
   d. proprietary

9. Many local alarms bring response only after the intruder has:
   a. broken in.
   b. gone.
   c. been caught.
   d. given up or died.

10. A _____ alarm may use an automatic telephone dialer to summon police.
    a. area
    b. local
    c. perimeter
    d. proprietary

11. _____, or point-of-entry, alarms place sensors at places such as doors, windows, and fences.
    a. Perimeter
    b. Spot
    c. Area
    d. Central

12. A(n) _____ protection system detects intruders in a specific room.
    a. local
    b. proprietary
    c. area
    d. spot

13. Intruder _____ include switches, photoelectric eyes, infrared detectors, and audio microphones.
   a. alarms
   b. protectors
   c. traps
   d. sensors

14. List the three main functional components of an alarm system.

15. "Boy who cried 'wolf'" refers to:
   a. fairy tales.
   b. apprehension of crooks.
   c. false alarms.
   d. emotional response to property loss.

Electromechanical Detectors

ABOUT THIS CHAPTER

Perhaps the oldest forms of intruder sensor are electromechanical switches on doors and windows. In this chapter, we will investigate the types of switches available, their proper installation, and the circuits in which they are used. We will also look at the advantages and disadvantages of typical electromechanical detectors.

CLOSED-CIRCUIT SYSTEMS

The simplest type of electronic intrusion alarm consists of a closed circuit around the area to be protected. An intruder entering the area will, at least in theory, break the circuit and set off the alarm.

A transistor can be used as an electronic switch. Normally, a closed loop keeps the transistor biased off. Intrusion breaks the circuit, removing reverse bias, and allows the transistor to turn on.

A typical circuit for an alarm of this type is shown in *Figure 4-1*. Normally, the 1.5-V battery keeps transistor Q1 cut off so that there is negligible current in its collector circuit. Since the transistor is cut off, there is only a very small current, usually less than a milliampere, in the protective circuit. When the protective circuit is broken, the reverse bias from the 1.5-V battery is removed and the transistor is biased in the forward direction through resistor R1. This causes the transistor to conduct and the voltage at its collector to drop rapidly. Since the collector is connected to the negative side of the supply, its voltage actually becomes more positive. This positive-going signal is coupled through capacitor C1 to the gate of the SCR, causing it to fire. The resulting voltage drop across resistor R4 actuates the alarm. Once the SCR has fired, it will continue to conduct until the circuit is reset by momentarily interrupting the power supply.

A protection diode prevents foiling the alarm with external jumpers across the protection path.

This circuit cannot be foiled merely by placing a jumper across the protective circuit. Suppose, for example, that an intruder attempted to place a jumper between points A and B in the circuit, hoping to break the protective circuit without tripping the alarm. If this were done, current would flow through resistor R1 and diode D1 to ground. Diode D1 is a silicon diode that has a forward voltage drop of about 0.7 V. Transistor Q1, on the other hand, is a germanium transistor that has a base-to-1 emitter voltage of only about 0.2 V. Thus, the voltage drop across diode D1 would be great enough to turn on transistor Q1 and trip the alarm.

TYPICAL DETECTORS

The electromechanical detector is the oldest type of electronic intrusion detector, and its effectiveness depends on the type of detector that is used and how well it is applied to the particular problem.

**Figure 4-1.
Typical
Electromechanical
Intrusion Alarm**

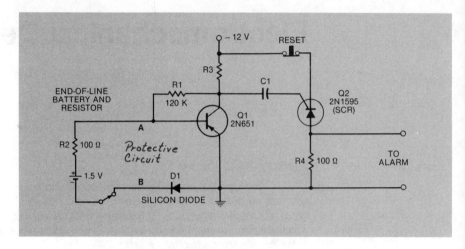

The most common detector is metallic foil taped to glass windows and doors.

The electromechanical detector most commonly seen is a metallic foil or tape applied to windows and doors in such a way that an intruder will break the foil when attempting an entry. The effectiveness of foil depends on how well it is installed and maintained. Unfortunately, in many instances, the foil is installed as shown in *Figure 4-2*. Here the points where the foil enters and leaves the window are obvious. A skilled burglar would realize that by connecting a jumper between points A and B, the window could be broken without disturbing the circuit. A skilled operator can usually cut a hole in the window large enough to permit installing the jumper. It takes only a little more time to install the foil as shown in *Figure 4-3*. Here, the actual configuration of the circuit is not at all obvious. Installing a jumper between two sections of the foil might actually trigger the alarm rather than frustrate it.

**Figure 4-2.
Poor Window Foil
Arrangement**

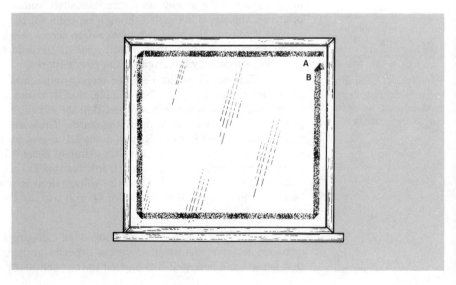

**Figure 4-3.
Proper Window Foil
Arrangement**

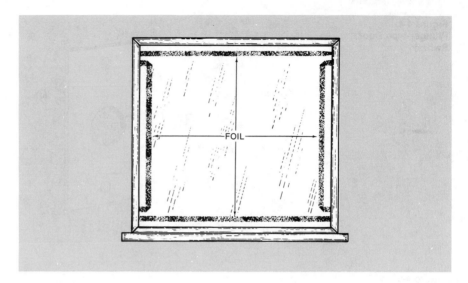

**Figure 4-3.
Proper Window Foil
Arrangement**

Problems with Foil Tape

The most common problem with foil or tape is that it is not properly maintained. The foil is subject to wear and abrasion from normal window washing, and after a while it will become ragged and break. Usually the break occurs at a most inconvenient hour and causes a false alarm.

For foil to be effective, it must be inspected frequently and any section that shows signs of wear must be replaced.

Connections to foil should be made through blocks designed for the purpose. If connections are made by soldering lead wires directly to the foil or by soldering the end of the foil to a wire, the connection will be unreliable and a potential source of false alarms.

DOOR AND WINDOW SWITCHES

Several very reliable door and window switches are available for use with electromechanical intrusion alarms. The U.S. Bureau of Standards has published standards governing such switches. Switches that meet these standards will prove to be reliable and not subject to changes in ambient conditions.

The plunger-type door switch, shown in *Figure 4-4*, is commonly used to initiate an alarm when a door is opened. To be effective, the switch must be installed so that it cannot be seen or tampered with. This is usually accomplished by mounting the switch on the jamb side of the door, as shown in *Figure 4-5*. Even with this arrangement it may be possible for an intruder who is aware of the location of the switch to slip a thin piece of steel between the door and the jamb in such a way as to keep the plunger depressed when the door is opened.

**Figure 4-4.
Plunger-type Door
Switch**

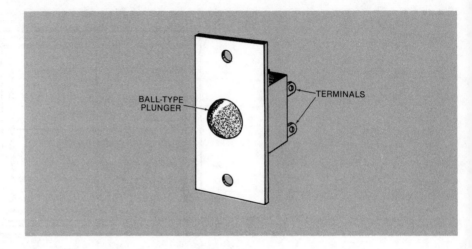

**Figure 4-5.
Plunger Switch
Mounted Behind Door**

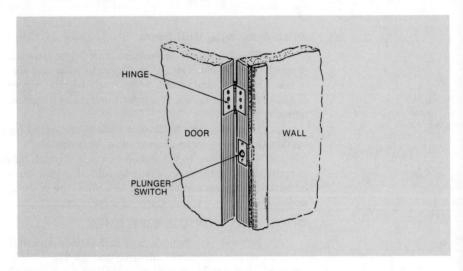

Magnetic switches are the most reliable sensors for protecting doors.

A more reliable door switch is the magnetic switch shown in *Figure 4-6.* Here a reed switch operated by a magnet is mounted on the door casing, and the operating magnet is mounted on the door. The usual arrangement is for the magnet to keep the switch closed while the door is closed. Then when the door is opened, the protective circuit will be opened and the alarm triggered.

**Figure 4-6.
Magnetic Door or
Window Switch**

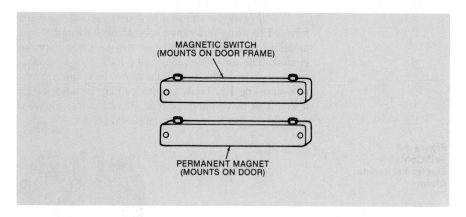

Many different types of magnetic door and window switches are available for various applications. The number of places where switches can be installed to detect tampering or intrusion is limited only by one's imagination. Switches can even be installed in cash registers so that when money is removed, the switch will be actuated.

Another frequently used switch is a pressure-sensitive floor mat that will open a switch if it is stepped on. This arrangement is often used to provide spot protection for sensitive objects such as file cabinets, safes, or jewelry cases. If an intruder steps on the mat, the alarm will be set off.

TILT AND VIBRATION SWITCHES

Vibration and tilt switches are often used to protect automobiles from thieves and vandals.

Switches are available that will open or close whenever they are tilted or vibrated. The vibration switch has a mass or weight suspended on a spring as shown in *Figure 4-7*. When the switch is at rest, the switch will be closed. When the switch is vibrated, the mass will move and momentarily open the switch and trigger the alarm. Vibration switches are frequently used to protect automobiles. The switch will open if the car is started or if it is jacked up so that a tire can be stolen.

**Figure 4-7.
Vibration-actuated
Switch**

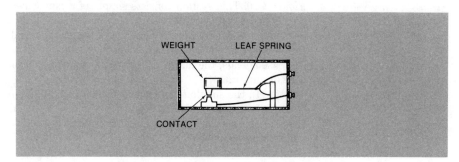

Mercury switches are often used to initiate an alarm when they are tilted. Thus, a mercury switch located inside a safe or cabinet will not be actuated if a door or drawer is opened in normal use, but will initiate an alarm if an attempt is made to carry it off.

Figure 4-8 shows a self-contained intrusion alarm that can be easily adapted to many different applications. The unit shown contains its own amplifier and alarm oscillator as well as a small speaker and triggering circuits. The connection diagram for the unit is shown in *Figure 4-9*. With the connections shown, the alarm can be triggered by either increasing R2 or decreasing R1. Thus, the device may be used to trigger either by closing a circuit or by opening a circuit. Its small size makes this unit particularly suitable for use in homes, camps, and offices.

**Figure 4-8.
Self-Contained
Electromechanical
Alarm**

**Figure 4-9.
Circuit of Alarm
Pictured in Figure 4-8**

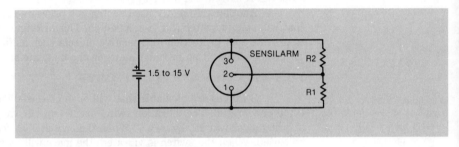

THE TAUT-WIRE INTRUSION ALARM

Taut-wire sensors stretched across the protected area trip a mechanical switch when tension increases or decreases.

Another form of electromechancial intrusion alarm is shown in *Figure 4-10*. This system consists simply of a taut wire strung around the area to be protected. The wire, which may be so small as to be nearly invisible, is connected mechanically to a snap-action switch in such a way that the switch will be thrown when the tension is either increased or decreased. Thus, the alarm will go off if an intruder brushes against the wire or cuts it.

In the simple form shown, the taut-wire system would be subject to many false alarms due to expansion and contraction of the wire. Commercial units are available that automatically compensate for temperature changes.

Figure 4-10.
Taut-Wire Alarm System

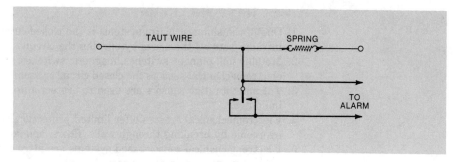

ADVANTAGES AND LIMITATIONS

Simple and low in cost, electromechanical sensors provide protection where more sophisticated sensors would be infeasible.

Because the electromechanical system lacks the glamor of some of the more sophisticated systems to be described later, its advantages are often overlooked. The principle of operation is simple, and the circuits have few components. This leads to a highly reliable system. If properly installed and maintained with redundant hidden switches, the system can provide good protection at low cost. The electromechanical system is an excellent backup system for a more sophisticated system. The fact that it can be seen and easily identified will tend to discourage amateur burglars and vandals. The skilled burglar, on the other hand, may manage to thwart the system and, feeling safe, walk right into a more advanced system that will alert the police.

Another advantage of this system is that it makes an excellent holdup alarm. In this use, during normal business hours, the regular protective circuit is disconnected. In its place is connected a loop containing switches that are hidden at various locations. If a holdup begins in the area, one of the employees may manage to trip one of the hidden switches.

An ingenious holdup switch that may be thrown by the person committing the holdup is sometimes used. This pressure switch is part of the weight that normally rests on the money in a cash drawer. Whenever the weight is lifted more than a normal amount, the switch will be thrown. Usually a holdup person is in a hurry and will throw the switch when taking money out of the drawer.

Electromechanical sensors are limited in that they cannot protect all areas of entrance.

The major limitation of the electromechanical intrusion detector is that it is usually not practical to protect all possible avenues of approach to the protected area. Even if all the doors and windows are protected, it is still possible for an intruder to enter through the walls, roof, or floor, if the expected reward is great enough. For this reason, the electromechanical system is rarely used when maximum security is required.

Another limitation of many systems of this type is that they are poorly installed, without imagination. The sensors are clearly visible, and with a little ingenuity they can be frustrated. Of course, this is a limitation of the particular installation and not of the principle itself.

WHAT HAVE WE LEARNED?

1. One of the simplest alarm systems is the closed-circuit alarm in which an intruder sets off the alarm by opening the circuit.
2. Metallic foil, plunger switches, magnetic switches, and taut wires are typical electromechanical sensors for closed-circuit systems.
3. Tilt and vibration sensors are used to protect automobiles and the roofs of buildings.
4. Electromechanical sensors offer limited protection because they can be overcome by breaking through walls, floors, and so forth.
5. Electromechanical sensor-based systems are attractive mostly because they offer some protection at low cost.

Quiz for Chapter 4

1. In a closed circuit protection system, an intruder will _____ the circuit and set off the alarm.
   a. complete
   b. close
   c. open
   d. turn off

2. Diode D1 in Figure 4-1 prevents defeating the alarm by:
   a. opening the circuit.
   b. avoiding the sensor.
   c. shorting the protection loop.
   d. destroying Q1.

3. The _____ detector is the oldest form of electrical intrusion detector.
   a. photoelectric
   b. electromechanical
   c. infrared
   d. plunger

4. A plunger switch is typically used to protect:
   a. windows.
   b. automobiles.
   c. attics.
   d. doors.

5. A "reed switch" is used on doors and windows and operates on:
   a. magnetism.
   b. electricity.
   c. light.
   d. vibration.

6. Tilt and vibration switches are typically used to protect:
   a. doors.
   b. automobiles.
   c. windows.
   d. internal areas.

7. Mercury switches are used as part of _____ sensors.
   a. tilt
   b. vibrations
   c. magnetic
   d. plunger

8. An advantage of electromechanical intrusion detectors is that they can protect all avenues of approach at low cost. True or false?

9. A _____ switch is used in cash drawer hold-up alarm systems.
   a. magnetic
   b. mercury
   c. plunger
   d. pressure

Photoelectric and Infrared Detectors

ABOUT THIS CHAPTER

Photoelectric detector devices have been around for more than six decades, and one of their first applications was in intruder alarms and store customer annunciator systems. In this chapter, you will learn the details of photoelectric systems for both the visible light and infrared regions.

BACKGROUND OF PHOTOELECTRIC SYSTEMS

The photoelectric intrusion detector represents one of the earliest applications of electronics to security. Early systems used visible light sources that focused a beam of light on a vacuum-tube photocell. The alarm was tripped when an intruder interrupted the light beam.

Older visible light systems could be either avoided, or they could be defeated with an ordinary flashlight.

These early systems were novel, but had many limitations. In the first place, the beam of light was usually visible. This provided the intruder with warning enough to avoid the beam by crawling under, or jumping over, it. Furthermore, many of the systems could be defeated by simply shining an ordinary flashlight into the photocell.

Because of these limitations, the photoelectric system was supplanted in many applications by other systems. Many refinements were made in the system, but it still wasn't extremely popular.

Modern technology has changed the situation considerably. Photoelectric systems that use infrared (IR), rather than visible, light are among the finest systems available. Much of this advance is due to developments in solid-state devices. Both light sources and detectors are now solid-state devices. The devices are efficient and sensitive. It is no longer necessary to use visible light in a photoelectric system, because infrared devices are available at a low cost.

THE LIGHT-EMITTING DIODE

An LED is a light source consisting of a forward-biased pn junction diode.

Figure 5-1 shows a sketch of a light-emitting diode, or LED, as it is commonly called. Technicians are familiar with one form of this device as a part of the readout of electronic instruments and calculators. The LED is essentially a pn diode that will emit light or infrared when it is biased in a forward direction.

LEDs can be made to emit infrared energy that is invisible to the human eye.

The state of the art is such that the wavelength of the emitted energy can be controlled closely, so it is possible to get an LED that will only emit energy over a restricted portion of the infrared part of the spectrum. This means that the emission from such a source will not be

Figure 5-1.
Light-emitting Diode

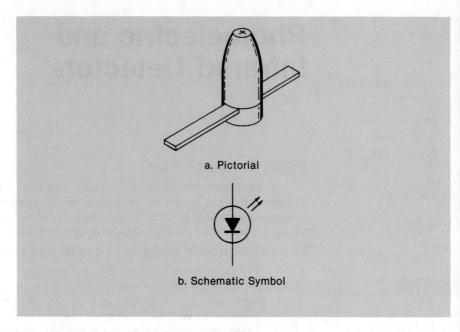

a. Pictorial

b. Schematic Symbol

visible to the human eye. This, in turn, makes it possible to build infrared alarm systems that are very easy to conceal as compared to the older systems that used visible light.

Light-emitting diodes are available that have focusing lenses built right into the case. These units can focus the infrared energy into a reasonably narrow beam.

THE PHOTOTRANSISTOR AND PHOTODIODE

Photodiodes and photo-transistors are used as sensors in modern systems. Other photodetectors exist but are rarely used in alarm systems.

The modern detector for an infrared alarm system is either a photodiode or a phototransistor. The photodiode is a back-biased diode that will conduct when it is exposed to infrared energy. Modern diodes are very sensitive and there is a drastic change in current when the device is exposed to infrared.

As shown in *Figure 5-2*, the phototransistor operates on a similar principle. Usually, there is no base connection to the device, and base current is caused by allowing light or infrared to fall on the base region.

Both photodiodes and phototransistors are available with built-in lenses that focus light or infrared on the sensitive area of the device.

There are other photodetectors available on the market, but these are only occasionally used in alarm systems. The photoresistor is a special ohmic resistance element that changes dc resistance when light hits it. The photovoltaic cell (or solar cell) generates a small dc voltage when illuminated. Although the photoresistor element finds some uses, photovoltaic cells have not been used for years.

**Figure 5-2.
Phototransistor (No
Base Connection)**

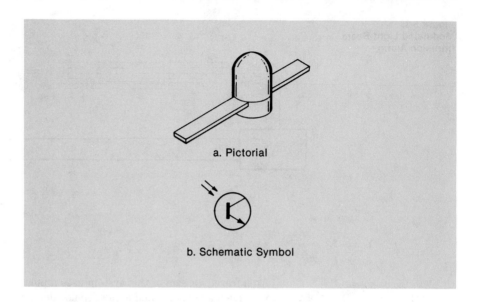

a. Pictorial

b. Schematic Symbol

PULSE AND MODULATED SYSTEMS

Simple photoelectric alarm systems can be foiled with a common flashlight. Even IR-based systems can be foiled this way.

One of the limitations of a simple photoelectric system is that it can be foiled by simply shining a flashlight into the photodetector. The system has no way of distinguishing between the light from the flashlight and that from the light beam of the system. Some infrared systems have enough sensitivity in the visible portion of the spectrum that they can be foiled in the same way.

By modulating the light beam with a low-frequency ac signal and applying the signal to a synchronous phase detector, we can prevent foiling of the alarm by any simple means.

Figure 5-3 shows the block diagram of a photoelectric system that cannot be foiled in this way. Here, the light source of the system is driven by a low-frequency oscillator so that the light beam will be modulated at the frequency of the oscillator. The oscillator also provides a reference signal for a phase detector circuit. The other side of the phase detector is connected to the photodetector. When the reference signal from the oscillator is in phase with the signal from the photodetector, the output of the phase detector circuit will be maximum. A resistance-capacitance (RC) phase-shifting circuit connected to the output of the photodetector compensates for the inevitable phase shifts in the system. If the light beam is interrupted, only the reference input of the phase detector will be excited, and the output will drop to zero, de-energizing the relay and setting off the alarm. Similarly, the alarm will be set off if a steady light, or even a modulated light that is not in phase, is applied to the photodetector. The frequency of the oscillator is usually quite low: 50 to 100 Hz. Multiples of the power line frequency are not used to prevent foiling the system with a light synchronized to the power line.

**Figure 5-3.
Modulated Light-Beam
Intrusion Alarm**

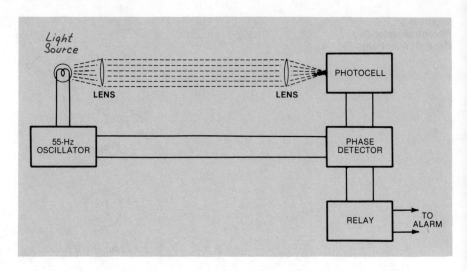

IR LEDs can be pulsed instead of ac modulated, resulting in the same protection and higher peak power.

An infrared version of this system uses a pulse generator instead of the low-frequency oscillator and a gated pulse detector instead of the phase detector. Otherwise the operation of the circuit is the same. It is very difficult to foil using an external source. The circuit has the added advantage that it is possible to get a much greater output from an LED if it is pulsed rather than being driven by a constant current.

The output of an LED is limited by its internal power dissipation. When used in a pulsed mode, it is possible to get high peak power without exceeding the average power rating of the device.

The LED power dissipation limits are based on average power, while detectors can be designed to respond to peak power. In a pulsed system, the average power is the product of the power in each pulse, the pulse width, and the number of pulses per second (i.e., the "pulse repetition rate" or PRR): $P_{av} = P_{peak} \times PRR$. The higher peak power is available because the LED is not turned on all the time. The percentage of each second that the LED is on is called the "duty cycle" of the LED.

Applications

Light beams travel in straight lines, so they are useful for entrance protection. Area protection is afforded by arranging a system of mirrors.

By its very nature, the light beam will travel only in a straight line. This makes it well suited for detecting entrance to an area where there is open space and nothing will normally interfere with the beam. Coverage of larger areas can be provided by an arrangement of mirrors to deflect the light beam as shown in *Figure 5-4*. With this arrangement, an intruder will be detected either when entering an area or when moving around.

Figure 5-4.
Light Beam Deflected
by Mirrors

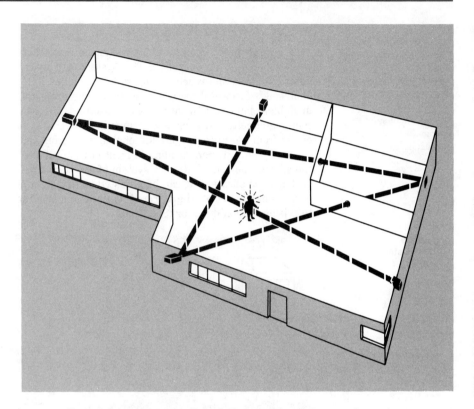

Some businesses use a light or infrared beam from an intrusion alarm as a customer annunciator. This system is especially useful in low-traffic small businesses where personnel who would normally wait on customers have other duties away from the sales counter.

Limitations

The principal limitations of the photoelectric system are:

1. It is difficult to apply to areas where there are no long, straight paths for the light beam. In such cases, many mirrors must be used and they will cause false alarms if they get out of alignment or become dirty.
2. It is possible (although difficult) for an intruder to enter a protected area without detection by using mirrors to deflect the beam.

PASSIVE OPTICAL DETECTORS

Slow changes in scene illumination can set off a false alarm. By using an RC coupling system, however, we can eliminate the effects of slow changes while retaining sensitivity to rapid changes in illumination.

Figure 5-5 shows a photoelectric detector that does not depend on a light source for its operation. This system actually measures the ambient light in an area and reacts to any sudden changes. In operation, the photocell is focused directly on the area to be protected. Very slow changes in ambient light have little effect because they are averaged out in the RC coupling circuit. However, any change in level that occurs more rapidly— either from the presence of additional light or from the decrease in light caused by an intruder standing in front of the protected object—will trip the alarm. The sensitivity of a system of this sort must be adjusted for the particular application. It can be adjusted so that lighting a single match in a dark room will set off the alarm. A variation on this theme is the modern television motion detector (See Chapter 9).

Figure 5-5.
Optical Detector
System

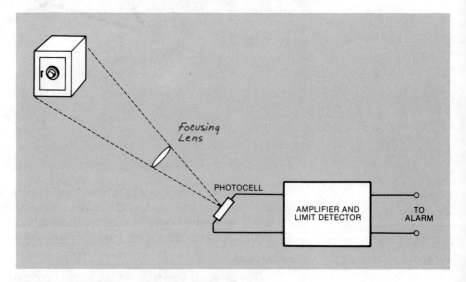

INFRARED BODY-HEAT DETECTORS

Infrared detectors can be made to detect the heat of human bodies, so they can be used as passive intrusion detectors.

The infrared body-heat detector is a variation of the optical detector. It is triggered by the heat from an intruder's body. The arrangement of the equipment is similar to the one shown in *Figure 5-5*, except that the detector responds to infrared radiation. The detector actually consists of several detectors arranged so that the device has a pattern of sensitivity, as shown in *Figure 5-6*. The detectors are adjusted so that they are most sensitive to radiation from a source having a temperature of 98.6°F, the normal temperature of the human body.

**Figure 5-6.
Sensitivity Pattern of
Infrared Body-Heat
Detector**

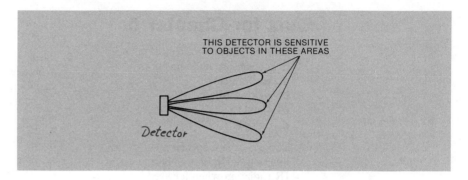

THIS DETECTOR IS SENSITIVE
TO OBJECTS IN THESE AREAS

Detector

If the temperature of the entire room should vary (up or down), the detector would not respond to the change. But if an object (such as an intruder) having a temperature approximately equal to body temperature were to pass through the pattern from a sensitive area to a non-sensitive area, the device would detect the difference in radiation and initiate an alarm.

Infrared body-heat detectors are quite sensitive and not as easy to foil as they might seem. Superficially, it would seem that an intruder completely covered with something like a sheet, would frustrate the alarm. Theoretically, this would work, but the sheet would have to be at the same temperature as the background temperature in the room, which would be hard to accomplish. The most effective way to frustrate an alarm of this type is for the intruder to move very slowly through the area.

WHAT HAVE WE LEARNED?

1. Modern photoelectric alarm systems use infrared (IR) rather than visible light.
2. The light-emitting diode (LED) is a common emitter for both visible and IR systems.
3. Available photoelectric sensors include photoresistors, photovoltaic cells, phototransistors, and photodiodes (with the latter two dominant).
4. Pulsed or low-frequency ac amplitude modulation of the IR beam counteracts simple countermeasures.
5. A simple light beam will protect an entranceway, while mirror systems can enable the system to protect larger areas.
6. Passive optical detectors monitor the average visible or IR illumination of the protected area and trigger the alarm if there is a substantial change in light level.

Quiz for Chapter 5

1. Modern photoelectric systems use _____ sensors and emitters.
   a. vacuum tube
   b. solid-state
   c. visible
   d. pulsed

2. The _____ is a special pn junction diode that emits light or IR radiation when forward biased.
   a. tunnel diode
   b. PIN diode
   c. LED
   d. Esaki diode

3. A phototransistor conducts current when light falls on the _____ region.
   a. output
   b. collector
   c. emitter
   d. base

4. AC modulated systems vary the light beam intensity at a _____ Hz rate.
   a. 40–50
   b. 10–50
   c. 40–100
   d. 100–200

5. An LED is operated in the pulsed mode. What is the average power dissipation if the LED has a pulse duration of 0.1 millisecond (0.0001 second), a peak power of 1 watt, and a pulse repetition rate (PRR) of 55 pps.
   a. 5.5 milliwatts (mW).
   b. 55 mW.

   c. 550 mW.
   d. 1000 mW.

6. Passive optical detectors overcome the effects of slow variation in scene illumination by averaging the signal output in a(n) _____ coupling circuit.
   a. RC
   b. RLC
   c. time-delay
   d. interfering

7. A certain type of passive optical detector uses IR sensors to detect:
   a. motion.
   b. body heat.
   c. IR beams.
   d. sound waves.

8. IR photoelectric systems are often _____ instead of ac modulated.
   a. shock excited
   b. gated
   c. monochromatic
   d. pulsed

9. _____ "light," used in modern alarm systems, is not visible to the human eye.
   a. Pulsed
   b. IR
   c. Ultraviolet
   d. Red

10. An advantage of _____ alarm systems is that they are easily concealed.
   a. visible light
   b. IR
   c. X-ray
   d. ultraviolet

Ultrasonic Intrusion Detectors

ABOUT THIS CHAPTER

One of the most successful intrusion alarms is the ultrasonic Doppler system. Acting something like an acoustical radar, the ultrasonic system provides area protection against moving intruders. In this chapter, you will learn the principles behind the ultrasonic intrusion system.

WHAT ARE ULTRASONIC WAVES?

The ultrasonic detector uses a beam of ultrasonic energy to detect the presence of an intruder. Ultrasonic energy is merely sound waves that have a frequency too high to be detected by the human ear—usually in the range of 20 to 50 kilohertz (kHz). Since ultrasonic energy cannot be heard, seen, or felt, the system has the obvious advantage of not being easily detected.

RADIO OR SOUND WAVES?

It is important to distinguish between radio waves and ultrasonic waves in the same frequency range. Some older texts refer to frequencies above 20 kHz as "radio frequencies," so we might assume that all 20 kHz- and-up signals are radio waves. This is not accurate. A radio wave is an electromagnetic wave consisting of alternating electric and magnetic fields. An ultrasonic wave, on the other hand, is an acoustical pressure wave in a transmission medium such as air, water, and so forth. In some medical applications, ultrasonic waves up to 10 megahertz (MHz) are used, even though many people automatically assume that any 10-MHz wave is a radio signal. If an ac oscillator produces a signal at, say, 50 kHz and feeds it to an antenna, then the result is an electromagnetic radio wave. But if that same 50-kHz ac oscillator is connected to an electromechanical ultrasonic transducer, then it will produce an ultrasonic wave. The difference is the energy conversion device: antenna or transducer. In Chapter 7, we will discuss alarm systems based on electromagnetic radio waves.

PRINCIPLE OF OPERATION

Direct and reflected ultrasonic waves combine at the receiver to either reinforce or cancel each other. An intruder affects the reflected wave and changes that relationship.

Figure 6-1 shows an ultrasonic detector unit, and *Figure 6-2* illustrates a typical installation to protect a small room. Ultrasonic waves from the transmitter reach all parts of the room and are reflected many times before arriving at the receiver. Most of the energy reaching the receiver comes directly from the transmitter, but a small portion of the reflected energy also reaches the receiver. The direct and reflected waves combine in the receiver and tend to either reinforce or cancel each other, depending on their phase relationship.

Figure 6-1.
Typical Ultrasonic
Intrusion Detector

Figure 6-2.
Ultrasonic Intrusion
Alarm

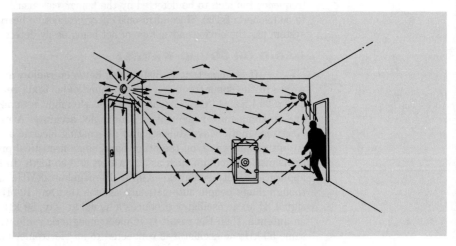

As long as nothing moves in the protected area, the signal at the receiver will be constant. If an intruder moves about in the protected room, the reflected signal will change in both amplitude and phase. This change in the reflected signal results in amplitude modulation of the signal at the receiver. This modulation is detected, and the alarm is initiated.

ULTRASONIC WAVES

The direct and reflected waves combine in the room to set up a "standing wave" of ultrasonic energy. The generation of the standing wave can easily be understood by comparing it to the generation of waves of motion along a rope. Suppose that the far end of a rope is not attached to anything and the rope is given a shake at the near end. A single wave of

A "standing wave" is created from the algebraic sum of direct and reflected waves.

motion will travel along the rope as shown in *Figure 6-3a*. If the shaking is continued rhythmically, a continuous traveling wave will be sent down the rope, as in *Figure 6-3b*. Suppose that the far end of the rope is securely fastened, as in *Figure 6-3c*, and it is given a single shake. As shown in *Figure 6-3c*, the single wave will now travel down the rope to the end, be reflected, and travel back to the starting end.

If the rope is shaken rhythmically, its motion will be the sum of the motion due to the direct wave and the motion due to the reflected wave. Since the two waves travel at the same speed, one going toward the far end and one coming back, the net result is that the waves do not move at all. There is a standing wave on the rope. The rope vibrates between nodes which do not move at all, as shown in *Figure 6-3d*.

The standing wave consists of nodes and antinodes. Ultrasonic waves combine in this way within a protected area.

At every point along the rope, the actual displacement is due to the combined effects of the direct and the reflected waves. The actual displacement at any point can be found by algebraically adding the displacement due to the direct wave alone and the displacement due to the reflected wave alone. The nodes occur when the algebraic sum of the two waves is zero. Ultrasonic direct and reflected waves combine in the same way to provide standing waves in a room.

Standing Wave Length

The length of the standing waves depends on the wavelength, and hence, on the frequency of the ultrasonic energy used in a particular installation. Since the velocity of sound in air is approximately 1040 feet per second, or 12,480 inches per second, we can compute the wavelength from the frequency, using the following formula.

$$\lambda = \frac{V_s}{f_s}$$

where,

λ is the wavelength of sound in inches,
V_s is the velocity of sound in inches per second,
f_s is the frequency of sound in hertz.

Since the standing waves are produced by the interaction of the direct and reflected waves, they will have a wavelength one-half that given by the preceding equation. Thus, if an ultrasonic signal has a frequency of 30 kHz, its wavelength will be

$$\frac{12,480}{30,000} = 0.416 \text{ inch}$$

and it will set up standing waves having a wavelength of one-half this value, or 0.208 inch.

**Figure 6-3.
Wave Motions**

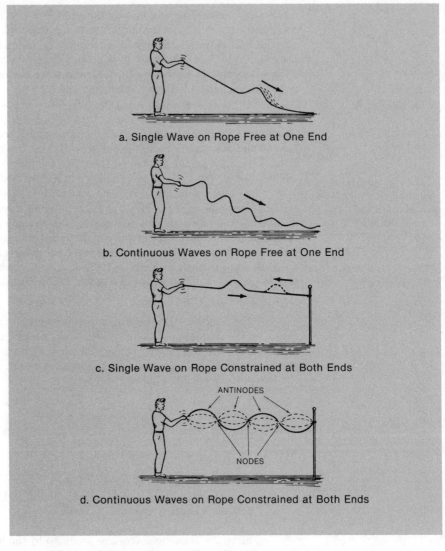

a. Single Wave on Rope Free at One End

b. Continuous Waves on Rope Free at One End

c. Single Wave on Rope Constrained at Both Ends

ANTINODES

NODES

d. Continuous Waves on Rope Constrained at Both Ends

Figure 6-4 shows the wavelength in inches versus the frequency of an ultrasonic wave.

**Figure 6-4.
Wavelength Versus
Frequency**

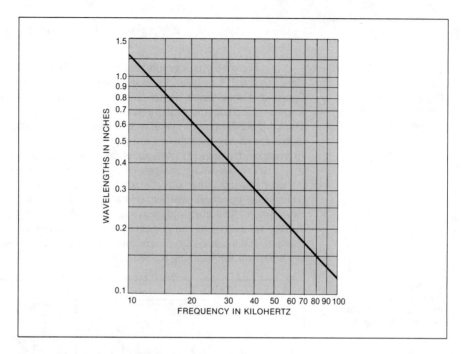

EFFECT OF MOTION IN THE ROOM

The effect of motion in the room is the same as moving the standing waves toward or away from the receiver. For example, if a frequency of 30 kHz is used, the pressure peaks are separated by 0.2 inch. Thus, if a reflecting surface moves toward the receiver at a rate of 0.2 inch per second, the signal at the receiver will appear to be modulated at a frequency of 1 Hz.

The ultrasonic alarm must be sensitive enough to detect small motions in the protected area but not be affected by changes caused by air current. The frequency of the "intrusion signal" generated by motion in the room can be calculated by the following formula.

$$f_i = 2\frac{V_i}{\lambda}$$

where,

f_i is the frequency of the intrusion signal in hertz,
V_i is the velocity of the intruder in inches per second,
λ is the wavelength of the system signal in inches.

Thus, if a system uses a frequency of 30 kHz (wavelength = 0.416 inch), an intruder moving at a rate of 20 inches per second will produce an intrusion signal having the following frequency.

$$2 \; \frac{20}{0.416} = 100 \text{ Hz, approximately}$$

The intrusion signal frequency is a function of the system frequency and the intruder's speed of passage through the protected area.

Figure 6-5 is a graph that gives the frequency of the intrusion signal that will be caused by various speeds of intruder motion. From this figure, it is seen that a higher-frequency system will produce higher-frequency intrusion signals for the same rate of motion of the intruder. Thus, higher-frequency systems are more sensitive, but, on the other hand, higher-frequency transducers are usually more expensive and less sensitive. In practice, frequencies from about 20 to 50 kHz are commonly used.

The preceding analysis of the intrusion signal is based on the intruder moving either directly toward or directly away from the transducer. In actual practice, this analysis is very close to what is actually experienced. The ultrasonic wave is reflected so many times from one surface to another in the protected area that motion in any direction will cause an intrusion signal. Therefore, the curves of of *Figures 6-4* and *6-5* are adequate for planning an actual system.

**Figure 6-5.
Relationship of Motion
of Intruder to Frequency
of Intrusion Signal**

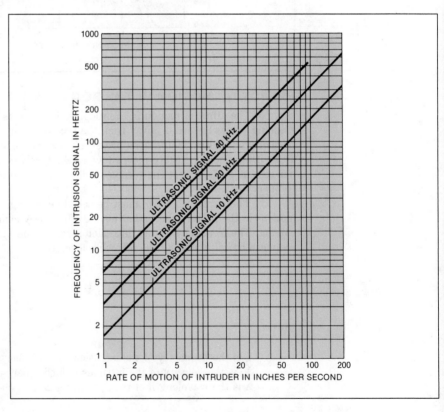

EFFECTIVENESS OF THE SYSTEM

The effectiveness of an ultrasonic system depends on the energy being reflected many times in the protected area so that standing waves will be set up everywhere in the room. Hard surfaces, such as walls, desks, and file cabinets, are good reflectors of sound. Soft materials, such as carpets, draperies, and clothing, are not good reflectors of sound. Therefore, a small area with hard walls and reflecting surfaces will require fewer transducers than an office with wall-to-wall carpeting and many draperies. An area that is completely filled with soft material would probably be better protected by some other type of system.

TRANSDUCERS

An ultrasonic transducer is much like either an audio loudspeaker or a microphone, except that it operates at much higher frequencies.

For a 20- to 50-kHz electrical signal to be converted into an ultrasonic acoustical pressure wave it must be passed through a device called a transducer. Two types of transducer are commonly used in ultrasonic systems: crystal and dynamic. The crystal type uses a vibrating piezoelectric resonator, while the dynamic uses a coil electromagnet/diaphragm system something like a loudspeaker or dynamic microphone. Since the function of the transmitting transducer is exactly the same as that of a speaker in a radio, it might appear that an ordinary speaker might be used as a transducer. Unfortunately, most speakers do not perform well at ultrasonic frequencies, so special transducers made for the purpose are used. These transducers work on the same principle as radio speakers, but they have small, stiff diaphragms so that they will operate well at ultrasonic frequencies. They more closely resemble a microphone in construction than a speaker. In fact, an ordinary crystal microphone cartridge may be used for a transducer in a home-constructed system.

The receiving transducer has the opposite function: it must convert sound pressure waves into electrical signals. Its function is the same as that of a microphone in a sound system. In actual practice, identical transducers are often used for both transmitting and receiving.

Just as regular sound microphones are made to have different direction patterns, ultrasonic transducers are available with different patterns. Highly directional units are available for use in long, narrow areas such as corridors. Omnidirectional units are used to protect rectangular areas. A typical ultrasonic transducer with cover is shown in *Figure 6-6.*

Figure 6-6.
Typical Ultrasonic
Transducer

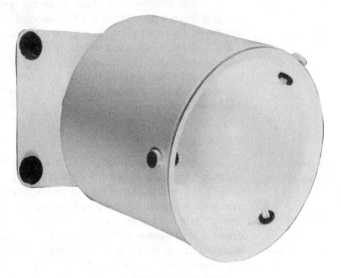

GENERATING ULTRASONIC ENERGY

The transmitter of an ultrasonic intrusion alarm is very simple, consisting merely of an oscillator operating at the desired frequency and a transducer. In modern systems, the oscillator is usually a small solid-state unit that can be mounted inside the transducer case. A typical oscillator circuit is shown in *Figure 6-7*. This is a simple emitter-coupled oscillator. The frequency is determined by the values of L and C in the circuit. Usually, the inductance is variable so that the frequency can be set at the desired value. Alternatively, RC networks or piezoelectric crystal resonators are also used to set the operating frequency.

Since the transmitter portion of the system is so simple, it is often mounted together with its transducer in the same case as the receiver. The unit in *Figure 6-1* uses this type of construction.

**Figure 6-7.
Ultrasonic Oscillator
Circuit**

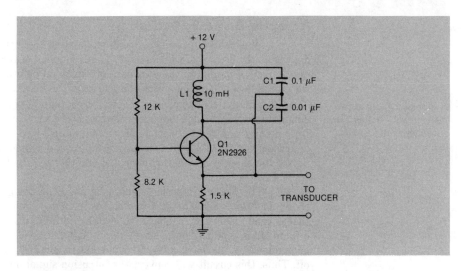

RECEIVER

An ultrasonic receiver typically consists of a transducer, tuned circuit, amplifiers, a detector, and an alarm trigger circuit.

Figure 6-8 shows a block diagram of a typical receiver. The first element is the transducer, which converts the ultrasonic energy to an electrical signal at the ultrasonic frequency. The input circuit is usually tuned to the frequency of the transmitter so that it will pass only frequencies close to the frequency of operation. This limiting of the bandwidth of the system is very effective in minimizing false alarms which might otherwise be caused by extraneous sounds.

**Figure 6-8.
Block Diagram of
Ultrasonic Receiver**

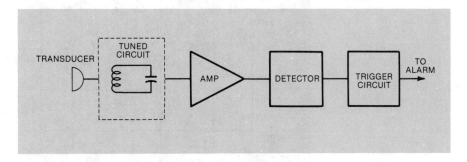

The signal is then amplified and applied to a detector. A gain control on the amplifier sets the sensitivity of the system. It should be remembered that at this point in the circuit the signal is a high-frequency audio voltage. If nothing is moving in the protected area, the amplitude of this signal will be constant, so there will be no output from the detector. When an intruder moves in the protected area, the ultrasonic signal is modulated by the low-frequency signal. Since this intrusion signal modulates the ultrasonic signal, the amplifier does not have to pass the low-frequency signal any more than the rf stages of a radio have to pass the audio signals.

Receiver Detector Output

When the ultrasonic signal is modulated, the intrusion signal will appear at the output of the detector. The frequency of this signal depends on the rate of motion of the intruder, as explained before. The amplitude of the signal depends on the obstructing area of the intruder.

The detector is usually followed by a high-pass filter that will eliminate very-low-frequency intrusion signals. This prevents the system from being triggered by normal air currents in the protected area. The adjustment of this filter is a compromise between a condition that will detect the slowest moving intruder and one that will be triggered by air currents.

The filtered intrusion signal is applied to a trigger circuit like that shown in *Figure 6-9*. The first two stages form a Schmitt trigger circuit that is really a sort of regenerative switch. Initially, transistor Q1 is shut off and Q2 is conducting. When the input signal exceeds a certain level, determined by the setting R1, Q1 will start to conduct and Q2 will be shut off. Thus, this circuit will convert the intrusion signal into a square wave-signal whenever it exceeds the threshold level set by R1. Below this signal level, there is no output. The output of the Schmitt trigger drives Q3, which drives the relay, which in turn actuates the alarm.

A high-pass filter in the receiver will eliminate false alarms due to normal air currents in the protected area, but only at the risk of failing to detect a slowly moving intruder.

**Figure 6-9.
Trigger Circuit for
Intrusion Alarm**

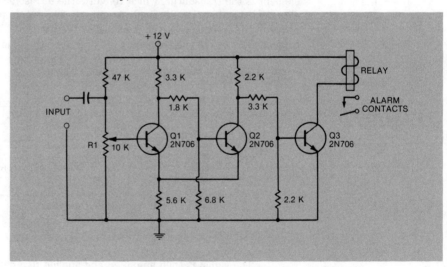

It is quite common to include a time delay in the circuit so that the alarm will not go off until the intrusion signal has been present for ten seconds, or even longer. This arrangement eliminates false alarms that might be caused by radio-frequency interference, curtains occasionally moving in the breeze, and transients on the power line.

Since the magnitude of the intrusion signal depends on the area of the intruder, the system can be adjusted so that it will set off the alarm if even a small person moves very slowly in the area, but will not be affected by the motion of insects, mice, and so on.

A time-delay circuit prevents false alarms from transient events such as rf interference, breezes, and so on.

APPLICATION ENGINEERING

The effectiveness of an ultrasonic intrusion alarm system depends very greatly on how well the particular application is engineered. The system must be made as foolproof as possible and yet produce a minimum number of false alarms. This is not an easy task. In general, the more sensitive a system is, the more likely it is to be triggered by some extraneous condition.

Optimization

The most important design feature of an ultrasonic system is the location of the transmit and receive transducers.

The first consideration in an installation is selection of an optimum location for the transducers. When the area to be protected is small, fairly open, and rectangular in shape, the problem is relatively easy to solve. The transducers should not be pointed directly at anything that might move or that has moving parts, such as electric fans. They should not be pointed directly through areas where air convection currents are apt to be strong, such as in front of air conditioners or over radiators. Otherwise, such an installation is straightforward.

Where the area to be protected is broken up by desks, cabinets, and other furniture, selecting a transducer location is often difficult. Even locations that appear to be adequate for complete coverage may leave large "blind" areas that are not sufficiently covered by the ultrasonic energy. The usual procedure in such a case is to select what appears to be the best location for the transducers and then test the system by walking through the protected area slowly. Another important part of the test is to determine if anything that normally moves or produces sound will trigger the circuit and cause a false alarm. Of course, it does not matter if something that should not be operated after the place is closed causes an alarm. If fact, this provides a measure of additional protection. For example, in an installation in a cocktail lounge, the cash register apparently produced some ultrasonic energy when it was operated. As a result, the alarm was triggered whenever the cash register was operated. This was no problem because the cash register should not have been opened after the place was closed. On the other hand, in another installation, a valve on a steam radiator generated ultrasonic energy at all times. This was the source of many annoying false alarms until the transducers were relocated.

Spurious Triggering

Spurious triggering of ultrasonic devices has resulted in some amusing and not-so-amusing events. For example, rattling a ring of keys can change the TV channel on ultrasonically based TV remote control systems. Bird calls have been known to unlock ultrasonic remote door locks. In one installation, service technicians were perplexed by a garage door that raised and lowered on its own, regardless of whether the owner's remote-equipped car was nearby. It was discovered that a neighbor was training dogs using a silent (ultrasonic) whistle, and the whistle was on a pitch close to the ultrasonic frequency used by the garage door receiver. A light adjustment of the tunable inductors in the transmitter and receiver moved the system frequency off the dog whistle frequency. Presumably, such diverse sources of interference also adversely affect intrusion alarms and should be suspect in the event of a series of inexplicable failures or false alarms in an otherwise healthy system.

Finding a Good Location

There are a few general considerations that will help in finding the best location for transducers.

1. Use a transducer with the proper pattern. If there are many normally moving objects in the area, it is best to use a directional transducer.
2. In small areas, mount the transducers near the corners of the area, preferably on the ceiling.
3. Mount the transducers on a surface that is free from vibration.
4. If the ceilings are more than 12 feet high, mount the transducers on the walls. Avoid walls that can be drilled through from the outside.
5. Keep the transducers at least 10 feet from objects that can emit high-pitched sounds, such as telephone bells, radiator valves, and steam pipes.
6. Locate transducers as far as possible from moving objects, such as drapes, curtains, fans, and machinery.

After the transducers have been placed in the optimum location, the system must be adjusted "tuned-up." This consists of adjusting the sensitivity controls to get optimum performance. Many systems also have time-delay controls and low-frequency response adjustments. These must be carefully adjusted in accordance with the manufacturer's instructions.

The final evaluation of the system is the "walk-through" test. After the system is installed and adjusted, the technician should try to fool it every way possible.

ADVANTAGES AND LIMITATIONS

The ultrasonic system has many advantages over the systems described in previous chapters. One of its big advantages is that it is not easy to identify. This makes it difficult for a burglar to attempt to foil it. Unlike the perimeter protection systems, it will spot the "stay-behind" the minute movement occurs in the area.

High-pitched sounds can create ultrasonic energy that may fool the alarm system. Large amounts of sound-absorbing material in the protected area limit the usefulness of the ultrasonic system.

There are certain limitations to the ultrasonic system. It is not suitable for use in areas that contain equipment that makes high-pitched noises. Since it is operated by ultrasonic energy, it can be jammed or triggered by ultrasonic energy. Because the system depends on reflection for its operation, it is hard to adapt to areas that contain large amounts of sound-absorbing material. For this same reason, it is not suitable for protection of completely open areas such as storage yards.

Many of the limitations and disadvantages that have been experienced in actual ultrasonic system installations arise because the application has not been properly engineered. In all but the simplest applications, it is not advisable simply to buy a system and put it in. Careful planning and engineering are needed to ensure an effective system.

WHAT HAVE WE LEARNED?

1. Ultrasonic signals are acoustical pressure waves at frequencies higher than the range of human hearing.
2. When ultrasonic waves are emitted into a room, at any given point the wave will consist of direct and reflected components.
3. Ultrasonic transducers are like microphones and loudspeakers, but have thin, stiff diaphragms to accommodate the high frequencies.
4. Limiting bandwidth of the receiver minimizes the false alarm rate.
5. A room with hard, highly reflective surfaces is easier to protect with ultrasonics than a room with many soft, absorbent surfaces.

Quiz for Chapter 6

1. Ultrasonic frequencies used in alarm systems are typically in the range of:
   a. less than 20 kHz.
   b. 100–1000 kHz.
   c. 1–10 MHz.
   d. 20–50 kHz.

2. Motion in the protected area disturbs both the amplitude and phase of the _____ signal.
   a. incident
   b. reflected
   c. standing
   d. nodal

3. Direct and reflected waves tend to either add or cancel each other depending upon their _____ relationship.
   a. standing wave
   b. frequency
   c. phase
   d. impedance

4. What is the wavelength in inches of a 50-kHz signal.
   a. 0.416 inch.
   b. 0.105 inch.
   c. 0.25 inch.
   d. 1.2 inches.

5. Two types of transducer are dynamic and:
   a. static.
   b. mechanical.
   c. crystal.
   d. moving coil.

6. The receiver input circuitry is tuned to the _____ frequency.
   a. intermediate
   b. Doppler
   c. reflected
   d. transmitter

7. The receiver detector is usually equipped with a _____ to eliminate false alarms due to air currents.
   a. high-pass filter
   b. low-pass filter
   c. notch filter
   d. bandpass filter

8. A _____ circuit is often included to prevent false alarms caused by rf interference, curtains moving in the breeze, or power line transients.
   a. filter
   b. canceller
   c. rejector
   d. time delay

9. Fans, air conditioners, and curtains can easily cause:
   a. false alarms.
   b. failure to detect.
   c. oscillations in the system.
   d. component failure.

10. _____ noises can cause false alarms.
    a. Low-frequency
    b. High-pitched
    c. Loud
    d. Soft

Microwave Intrusion Detectors

ABOUT THIS CHAPTER

Microwave radio waves can be used in a simple type of "Doppler radar" to form an intrusion detector. In this chapter, you will learn the basic principles of microwave energy generation and examine the use of microwave waves in an intrusion alarm system.

INTRODUCTION TO MICROWAVE SYSTEMS

Microwave intrusion detectors are a form of Doppler radar.

The microwave intrusion detector shown in *Figure 7-1* operates similarly to the ultrasonic intrusion detector described in the previous chapter. One principal difference is that the ultrasonic system utilizes sound pressure waves in air, whereas the microwave system uses very short radio waves. The microwave system is often called a radar alarm because it is actually a form of Doppler radar.

**Figure 7-1.
Microwave Intrusion
Detector**

PRINCIPLE OF OPERATION

The principle of operation of the microwave intrusion detector is exactly the same principle by which a moving airplane causes the picture on a television receiver to flutter on the screen. As shown in *Figure 7-2*, the signal from a television broadcasting station reaches a particular receiver through different paths. One is a direct path from the transmitter. In the other path, the signal is reflected from the plane before reaching the receiver. The received signal is the algebraic sum of the signals from the two paths. If the plane were not moving, the signal strength at the receiver would be constant. When the plane moves, however, the phase of the reflected signal changes with respect to that of the direct signal. It alternately reinforces and cancels the direct signal. The result is that the received signal is amplitude modulated at a frequency that depends on the speed and direction of the motion of the plane, causing the flutter of the picture on the receiver.

**Figure 7-2.
Microwave Intrusion
Detector Principle**

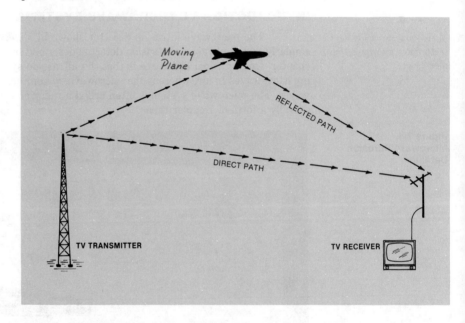

A typical system consists of transmit and receive antennas. Direct and reflected signals from the transmitter combine at the receiver to set up a system of standing waves.

In a typical microwave intrusion detector, microwave energy from the transmitter fills the protected area and sets up standing waves in much the same way as in the ultrasonic system. Two separate signals arrive at the receiver. One is a direct signal from the transmitter. This is received either by radiation from the transmitter or often by direct connection. The other signal is the complex signal reflected from many different surfaces in the protected area. As long as nothing moves that will reflect a signal, the signal strength at the receiver is constant and is the algebraic sum of the direct and reflected signals. An intruder entering the area upsets the standing wave pattern and causes the amplitude and phase of the received signal to vary at a rate that depends on the speed of motion. This has the effect of amplitude modulating the received signal by a low-frequency intrusion signal.

FREQUENCIES USED

The wavelength of a microwave signal depends on the speed of propagation of radio waves and the frequency of the signal. The wavelength is given by the following formula.

$$\lambda = \frac{300}{f}$$

where,

λ is the wavelength in meters,
f is the frequency in megahertz.

Use the following formula to find wavelength in inches.

$$\lambda = \frac{11,811}{f}$$

where,

λ is the wavelength in inches,
f is the frequency in megahertz.

Example 7-1

Calculate the wavelength in inches of a signal that has a frequency of 9000 MHz.

Solution

$$\lambda = \frac{11,811}{f}$$

$$\lambda = \frac{11,811}{9000}$$

$$\lambda = 1.31 \text{ inches}$$

Various commercial microwave intrusion detectors operate anywhere from 400 to 25,000 MHz. *Figure 7-3* gives the wavelength of microwave signals in inches for various frequencies. From this figure, we see that a signal of 10,000 MHz will have a wavelength of 1.2 inches.

Figure 7-3.
Frequency Versus
Wavelength of
Microwave Signals

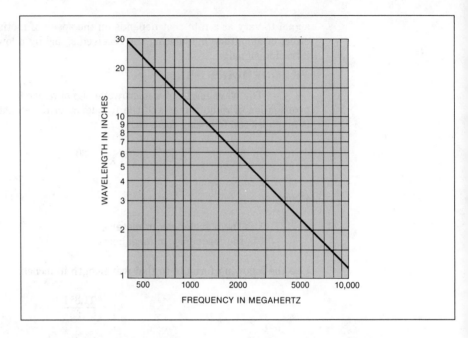

The frequency of the Doppler intrusion signal depends on the rate of motion of the intruder and the frequency operation of the system. The frequency is given by:

$$f_i = \frac{2f_s \times S_i}{11,811}$$

where,

f_i is the frequency of the intrusion signal in hertz,
f_s is the frequency of operation of the system in megahertz,
s_i is the rate of motion of the intruder in inches per second.

Example 7-2

Calculate the Doppler intrusion frequency in hertz if an intruder moves through a 9000-MHz field at 6 inches per second.

$$f_i = \frac{2F_s S_i}{11,811}$$

Solution

$$f_i = \frac{(2)(9000 \text{ MHz})(6 \text{ in/sec})}{11,811}$$

$$f_i = \frac{108,000}{11,811}$$

$$f_i = 9.15 \text{ Hz}$$

The factor of 2 is needed in the foregoing equation because the wavelength of the standing wave is one-half that of the system signal.

The intrusion frequency is directly proportional to the system transmit frequency and the intruder's speed of motion.

Thus, in a 10,000-MHz system, an intruder moving at a rate of 5 inches per second will generate an intrusion signal of 8.46 Hz. *Figure 7-4* gives the frequency of the intrusion signal for various rates of intruder motion in a 10,000-MHz system. Since the frequency of the intrusion signal is directly proportional to the system frequency, if the system frequency were cut in half, the frequency of the intrusion signal would also be cut in half. Thus, higher-frequency systems tend to be more sensitive to slower rates of intruder motion.

**Figure 7-4.
Intrusion Signal
Frequency Versus
Speed of Intruder
Movement**

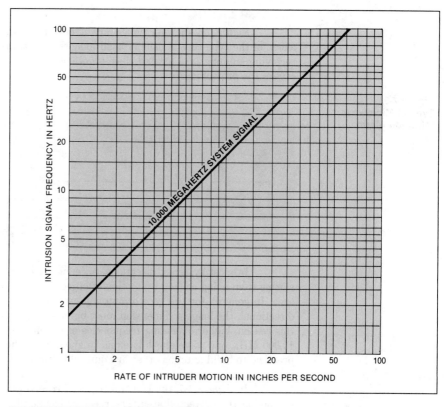

PROPERTIES OF MICROWAVES

Radio waves reflect easily from metallic surfaces, but they pass through non-metallic surfaces.

Although the principle of operation of the microwave system is somewhat similar to that of the ultrasonic system, the two systems differ in many important respects. The ultrasonic system uses sound waves in air. These waves are actually air-pressure waves. In general, they are reflected by hard surfaces and are absorbed by soft surfaces. Microwaves are actually high-frequency radio waves. They are reflected well by metal surfaces, but most interior building materials such as wood, glass, and wallboard are almost transparent to microwaves. The signal will go right through them. This is both an advantage and a limitation. As an advantage, it permits protecting several rooms or offices with one system—something that could not be done with an ultrasonic system. As a limitation, it is sometimes difficult to contain the microwave signal in the protected area. Since the signals will pass through glass easily, the signals may be reflected by a moving automobile outside, causing a false alarm. We will look at this again later in the chapter, under application engineering.

Since microwaves are radio waves, they are usually not affected by air currents such as would be produced by heaters or air conditioners. Of course, the microwave system is not affected at all by extraneous noises which could easily occur in the protected area.

SYSTEM LAYOUT

Figure 7-5 shows a typical arrangement of a microwave intrusion alarm of the type that is usually used indoors. The transmitting and receiving antennas are located close together and the microwave beam covers the protected area.

**Figure 7-5.
Typical Microwave
Intrusion Alarm**

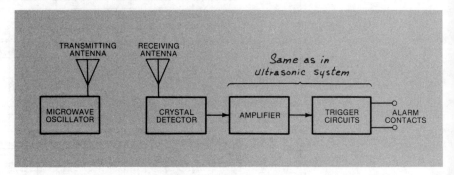

In most systems, directional antennas are used to prevent false alarms from being caused by motion of objects outside of the protected area. In general, for the type of antenna used in these systems to be directional, the longest dimension must be longer than one wavelength. For this reason, higher operating frequencies are preferred. At a frequency of 10,000 MHz, one wavelength is equal to about 1.2 inches. Therefore, it is practical to build antennas that are quite directional but only a few inches in diameter.

In *Figure 7-5*, the transmitting and receiving antennas are both beamed at the protected area. The receiver has an identical antenna pointed in the same direction as the transmitting antenna, so it picks up any microwave reflections from objects in the area. A small portion of the signal from the transmitter reaches the receiver antenna directly in most installations. In some cases, the signal is fed directly to the receiver through a small coaxial cable.

As long as nothing is moving in the protected area, the rf signal at the receiver antenna is constant. An intruder moving through the protected area will change both the amplitude and phase of the reflected signal. This causes the signal at the receiver to be amplitude modulated by the intrusion signal.

The output of the receiver crystal detector is a low-frequency version of the intrusion heterodyne signal.

In most microwave systems, the first stage of the receiver is a crystal detector that demodulates the signal so that its output is the low-frequency intrusion signal. The intrusion signal is amplified and applied to a trigger circuit in much the same way as it is in the ultrasonic system. Filters are sometimes used to filter out all signals except those that would be caused by human-like movements. Time-delay relays are usually provided so that the intrusion signal will have to persist for a few seconds before the alarm is set off. A gain control is provided in one of the amplifiers of some systems to permit setting the sensitivity of the complete system.

Use of Single Antenna

A directional coupler allows both receiver and transmitter to use the same antenna.

Some microwave systems are quite similar to the one just described except that they use the same antenna for transmitting and receiving. This arrangement is usually more convenient to install because it is not necessary to carefully align two separate antennas. The principle of operation is shown in *Figure 7-6.* The signal from the oscillator passes to the antenna through a directional coupler, which is also connected to the input of the receiver. A directional coupler is a microwave device that can distinguish between signals that are traveling in different directions. Very little of the signal traveling from the oscillator to the antenna is coupled to the receiver. On the other hand, a comparatively large amount of the reflected signal that is traveling in the opposite direction is coupled to the receiver. This system is otherwise the same as that shown in *Figure 7-5.*

**Figure 7-6.
Single Antenna for
Transmitting and
Receiving**

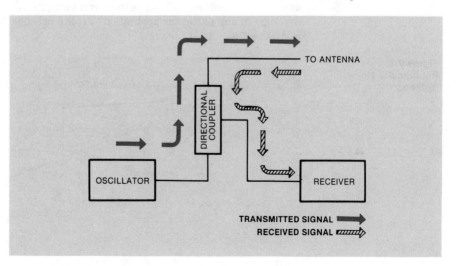

Bistatic Systems

A bistatic system has receiver and transmitter antennas located at different points in the protected area.

It is not necessary for the transmitting and receiving antennas to be located at the same point. Often in outdoor systems they are separated by some distance. As shown in *Figure 7-7*, the transmitting and receiving antennas can be located some distance apart to get appreciably greater range. The beam from the transmitter reaches the receiver through reflection from objects in the protected area. A system of this type can be arranged to trip not only on Doppler signals, but also whenever the microwave beam between the transmitter and receiver is interrupted.

**Figure 7-7.
Bistatic System**

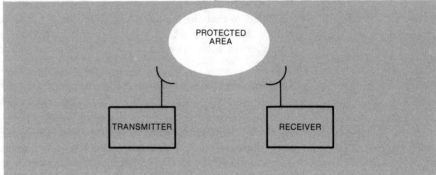

Antennas

Microwave intrusion detectors use horn and parabolic reflector antennas. Horns are preferred because of low sidelobes.

Most microwave alarms use either a horn antenna of the type shown in *Figure 7-8* or a parabolic reflector of the type used in microwave communication links. The horn is popular because it has very low sidelobes and this prevents interference from outside the protected area. Many alarm antennas are built so that the pattern can be adjusted to give optimum coverage in any particular application. Typical antenna patterns are shown in *Figure 7-9*.

**Figure 7-8.
Rectangular Horn
Antenna**

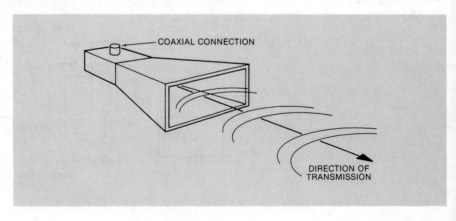

**Figure 7-9.
Typical Directional
Patterns of Alarm
Antennas**

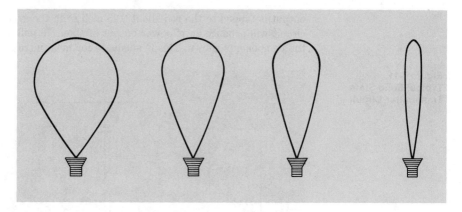

Figure 7-10 shows a photo of a 10-gigahertz (GHz) alarm antenna. In this system, the beam will provide coverage at ranges of 20 to 500 feet. By adjusting the pattern of the antenna, the width of the protected area can be adjusted from 1 to 40 feet.

**Figure 7-10.
Microwave Alarm
Antenna** *(Courtesy
Raycon, Inc.)*

TYPICAL SOLID-STATE SYSTEM

Intrusion alarms require only small power levels of rf energy. Therefore, it is possible to use several different solid-state technologies to generate the microwave signals. We can use bipolar transistor oscillators that are tuned by either LC resonant tank circuits or resonant cavities. Above 1 GHz we can use such devices as the gunn diode or the IMPATT diode.

Bipolar transistor LC-tuned oscillators are used to generate up to 10 mW at frequencies up to 900 MHz.

Figure 7-11 shows the schematic diagram of a typical microwave oscillator used in intrusion alarms. This is a conventional emitter-coupled oscillator that can be used to at least 900 MHz. At this frequency, the tank inductance, L1, does not have any turns. It is simply a rod about 1.5 inches long, connected directly from the collector of the transistor to ground. The output is tapped to the rod about 0.25 inch from the ground end. This circuit will produce an rf power output of about 10 milliwatts (mW) with the components shown. This is adequate for most intrusion alarms.

**Figure 7-11.
Typical Solid-State
Transmitter Circuit**

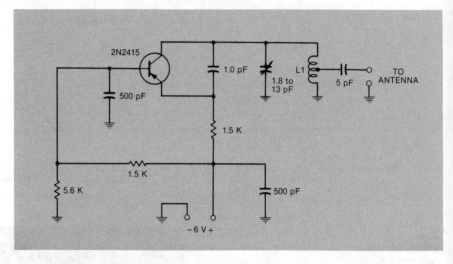

Solid-state units using special transistors that operate at higher frequencies are now on the market. In these units, the oscillator tank circuit is usually a cavity. *Figure 7-12* diagrams a transistor cavity oscillator that will provide about 0.5 watt (W) of power at frequencies over 1000 MHz. The tank circuit is a rectangular cavity about 1 inch square by 1.75 inches long.

**Figure 7-12.
Microwave Oscillator
Using Transistor in
Resonant Cavity**

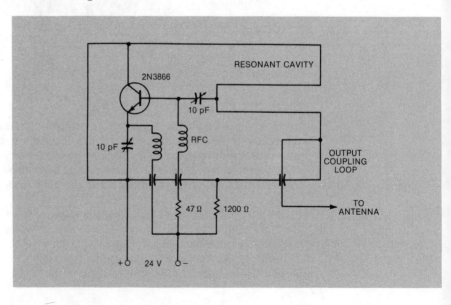

APPLICATION ENGINEERING

The microwave intrusion detector will provide a very effective protection system if the application is properly engineered. On the other hand, a poorly engineered installation will often be easy to foil or will cause a lot of false alarms. The details of installation vary from one location to another because the system must be adjusted to provide optimum protection for each particular area. The general principles given below must be taken into consideration in every installation.

Antenna Location

The intrusion detector antennas, located at least 8 feet off the floor, must be mounted on a vibration-free surface.

The location of the antennas is of paramount importance. Usually they are mounted at least 8 feet above the floor. This enables them to be oriented for good coverage and at the same time minimizes the chance that the antennas will be knocked out of alignment during normal business hours when the system is not operating. The antenna must be mounted on a surface that is free from vibration. As we saw earlier, the higher-frequency systems are well suited to directional antennas that permit concentrating the microwave energy in the desired area.

Since microwave energy will pass through most interior wall materials easily, it is possible to protect more than one room with a single system. The signal will pass through at least two plasterboard walls and even more plywood walls.

Most exterior wall materials, such as brick, concrete block, and masonry, are reasonably opaque to microwaves, but care must be taken to avoid wooden exterior walls and glass windows. The antennas must not be pointed at wooden doors, walls, or glass windows because reflections from objects passing by outside will cause false alarms. In installations where it is practical, a dead zone is often provided around the protected area. An intruder passing around this dead zone would not trip the alarm, but movement from the dead zone into the protected area would trigger the alarm.

Obstructions and Interference

Moving metallic objects, such as fans and venetian blinds, can cause false alarms in microwave intrusion detectors.

Although air currents will usually not affect a microwave alarm, moving objects will affect it. For example, a metal venetian blind swinging in the breeze could cause a false alarm, as could moving fan blades. It is good practice to see that the beam is not aimed directly at metallic objects that might move. Interference from a fan can be eliminated by placing a wire screen in front of the fan. The microwave signal will be reflected from the screen and will not "see" the fan blades at all. Of course, the screen must be firm enough that the fan will not cause it to vibrate.

Many microwave intrusion detectors have range or sensitivity controls. The setting of this control represents a compromise between providing adequate protection at the longest range from the system and avoiding false alarms because of too much sensitivity at close ranges. The range setting must be correlated with the location of the antennas. For example, it would not be wise to try to adjust the sensitivity of a system in such a way that it would be able to detect a person walking at one location and yet ignore a large moving object such as an elevator just behind a thin wall. This could be accomplished better by locating the antennas so that they would not "see" the elevator.

The fact that metal objects are opaque to microwaves means that objects such as desks, file cabinets, and storage cabinets can create "shadows" in the protected area. That is, there will be no microwave energy and hence no reflections from areas behind metal objects. Unless care is taken in properly positioning the antennas, there might be a shaded path along which a burglar could crawl without being detected.

Testing the Installation

A new system must be tested under realistic conditions: an "intruder" should try to defeat the system, and devices such as fans and blinds should be tried to see if they cause false alarms.

Regardless of how much care has been exercised in planning the installation, the final proof of performance is an actual test. In testing a system, anything that might produce a false alarm must be tried. Fans must be turned on, venetian blinds waved back and forth as they would wave in a breeze, and loose doors vibrated. If the protected building is near a street or sidewalk, the system should be tested to make sure that people or vehicles passing by outside will not cause false alarms.

The test should also include all possible attempts to foil the system, such as walking into the protected area very slowly or trying to reach a critical area by crawling under the beam or finding a "shaded" path.

ADVANTAGES AND LIMITATIONS

The microwave intrusion detector ranks with the ultrasonic detector as one of the most effective means of providing specific area protection. A properly installed system is very difficult to foil. It has the advantage that two or more separate rooms can often be protected by a single system.

The microwave alarm is very effective in trapping the "stay-behind," who will trip the alarm with any movement.

The principal limitation of the microwave system is that it requires adequate installation engineering. The fact that many outside walls contain large windows which are easily penetrated by microwaves can lead to frequent false alarms in poorly engineered installations.

Another limitation that must be considered concerns the power from a microwave system. The power must be held to levels that are not dangerous to human beings; under no condition should the power density be allowed to exceed 10 milliwatts per square centimeter (10 mW/cm^2).

RADAR INTERFERENCE

Radar from defense and air-traffic control sites can cause false alarms in microwave intrusion systems. Sometimes directional antennas can overcome this problem.

In some locations, microwave systems are subject to interference from high-powered radars such as those used in air-traffic control and defense establishments. This possibility should be checked out when a microwave system is being installed. In most cases, the interference can be eliminated by proper orientation of the antennas. In installations on the same property as radar systems, much more care must be taken. The system chosen should not be susceptible to radiation at the frequencies of the radars in use.

FCC RULES AND REGULATIONS

Any device that radiates rf energy, such as a microwave intrusion detector, can both cause interference and be susceptible to it. For this reason, the Federal Communications Commission (FCC) carefully regulates all such devices. In the FCC rules, a microwave intrusion alarm is called a "field disturbance sensor" because it operates on the basis of sensing a disturbance in an electromagnetic field. The rules covering field disturbance sensors are found in Part 15 of the *FCC Rules and Regulations*, available from the U.S. Government Printing Office, Washington, D.C. 20402.

Before any field disturbance sensor can be operated, it must be certificated and labeled in accordance with the FCC rules.

General Operating Frequencies

In general, a field disturbance sensor may be operated on any frequency as long as it does not cause interference to any other device or equipment. Unless special frequencies are used, however, the radiation on any frequency, including both the fundamental frequency and the harmonics, must be less than 15 microvolts per meter at a distance in meters from the sensor given by the following formula:

$$\text{Distance} = \frac{\lambda}{2\pi}$$

where,

λ is the wavelength in meters.

In more familiar units, the distance in feet is given in terms of frequency by the following formula:

$$\text{Distance} = \frac{157,000}{\text{frequency in kHz}}$$

Special Operating Frequencies

From an inspection of the foregoing equation, you can see that the radiation from a microwave alarm that meets these requirements will be rather seriously limited. This means that the receiving portion of the system must be very sensitive in order to detect an intruder at a distance. This high sensitivity in turn means that the receiver will be quite sensitive to interference from other radiating sources, and this interference may well cause false alarms.

To avoid this limitation, the FCC will allow much higher radiation if the alarm is operated on certain frequencies and the frequency is held constant. Table 7-1 lists these special frequencies and gives the frequency tolerances as well as the permissible radiation.

**Table 7-1.
Special Frequencies for
Microwave Alarms
(Field Disturbance
Sensors)**

Operating Frequency (MHz)	Band Limits (MHz)	Allowable Field Strength at 30 Meters*
915	±13	50,000 μV/m
2450	±15	50,000 μV/m
5800	±15	50,000 μV/m
10,525	±25	250,000 μV/m
24,125	±50	250,000 μV/m

*30 Meters = 98.4 Feet

In order to obtain FCC certification, a complete series of tests and measurements must be performed by a competent engineer and submitted to the FCC. Once the device has been certificated, no changes can be made that will affect the amount of radiation from the device. When repairs are made, tests must be made to ensure that the device will still meet the prescribed standards.

WHAT HAVE WE LEARNED?

1. Microwave intrusion detectors use very short radio waves and are basically a form of Doppler radar.
2. Radio waves are reflected by metal surfaces, but pass through materials such as wood, glass, and wallboard.
3. Three protection schemes use (a) co-located twin antennas for transmitter and receiver, (b) a single transmit/receive antenna, or (c) bistatic (i.e., non-colocated) transmit and receiver antennas.
4. Rf energy sources used in microwave intrusion alarms typically produce 10 to 500 milliwatts at frequencies between 400 and 25,000 MHz.
5. Microwave intrusion systems are called "field disturbance sensors" and are regulated by the FCC.

Quiz for Chapter 7

1. Microwave intrusion systems are a form of _____ radar.
   - **a.** PPI
   - **b.** A-scan
   - **c.** speed
   - **d.** Doppler

2. A microwave intrusion alarm system combines incident and reflected waves to set up _____ in the protected area.
   - **a.** field disturbances
   - **b.** standing waves
   - **c.** rf disturbances
   - **d.** EM fields

3. Find the wavelength of a 6000-MHz microwave signal.
   - **a.** 1.97 inches.
   - **b.** 2.10 inches.
   - **c.** 0.97 inch.
   - **d.** 0.05 inch.

4. What is the frequency of an intrusion signal if an intruder moves through a 6000-MHz field at 6 inches/second?
   - **a.** 3.05 Hz.
   - **b.** 11.811 Hz.
   - **c.** 6.1 Hz.
   - **d.** 100 Hz.

5. Increasing the frequency of the microwave system generator has what effect on the intrusion signal?
   - **a.** None.
   - **b.** Increases frequency.
   - **c.** Decreases frequency.
   - **d.** Changes its phase.

6. Reducing the rate of passage through a protected area by an intruder will have what effect on the intrusion signal?
   - **a.** None.
   - **b.** Increases frequency.
   - **c.** Decreases frequency.
   - **d.** Changes its phase.

7. If care is not used in system design, automobiles passing outside the protected area will cause false alarms. True or false?

8. Receive and transmit functions can be combined in a single antenna through use of:
   - **a.** coaxial cable.
   - **b.** directional coupler.
   - **c.** combiner.
   - **d.** resonant cavity.

9. A system in which receive and transmit antennas are separated by some distance is called a _____ system.
   - **a.** microwave
   - **b.** twin antenna
   - **c.** dual antenna
   - **d.** bistatic

10. A horn antenna is popular because it has:
    - **a.** directivity.
    - **b.** low sidelobes.
    - **c.** high gain.
    - **d.** low cost.

11. An LC oscillator can be used to generate about _____ mW of rf energy, up to a frequency of about 900 MHz.
    - **a.** 10
    - **b.** 100
    - **c.** 1000
    - **d.** 500

12. A cavity oscillator is used over frequencies of _____ MHz, and generates about 0.5 W of rf energy.
    a. 600
    b. 2500
    c. 1000
    d. 25,000

13. _____ metal objects can produce false alarms in microwave intrusion alarms.
    a. Static
    b. Grounded
    c. Moving
    d. Floating

Proximity Detectors

ABOUT THIS CHAPTER

Proximity detectors are a completely passive class of intrusion detectors that use body capacitance as the detection factor. These devices use several different types of capacitance-sensitive circuit, as we will see in this chapter.

INTRODUCTION TO PROXIMITY DETECTORS

The proximity detector, as its name implies, is a device that will trigger an alarm whenever an intruder comes close to it; the intruder need not actually touch any part of the system.

Most proximity detectors are uniquely designed—no two are exactly alike. Sensors can be wires, metal plates, or the protected object itself.

The proximity detector is unique among intrusion detectors because, in general, no two detectors are exactly alike. Other types of intrusion detectors are manufactured products, and the manufacturer has usually done a great deal of engineering to ensure that the detector will operate properly if it is properly installed. The proximity detector, on the other hand, is usually a wire of arbitrary length, or, in some cases, the actual object that is to be protected, such as a safe or file cabinet.

Unfortunately, many proximity detectors are not properly engineered for a particular application, with the result that they operate poorly or cause a lot of false alarms. A properly engineered proximity system, however, is very reliable.

To select and install a proximity detector properly, it is essential to understand the principle of operation of the device. The most critical part of the system is the sensing wire or the object selected to be protected. This choice is made at the time of installation rather than at the time of manufacture.

PRINCIPLE OF OPERATION

The proximity sensor is one plate of a capacitor; the other plate is ground.

The sensing circuit of a proximity detector is actually a capacitor but, as we will see, this capacitor differs considerably from the capacitors normally used in electronic circuits. A typical arrangement is shown in *Figure 8-1*. When no intruder is in the vicinity of the system, the electric flux passes from the sensing wire to the ground. The air between the two points acts as the dielectric and has a dielectric constant of 1 (*Figure 8-1a*).

The dielectric constant of the human body is 80 times that of air, so a human entering the field of a capacitor drastically changes the capacitance.

**Figure 8-1.
Flux Lines in Proximity Detector**

The dielectric constant of the human body is approximately the same as that of water—about 80. Thus, when intruders approach the system, some of the electric flux will pass through their bodies, as shown in *Figure 8-1b*. This has the effect of increasing the capacitance of the system. Since most of the body fluids are electrolytes, the human body is a rather poor dielectric. Thus, the losses of the system also increase in the presence of an intruder.

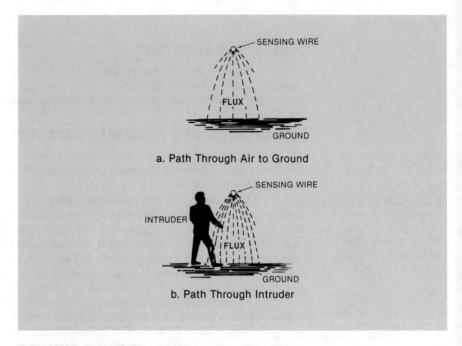

a. Path Through Air to Ground

b. Path Through Intruder

SENSING DEVICES

The actual sensing device may be a straight wire, a wire that follows some path around the wall of a building, or a cabinet of almost any shape. An exact analysis of the situation involves electric field theory and can become very complicated. There are a few general principles, however, that can be used to improve the design of a system without involving much mathematical analysis.

The requirements for a sensing circuit for a proximity detector include the following:

1. The capacitance of the system, without an intruder present, should be as stable as practical.
2. The change in capacitance caused by the presence of an intruder must be great enough to trigger an alarm.
3. The system must not radiate enough energy to cause interference in the operation of other equipment.
4. The system should have minimum sensitivity to interference from other sources such as nearby radio stations.

In connection with the requirements of minimum radiation and susceptibility to radiation, it should be noted that the term "antenna" sometimes applied to the sensing wire is actually a misnomer. The sensing wire should not act at all like an antenna, which both radiates and receives electromagnetic energy.

Antenna-like Operation

Any wire longer than one-tenth wavelength will try to act as an antenna— which is disastrous for proximity detector circuits.

Any wire longer than about one-tenth of a wavelength at the frequency of operation will try to act as an antenna. To minimize this effect, most intrusion detectors operate at frequencies below about 50 kHz. At this frequency, one-tenth wavelength is nearly 2000 feet, so a reasonably long sensing circuit will not radiate significant energy.

Flux Density

In order for the presence of an intruder to increase the capacitance of a system, some of the electric flux that flows between the "plates" of the capacitor must pass through the intruder. As a rule of thumb, the flux density varies inversely with the distance from the sensing wire. Thus, if the distance from the sensing wire to an intruder is cut in half, the change in capacitance will be 4 times as great.

This is not a serious limitation because there is usually no reason to make the sensitivity of a proximity detector greater than that necessary to detect the presence of an intruder. In most installations, just as much protection will be provided by a system that triggers an alarm when an intruder comes within a few inches of the sensor as by a system that triggers an alarm when an intruder comes within 20 feet of the system. Some systems are purposely made so insensitive that the intruder must actually touch the protected object to trigger the alarm.

Capacitance

Some idea of the capacitance of various arrangements of sensing circuits can be obtained from the formulas in *Figure 8-2*. These formulas are approximate because the sensing circuit rarely has a neat geometry that will fit the equations closely. They will nevertheless give an idea of the order of capacitance that can be expected from various arrangements.

Many different circuits have been used to detect the change in capacitance of the sensing circuit of a proximity alarm. However, all of these arrangements operate on one of two principles. They either detect the change in capacitive reactance resulting from the capacitance change, or they detect the change in voltage across the capacitor that results from the capacitance change.

Capacitive Reactance

The capacitive reactance of any capacitor is given by the following expression.

$$X_c = \frac{1}{2\pi fC}$$

where,

C is the capacitance in farads,
X_c is the capacitive reactance in ohms,
f is the frequency in hertz.

Another form of this equation using the more familiar microfarads, is shown here:

$$X_c = \frac{1,000,000}{2\pi fC}$$

where,

X_c is in ohms,
f is in hertz,
C is in microfarads.

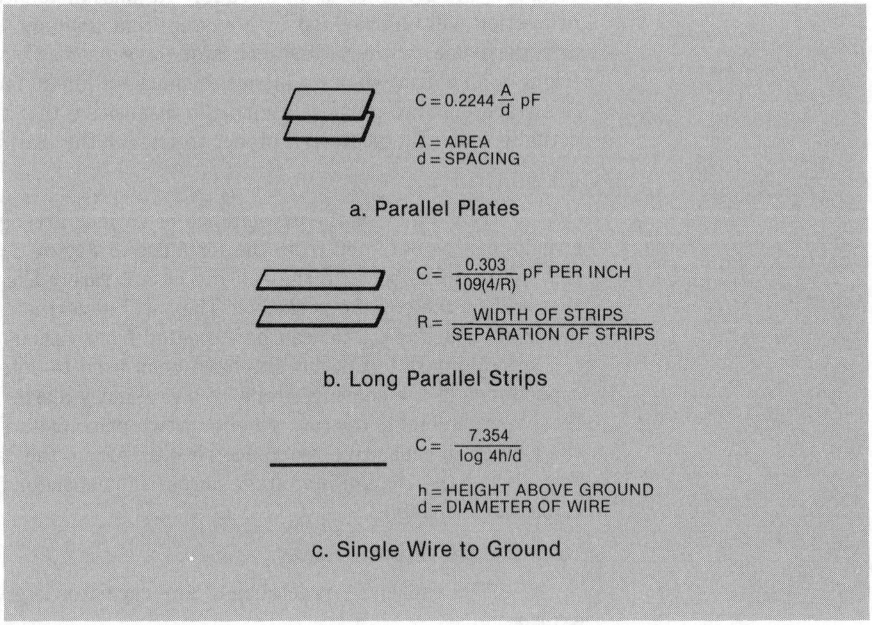

Figure 8-2.
Capacitance Equations

$$C = 0.2244 \frac{A}{d} \text{ pF}$$

A = AREA
d = SPACING

a. Parallel Plates

$$C = \frac{0.303}{109(4/R)} \text{ pF PER INCH}$$

$$R = \frac{\text{WIDTH OF STRIPS}}{\text{SEPARATION OF STRIPS}}$$

b. Long Parallel Strips

$$C = \frac{7.354}{\log 4h/d}$$

h = HEIGHT ABOVE GROUND
d = DIAMETER OF WIRE

c. Single Wire to Ground

Example 8-1

Find the capacitive reactance (X_c) a 0.0001 μF capacitor operated at 40 kHz.

Solution

$$X_c = \frac{1,000,000}{2\pi fC}$$

$$X_c = \frac{1,000,000}{(2)(3.14)(40,000)(0.00001)}$$

$$X_c = \frac{1,000,000}{25.12} = 39.8 \text{ ohms}$$

(Note: To convert picofarads [pF] to microfarads [μF], divide picofarads by 1,000,000. To convert μF to pF, multiply μF by 1,000,000.)

It is not immediately obvious, but an inspection of this equation will show that the percentage change in capacitive reactance is the same as the percentage change in capacitance, regardless of what the capacitance is to start with or what frequency is used.

The most common way to detect the change in capacitive reactance is to connect the sensing circuit into the tank circuit of an oscillator. Then, any change in capacitance will result in a change in frequency, which is easy to detect.

Detection by Applied Voltage

Another way of detecting a change in capacitance is to apply a charge to the capacitor and detect the change in voltage that results from a change in capacitance. As shown in *Figure 8-3*, the voltage across a capacitor is given by the following formula.

$$E = \frac{Q}{C}$$

where,

E is the voltage in volts,
Q is the charge in coulombs,
C is the capacitance in farads.

Example 8-2

What is the voltage appearing across a 1000-pF capacitor that is charged with 4×10^{-8} coulombs?

Solution

$$E = \frac{Q}{C}$$

$$E = \frac{0.00000004}{100 \text{ pF} \times \frac{1 \text{ pF}}{10^{12}}}$$

$$E = \frac{0.00000004}{0.000000001}$$

$$E = 40 \text{ volts (V)}$$

**Figure 8-3.
Voltage, Charge,
Capacitance**

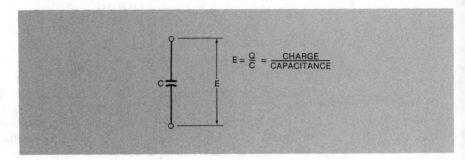

Therefore, if we increase the capacitance of the capacitor, the voltage across it will decrease, and vice versa.

ADVERSE INFLUENCES

Sense capacitances can change by 50 pF due to daily changes in temperature and humidity.

The capacitance between a wire and ground is influenced by any changes in the dielectric constant of the air between them. The most common influence is a change in either the temperature or humidity of the air. A sensing circuit having a capacitance of 2000 pF may change as much as 50 pF at sunrise or sunset. In many systems, this is a greater change than would be produced by an intruder.

To avoid false alarms resulting from changes in the quiescent capacitance of a system, ac coupling is usually incorporated at some point in the system. Such a system will not respond to very slow changes in capacitance but will respond to the faster change that occurs when an intruder suddenly approaches the sensing circuit.

Stray Signals

Stray signals picked up by the sensing circuit are another influence. Although the sensing circuit is designed to be a rather poor antenna, it may still pick up a substantial signal from a nearby radio transmitter. Even though there may not be a radio station nearby, the increasing use of mobile radio means that a transmitter may suddenly show up at almost any location. To minimize this influence, a low-pass filter should be included in the system at the point where the sensing wire is connected to the remainder of the system.

Still another adverse influence is ordinary electrical noise of the type that causes interference with radio and television reception. Any electrical device, such as a motor or a neon sign, can cause enough electrical noise to produce false alarms. The alarm not only should have a low-pass filter at the point where the sensing wire connects to the remaining circuit, but should also have an interference filter at the point where the power line enters the unit.

BEAT-FREQUENCY PROXIMITY DETECTORS

Beat-frequency proximity detectors use two sense wires that are driven by two different oscillators operating in a heterodyne system.

Figure 8-4 shows a block diagram of a proximity detector designed to compensate for the effects of temperature and humidity. This circuit uses two oscillators with two separate sensing wires. The oscillators are tuned to provide a predetermined beat, or difference, frequency. This beat frequency is amplified in a highly selective circuit and is applied to a trigger circuit. As long as the beat frequency remains at its original value, the alarm will not be initiated. If the frequency of one of the oscillators is changed, the beat frequency will no longer fall within the passband of the selective amplifier, and the input to the trigger circuit will decrease. This, in turn, will initiate the alarm.

Figure 8-4.
Proximity Detector with Temperature and Humidity Compensation

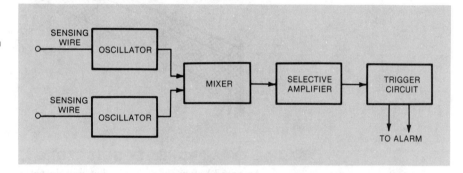

Beat-frequency systems depend upon changes in sensor capacitance to change the frequency of one or both oscillators.

The tuned circuits in the oscillators are designed so that when the third harmonic of one oscillator is heterodyned with the fourth harmonic of the other, equal changes in the capacitance of both circuits will not change the beat frequency. If, on the other hand, the capacitance of one of the circuits is changed slightly, the beat frequency will change by a larger percentage. Suppose, for example, one oscillator is tuned to 100,000 Hz and the other is tuned to 74,875 Hz. The third harmonic of the first oscillator has a frequency of 300,000 Hz, and the fourth harmonic of the other oscillator has a frequency of 299,500 Hz. The beat frequency is then 500 Hz. If the frequency of the first oscillator changes to 100,010 Hz (a 0.01% change), the beat frequency will change to 530 Hz (a 6% change). Thus, the percentage of change in the beat frequency is 600 times as great as the percentage of change in the frequency of the 100,000-Hz oscillator.

Applications of the Beat Technique

Changes in temperature and humidity affect both wires equally, so the net adverse effect is nearly zero.

The beat circuit may be used in an outdoor application such as that shown in *Figure 8-5*, where the two sensing wires are run close to a fence to provide perimeter protection. Changes in temperature, humidity, and motion of the fence will produce equal capacitance changes so that the beat frequency will not change and false alarms will be prevented. On the other hand, an intruder will have more influence on the lower sensing wire and will trigger the alarm. This system may detect intruders approaching within 7 feet of the sensing wire. This system actually provides some protection beneath the surface of the earth, depending on soil conductivity, so it gives some protection against an intruder tunneling under the fence. *Figure 8-6* shows a modern solid-state proximity system for fence protection.

**Figure 8-5.
Proximity Detector
Along a Fence**

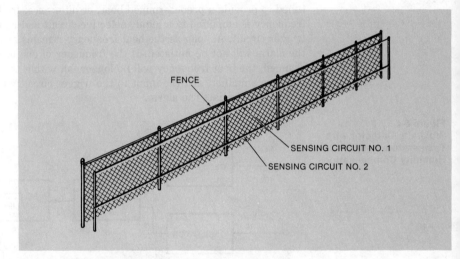

BRIDGE-TYPE PROXIMITY DETECTORS

As noted before, any circuit that will detect a change in capacitance can be used as a proximity detector. One of the oldest systems for measuring capacitance is the impedance bridge shown in *Figure 8-7*. This circuit is balanced—that is, there is no voltage between points A and B when the values of resistance and capacitance are such that the following equation is true.

$$\frac{C1}{C2} = \frac{R2}{R1}$$

When R1 = R2, the bridge is balanced when the two capacitances are equal. This is called the null condition. When the bridge is not balanced, an ac voltage appears between points A and B.

**Figure 8-6.
Console of Fence-
Protection Detector**
*(Courtesy GTE Sylvania,
Inc.)*

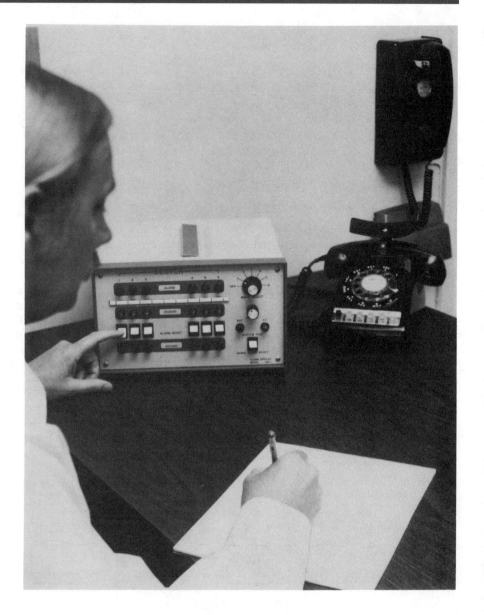

**Figure 8-7.
Basic Capacitance
Bridge**

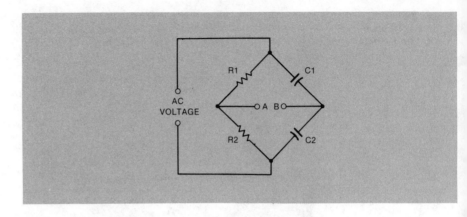

Practical Circuits

A practical version of this arrangement is shown in *Figure 8-8*. Here, one of the capacitors is actually the sensing circuit. When the capacitance of the sensing circuit is equal to the capacitance of C1, the bridge is balanced and there is no voltage at the input of the trigger circuit. When an intruder approaches the sensing circuit, he causes its capacitance to change, unbalancing the bridge circuit. Then an ac voltage appears at the output of the bridge circuit. This voltage is rectified and fed to a trigger circuit, which initiates an alarm. The circuit of *Figure 8-8* is commonly used in proximity alarms, but it has several limitations. In order to get good coverage, a fairly large signal is required from the oscillator. This may cause interference to radio or television receivers. The circuit is also subject to false alarms caused by stray signals picked up by the sensing circuit. If a strong signal is picked up by the sensing circuit, some of it may appear at the rectifier and trigger the alarm.

**Figure 8-8.
Bridge-type Proximity
Detector**

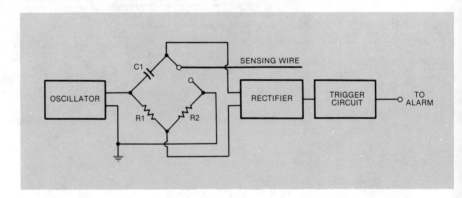

A tuned amplifier ahead of the rectifier reduces system susceptibility to interference.

The circuit shown in *Figure 8-9* is very similar to that of *Figure 8-8*. The difference is that a tuned amplifier is used ahead of the rectifier and trigger circuit. This makes it possible to use a very low-level signal on the bridge circuit, reducing the probability that the system will cause interference. Since the amplifier ahead of the trigger circuit is sharply tuned, the circuit is also much less susceptible to interference. And since the components of the oscillator, tuned amplifier, and bridge circuit can be made highly stable, changes in the sensing circuit itself are the chief cause of false alarms. These can be minimized by careful installation and by not making the circuit any more sensitive than necessary.

Figure 8-9.
Advanced Bridge-type
Proximity Detector

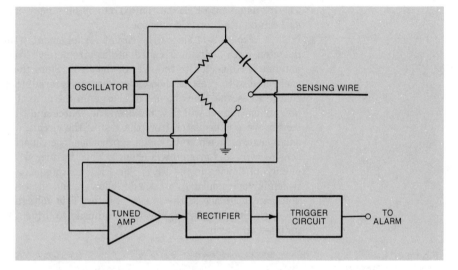

Figure 8-10 shows a bridge-type proximity detector that is designed particularly for outdoor applications, such as fence protection, where large changes in capacitance can be expected because of changes in temperature and humidity. In this circuit, two sensing circuits are used, one in each side of the bridge circuit. Equal changes in capacitance will not unbalance the bridge and initiate the alarm. In installation, the sensing wires are positioned so that temperature and humidity changes will affect the two circuits in the same way, but an intruder will affect one circuit more than the other.

Figure 8-10.
Bridge-type Detector
with Temperature and
Humidity Compensation

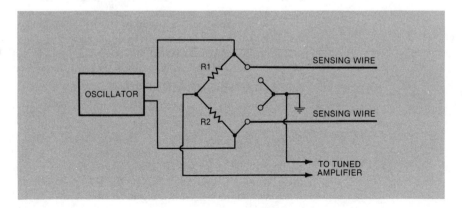

FET PROXIMITY DETECTORS

We can detect changes in sensor capacitance by measuring the value of the dc charge voltage across it.

Earlier in this chapter we saw that if we increased the value of the capacitance, the voltage across it would decrease, and vice versa. This suggests that we could make an intrusion alarm by merely measuring the voltage across a charged capacitor, which indeed we could, except that most voltage-measuring circuits would drain the charge from the capacitor. The insulated-gate FET has an extremely high input impedance, however, and can be used for this purpose.

Figure 8-11 shows the circuit arrangement of an FET proximity detector. Such a circuit is called an "electrometer." The sensing wire or antenna is connected to the gate of the FET. Since the gate is not directly connected to the rest of the semiconductor material, there is no way for the charge to escape. The amount of charge on the gate of the FET determines how much current will flow between the source and the drain. Since the sensing wire is insulated from the rest of the circuit, it will accumulate a small charge. When an intruder approaches, the capacitance between the sensing wire and ground will change. This, in turn, will change the amount of current flowing in the FET. The FET operates as a source follower, which is very similar to a cathode follower, and the current change causes a voltage change across the source resistor. This voltage is passed through a low-pass filter, amplified, rectified, and used to drive a trigger circuit that initiates an alarm.

Figure 8-11. Proximity Detector Using an FET

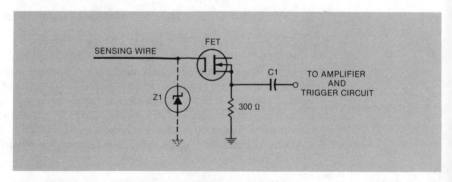

The principal limitation of the FET proximity detector is its high sensitivity. It can be made extremely sensitive and is then subject to false alarms from temperature and humidity changes. Nevertheless, when properly installed and adjusted, it is a very effective proximity detector.

APPLICATION ENGINEERING

Proximity detectors can provide perimeter, area, and spot protection, depending upon design.

The proximity detector is well suited for both perimeter protection and protection of specific objects or small areas. In perimter protection, the sensing wire is run around the protected area. In a typical example, it might actually be a part of a fence. The sensitivity can be adjusted so that the alarm will be triggered whenever anyone tries to enter the protected area. When properly adjusted, it will detect an intruder who tries to scale a fence without actually touching it.

Outdoor applications are subject to frequent false alarms unless great care is exercised in the application. The most common causes of false alarms are changes in temperature and humidity. Rain is particularly troublesome, but the effects of rain can be minimized by the use of high-grade insulators to support the sensing wire. The sensing wire must be strategically located where it will detect intruders but will not be influenced by small animals. It must not be located close to bushes or tree branches that will sway in the wind.

AUTO-PROTECTION SCHEMES

Proximity detectors are widely used indoors to provide protection for specific objects such as desks and file cabinets. Often, the objects that are to be protected are metal and can actually be made a part of the protective circuit. This arrangement is called "auto protection." *Figure 8-12* shows a system in which the sensing wire is connected to a row of file cabinets that act as one plate of the capacitor in the sensing circuit. In most systems, the number of objects that can be protected by a single system is limited by the maximum capacitance that can be tolerated in the sensing circuit. Commercially available systems can protect up to forty file cabinets connected together.

**Figure 8-12.
Proximity Detector to
Protect File Cabinets**

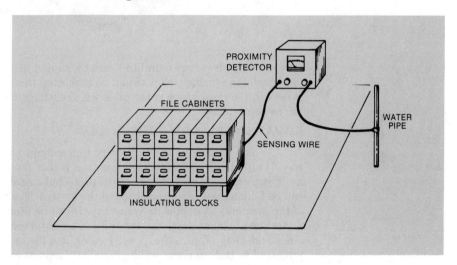

GROUNDS

A wire screen can be used as a counterpoise ground when the real ground is difficult or impossible to use.

In the arrangement of *Figure 8-12*, one side of the system should be connected to a good earth ground or a cold-water pipe. In cases where a good ground is not available, it is desirable to make a counterpoise ground of wire screen on the floor under and around the protected objects, as shown in *Figure 8-13*. The protected objects should not be any closer than 6 inches to the walls and should be mounted on insulating blocks. Loose wires such as lamp or telephone cords must be kept away from the protected objects because they are apt to be the cause of false alarms.

**Figure 8-13.
Wire Screen Used as
Ground**

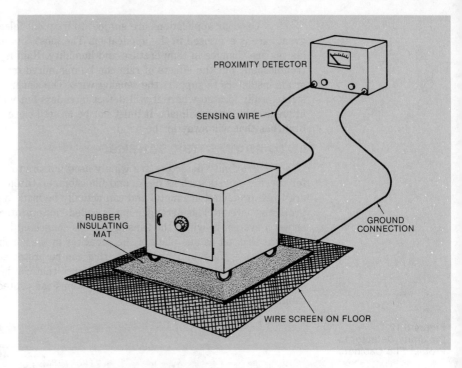

When it is impractical to locate the unit close to the area to be
protected, the sensing circuit should be connected through coaxial cable.
However, the capacitance of the cable will limit the number of objects that
can be protected.

ADVANTAGES AND LIMITATIONS

Versatility is the principal
advantage of proximity
detectors.

    The proximity detector is very well suited to the protection of
specific objects. One outstanding advantage is that the case of the unit
itself may easily be made a part of the protected circuit so that the alarm
will be initiated by any attempt to foil the system. The principal advantage
of the proximity system is its versatility. It can be used to provide
protection of almost anything, but will not be disturbed by normal activities
a few feet away. Thus, safes, jewelry cases, and file cabinets can be
protected so that an alarm will be initiated if anyone comes close to them,
but normal business can be conducted close by.

    The chief limitation of proximity systems is that they are very
sensitive, and if the sensitivity in a particular application is made too high,
there are apt to be frequent false alarms. Unlike some other systems, they
cannot be simply plugged in and expected to operate properly. The
application must be planned to provide adequate protection with a
minimum probability of false alarms.

WHAT HAVE WE LEARNED?

1. Proximity detector sensors are basically capacitors in which one plate is ground and the other plate is a sensor wire, metal plate, or even the protected object itself.
2. Several techniques are used to detect change of sensor capacitance: (a) LC oscillator, (b) capacitor charge voltage, (c) bridge null, and (d) beat frequency.
3. Two-wire sensors are used to protect perimeter barriers like fences.
4. Area protection can be afforded by single-wire detectors.
5. Objects made of metal or other conductive materials can be spot protected by making the object the sensor plate of the capacitor; the other plate is ground or a wire screen on the floor.
6. Temperature and humidity effects are minimized by two-wire sensors.

Quiz for Chapter 8

1. A(n) _____ detector triggers an alarm when an intruder comes close to it.
   a. microwave
   b. proximity
   c. IR
   d. field disturbance

2. Proximity detectors depend upon the _____ between the sensor element and ground.
   a. distance
   b. resistance
   c. inductance
   d. capacitance

3. The presence of a human body close to the proximity detector (increases/decreases) its capacitance.

4. Any wire longer than about 1/10 wavelength will try to act as a(n):
   a. sensor.
   b. antenna.
   c. capacitor.
   d. bridge.

5. What is the reactance of a 1000-pF (0.001-μF) capacitor operated at 30 kHz?
   a. 10,000 ohms.
   b. 8200 ohms.
   c. 2000 ohms.
   d. 5308 ohms.

6. What voltage appears across a 0.01 μF capacitor that is charged to 0.01 coulombs?
   a. 100 V.
   b. 1 V.
   c. 10 V.
   d. 1000 V.

7. _____ is/are often employed in proximity alarm systems to reduce the effects of changes in quiescent capacitance.
   a. DC-coupling
   b. Resistance coupling
   c. Tuned circuits
   d. AC-coupling

8. A beat-frequency system using two wires overcomes _____ effects.
   a. temperature/humidity
   b. drift
   c. frequency
   d. interference

9. No voltage appears at the output of a bridge-type proximity detector in the _____ condition.
   a. quiescent
   b. alarm
   c. null
   d. operating

10. An FET _____ is sometimes used to measure the dc charge voltage across a sensing capacitor.
    a. electrometer
    b. amplifier
    c. oscillator
    d. voltmeter

11. In cases where there is no good ground, a _____ can be used as a counter poise ground.
    a. water pipe
    b. wire screen
    c. drain pipe
    d. gutter

Audio and Video Monitoring

ABOUT THIS CHAPTER

In this chapter, you will learn about audio and video intruder alarms. We will examine both passive monitoring systems that function like any intruder alarm and interactive gatekeeper systems that permit controlled entry into the protected space.

WHY ARE AV SYSTEMS NEEDED?

Audio and visual monitoring is best suited to areas where only a few security personnel are available.

One obvious way to make an area secure is to post guards in the area and at every entrance and exit so that they can watch and listen for any attempt to enter the area. In fact, this is done in many facilities where highly sensitive, classified work is being carried on. In most facilities, it is not economical to post guards so that all of the protected area is under their surveillance. It is both possible and practical, however, to use electronic systems to extend the listening and watching area of a security guard. Audio and video systems are widely used for this purpose. In many applications, audio and video systems are used not only for monitoring but also as an intrusion detector to trip an alarm whenever anyone enters the protected area.

APARTMENT BUILDING INTERCOM SYSTEMS

Apartment house intercoms are used for visitor control. Tenants have keys to the door, but non-tenants must be recognized to gain entry.

Audio-monitoring systems are widely used to protect apartment buildings from intruders. The common arrangement is a simple intercom system used in conjunction with an electrically operated door latch. With this system, shown in *Figure 9-1*, the door of the apartment building is kept locked at all times. All tenants, and others who are authorized to enter, have keys. A visitor not having a key who desires to enter the building must press the doorbell button of one of the apartments. The tenant and visitor can then talk over the intercom to establish the visitor's identity. When the tenant is satisfied that it is safe to admit the visitor, he or she can press a button that operates the electric door latch.

The simple system has many limitations. Probably its greatest disadvantage is that a single, careless tenant who will admit anyone who sounds the bell will jeopardize the security of the entire building. In most large apartment buildings, the tenants do not know each other personally. So, in these, another limitation is that, posing as a tenant who has misplaced a key, a visitor can wait until another tenant opens the door and then enter the building at the same time.

**Figure 9-1.
Apartment Building
Intercom**

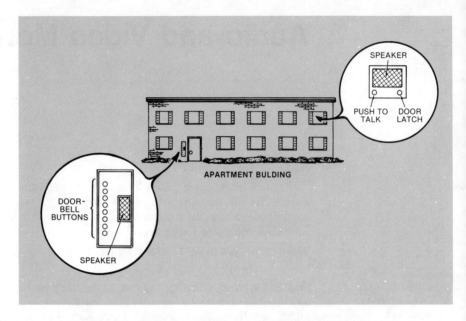

In spite of its limitations, the apartment building intercom does provide some control over the number of people who enter and leave the building. If all of the tenants are security-minded, the system can be made very effective. It also acts as a deterrent to the burglar or vandal who does not wish to call attention to his or her presence when entering a place.

GATE-MONITORING SYSTEMS

A limitation of audio systems is that silent visitors can slip in with careless tenants.

A very similar system is frequently used to control access to industrial plants. With such an arrangement, a single guard can control access to several different entrances. Naturally, this system has many limitations. It is very difficult to positively identify a visitor by merely hearing the voice. Furthermore, a silent intruder may slip in with an authorized visitor. The effectiveness of the system is increased by proper procedures. For example, an identified visitor may be permitted to enter the plant but told to report to a receptionist or security guard immediately. In this way, a security guard can immediately start searching for anyone who enters but does not report.

Gate-monitoring systems can be improved substantially by a closed-circuit TV system that allows the visitor to be examined before he or she is admitted. Today the lower cost of home video equipment makes video monitoring of gates and doors economically feasible, even though the cost was once prohibitive.

AUDIO INTRUSION DETECTORS

In addition to being used for controlling access to doors or gates, audio intercom systems can be used to monitor an area for the presence of intruders. The regular intercom can be used for this purpose and, in fact, is often used in this way, but it has a disadvantage in that a guard must constantly listen for an intruder who is trying to be as quiet as possible. This is particularly difficult when one security guard must monitor several different areas. This disadvantage is overcome by adding a trigger circuit as shown in *Figure 9-2*.

A trigger circuit following the microphone amplifier can automatically monitor the situation and alert security personnel when noises are detected.

In this system, a microphone (often a permanent-magnet speaker) located in the protected area is connected to an amplifier as in an ordinary intercom system, but instead of being connected to a monitoring speaker, the output of the amplifier is connected to a diode rectifier and a trigger circuit. Whenever the sound level in the protected area exceeds a preset level, the trigger circuit will operate, initiating an alarm.

Figure 9-2.
Audio Intrusion Alarm

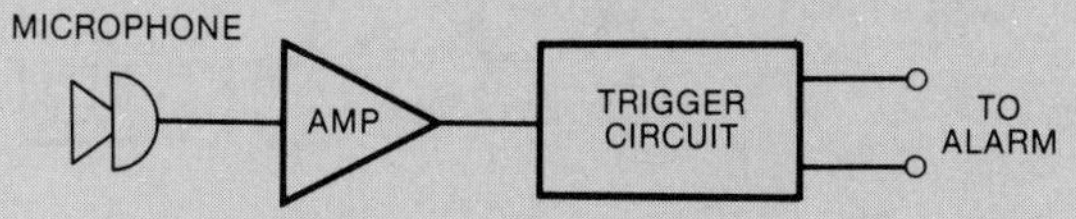

Limitations

The audio intrusion detector has many limitations. It is very susceptible to false alarms in locations where the background noise may vary over a wide range under normal conditions. Thus, it is not well suited for use in an area where machinery that operates all night turns on and off automatically, producing all sorts of different sounds. Neither is it suitable for protecting an area that has heavy drapes and thick carpeting. For example, a burglar might steal a typewriter from an office, making hardly any sound at all. The effectiveness of this system may be increased considerably by using doors, locks, and cabinets that cannot be broken without making a great deal of noise.

An Advantage

An advantage of audio or video monitoring is that it allows security personnel to evaluate the situation before summoning police.

One outstanding advantage of the audio intrusion detector over other types is that it can be used to evaluate the situation causing the alarm. For example, a guard at a central location monitoring several areas can turn up the monitor speaker whenever an alarm is triggered. The guard can then listen carefully to the sounds in the protected area and determine whether or not there is an intruder in the area. If the alarm were triggered by some natural sound, such as a loose window rattling, the guard could probably recognize the situation. On the other hand, if sounds were made that would not normally occur in the protected area, the guard could immediately send someone to investigate or call the police. This system has the advantage of detecting abnormal conditions other than intrusions. For example, the alarm would be triggered if a piece of machinery were to make an unusual noise because of a bearing failure.

An Improved System

    A more sophisticated audio intrusion detector is shown in *Figure 9-3*. This system has two additional features that will minimize false alarms as well as increase the versatility of the system. The first of these is a system of audio filters that can be adjusted to discriminate against the sounds that normally occur in the protected area. In addition, a time-delay circuit is provided that can be adjusted so that the alarm will not be triggered unless the abnormal sound persists for a certain period of time. This helps to avoid false alarms that would be caused by sounds such as thunder or a passing truck.

**Figure 9-3.
Improved Audio
Intrusion Alarm**

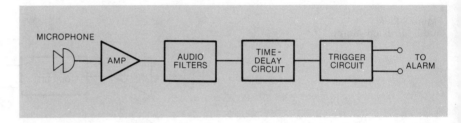

Sound Cancellation

    Some audio intrusion systems use a circuit that will not trigger the alarm if the sound that is picked up originates outside of the building. This system, shown in *Figure 9-4*, has two microphones—one in the protected area and another outside the building. Any loud sound originating outside the building, such as the sound of a passing truck, will be picked up by both microphones, but the circuit is arranged so that when the same sound is picked up by both microphones, the alarm will not be triggered if the signal from the outside microphone is stronger. Thus, the circuit would not be triggered by a clap of thunder, but would be triggered by the sound of a safe being blasted inside the building.

**Figure 9-4.
Sound Cancellation
System**

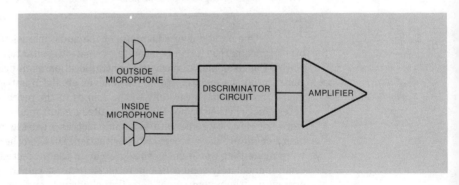

    By proper use of sound cancellation, filters, and time-delay circuits, the audio alarm can be adapted to many different applications. It must, however, be carefully tailored to the application. Before adjusting the system, the installer must know every sound that will normally be present in the protected area at any time. If the installation is made when air conditioning is in use, care must be taken to ensure that false alarms will not be caused by the heating system later on. As with other systems, the final proof of effectiveness is a "walk through" test where every effort is made to foil the system.

Portable Audio Alarm

The audio alarm system can be made very compact. All that is required is a permanent-magnet (pm) speaker and a simple circuit that may consist of a few transistors. The operating power may be supplied be a small battery. For these reasons, the audio detector is often used to provide temporary protection for an area that normally does not need protection. Suppose, for example, that a truck arrives at a plant too late to be unloaded and must remain overnight outside the building. An audio alarm can be mounted on the truck to provide protection. If the truck is properly secured, it cannot be opened without causing enough noise to trigger the alarm.

VIBRATION INTRUSION DETECTORS

The vibration detector is practically identical to the audio intrusion detector except for the pickup device. Whereas an audio detector uses a microphone that will pick up sounds in the protected area, the vibration system uses a vibration detector that must be moved physically before it will produce a signal. The vibration detector is electrically about the same as a microphone, but it does not have a diaphragm.

Figure 9-5 shows a sketch of a typical vibration detector. The mechanism is very similar to a pm speaker. A mass suspended from a spring holds a coil in the strong field of a permanent magnet. Normally, the mass is at rest and there is no output from the device. Whenever the case is subject to vibration, the mass will not move because of its inertia and the magnet is moved with respect to the coil. This motion results in the magnetic field being cut by the coil, which in turn induces a voltage in the coil. A smaller transistor amplifier increases the strength of the signal to a level suitable for transmission to a remote amplifier and trigger circuit.

The circuitry used with vibration detectors is identical to that used with audio detectors, except that speakers are not used for monitoring. The sensitivity of a vibration detector can be adjusted over a wide range. It may be adjusted so that the alarm will be tripped by vibration ranging anywhere from a light touch to a hammer blow.

All of the accessory circuits, such as filters and time delays that are used with audio intrusion detectors, may be used with vibration detectors. Vibration cancellation can also be used in the same way as sound cancellation to cancel out the effects of things that vibrate an entire building, such as the rumble of a passing train.

Figure 9-5.
Vibration Detector

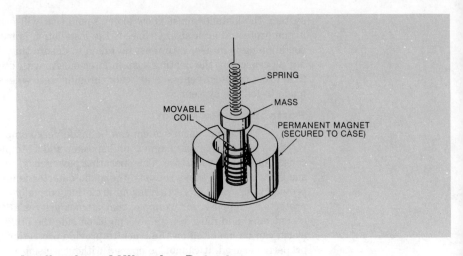

SPRING

MOVABLE
COIL

MASS

PERMANENT MAGNET
(SECURED TO CASE)

Application of Vibration Detectors

Vibration detectors are well suited to spot protection of specific objects such as file cabinets and safes.

Although the principle and circuitry of the vibration intrusion detector are very similar to those of the audio detector, the application is completely different. Whereas the audio system is used primarily for area protection, the vibration detector is best suited for protection of specific objects such as file cabinets, safes, and similar objects. It is also well suited for use with other systems to protect against a burglar breaking through the walls of a facility not otherwise protected.

The effectiveness of the vibration detector depends upon proper application. It is often used to provide protection for a specific object is an area that might normally be occupied by people. For example, *Figure 9-6* shows a vibration detector mounted in a file cabinet to provide protection against anyone tampering with it. The file cabinet might be located in an office where cleaning people come in and out when the office is not open for business. As long as they do not jar the cabinet excessively, the alarm will not be triggered. But if anyone tries to force the cabinet open, the alarm will be triggered. Proper adjustment of the sensitivity of the system is necessary to avoid false alarms.

Figure 9-6.
Vibration Detector
Mounted in File Cabinet

VIDEO-MONITORING SYSTEMS

Video monitoring enables security personnel to see silent intruders who could evade audio monitoring.

Many of the limitations of audio-monitoring systems can be overcome by the use of closed-circuit TV systems. The intruder who could remain perfectly still for a while without making any sound is still visible and could be seen on the television system. Monitoring of gates and doors is much more effective with video than with audio systems. *Figure 9-7* shows a typical camera installation in a museum. With several such cameras, a guard at a central location can monitor several parts of the museum. *Figure 9-8* shows a television-monitoring system that allows a security guard to monitor several warehouses.

**Figure 9-7.
TV Camera Monitoring
Museum Hallway**

**Figure 9-8.
Television-Monitoring
System**

When used in conjunction with other systems, such as audio detectors, video systems are very effective for many applications, particularly when guards are on the premises. They are not suited for very remote locations because of the cost and complexity of transmitting television signals over long paths.

As an intrusion detector, the television system has the disadvantage that it must be watched continuously if an intruder is to be spotted when passing the camera. This disadvantage can be overcome by using some other form of intrusion detector to detect the presence of an intruder, then evaluating the situation by watching the area on the television system.

Television-monitoring systems are being used increasingly for areas such as department stores where shoplifting and pilferage by employees are constant headaches. This arrangement permits a security officer to spot-check an area without alerting those being watched. This is a very effective deterrent. In fact, many dummy television cameras are in current use to discourage shoplifting. But, as we noted earlier, while these systems may discourage amateurs they are an open invitation to experienced shoplifters who know that they are inoperative.

Dummy TV cameras are effective against amateur thieves but rarely fool professionals who can distinguish genuine from counterfeit equipment.

Video Motion Detectors

The requirement that a television monitor be watched continuously to detect an intruder can be overcome by the use of a video motion detector. The video motion detector operates in the following way. The video signal from the television camera at a particular period of time is sampled and stored in a memory circuit. At a later time when the camera is scanning the same area, the signal is sampled again and compared with the first sample. If nothing has moved in the area being scanned between the two samplings, the two samples will be the same. If, however, the picture has been changed by an intruder entering the area, the two samples will not be the same, and the alarm will be triggered. *Figure 9-9* is a block diagram of such a system.

Video motion detectors sample video signals in a protected area and compare them with a signal stored when the area was known to be secure.

Figure 9-9.
Video Motion Detector
Block Diagram

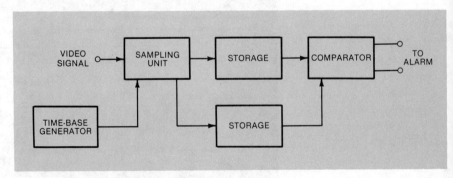

The number of areas of the television screen that can be covered by a motion detector depends on the amount of storage capacity available. It is usually not considered practical to try to cover the entire screen. One way of showing the portion of the picture covered by a motion detector is to brighten that portion of the screen, as shown in *Figure 9-10*. The sensitivity of the system is great enough to detect the motion of a person several feet from the camera.

Figure 9-10.
Video Motion Detector
Display

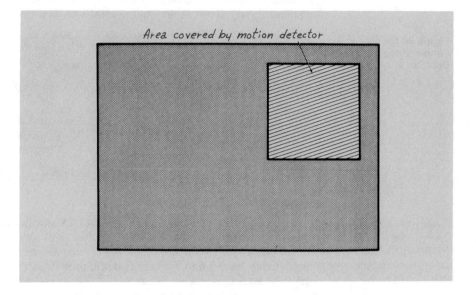

Area covered by motion detector

A newer version of this type of system uses a "frame freezer" device. These electronic devices digitize a single frame of video. The digital gray-scale values are stored in a computer memory as a reference. Subsequent frames are digitized and compared with the stored values. An alarm is sounded if the new frame differs significantly from the reference value. If the scene changes naturally, the operator can freeze and store a new reference frame.

A simpler form of video motion detector that is popular is shown in *Figure 9-11*. This system is not electrically connected to the television system. The detector (or detectors, since more than one can be used) is a photoelectric cell mounted within a container that is equipped with a suction cup so that it can be attached to the face of a television monitoring tube. The photocell integrates the light over the area covered by the suction cup. As long as the average light over this small area remains constant, the output of the detector remains constant. If the light changes (as it will if anything in the picture moves), the output will become either higher or lower. The output of the detector is connected to a trigger circuit that will initiate an alarm when the signal either increases or decreases.

In use, the detectors are mounted so that they will cover entrances to an area or a highly sensitive area. For example, in a building, the closed-circuit television camera may be oriented so that the picture will give an overall view of the area, including both the door and a safe. Detectors may be mounted over that portion of the picture showing the door and the safe. Thus, if anyone enters the area or approaches the safe, an alarm will be sounded. A security guard can then watch the area to determine whether or not an emergency exists and take appropriate action.

The television system has the added advantage that it can be used to monitor conditions other than security, such as the operation of equipment, and detect other emergencies, such as a fire.

**Figure 9-11.
Simple Video Motion
Detector**

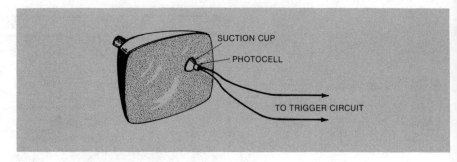

SUCTION CUP

PHOTOCELL

TO TRIGGER CIRCUIT

Low-Light–Level Television

Modern low-light TV cameras provide good quality images without the need for special lighting in the protected area.

One of the traditional limitations of TV monitoring systems is that they are not very effective when the ambient light level is low. Developments in TV camera tubes, particularly silicon target and diode array tubes, have led to cameras that will provide satisfactory images when the light level is very low.

Figure 9-12 shows a diode-array camera that contains a low-noise preamplifier. This camera is particularly well suited to surveillance and monitoring.

**Figure 9-12.
Diode-array Camera**
*(Courtesy Motorola Inc.,
Communications Sector)*

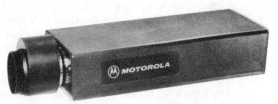

MOTOROLA

An image-intensifier device amplifies available light to reproduce a low-light scene for hand-held manual or TV camera use.

A device that can be used in situations where there is little light is the infrared image intensifier shown in *Figure 9-13*. This device is somewhat similar to a television camera tube and picture tube in the same package. When infrared energy strikes the photosensitive surface, electrons are released. The electrons are focused by a magnetic field onto a fluorescent screen at the opposite tube. This screen emits visible light. Thus, infrared energy, which is not normally visible, is converted into visible light.

**Figure 9-13.
Sectional Drawing of
Image Intensifier**

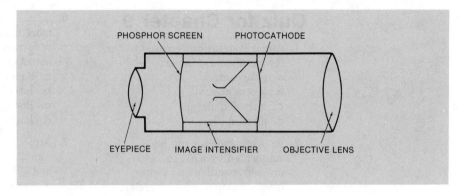

PHOSPHOR SCREEN   PHOTOCATHODE

EYEPIECE   IMAGE INTENSIFIER   OBJECTIVE LENS

When incorporated into a portable hand-held unit, the image intensifier system may be used to enable a security guard to inspect an otherwise dark area at night. The unit may also be used with a TV camera to permit viewing activities in dark areas or (with a film camera) to photograph surreptitious activities for evidence or identification. In areas where there is little illumination of any type, including infrared, an infrared spotlight may be used to provide the necessary illumination. The use of infrared, which is not visible, allows intruders to think they are operating in total darkness when, in fact, they are under observation.

WHAT HAVE WE LEARNED?

1. Audio and video monitoring equipment can be used to protect areas where it is not feasible or economical to post guards.
2. Ordinary apartment house intercoms can be used for both audio monitoring and gate control.
3. Audio intrusion detectors consist of a microphone (or vibration sensor), amplifier, and trigger circuit to detect sound in a protected area.
4. Audio monitoring is useful for most areas, except very noisy environments and those with thick, heavy drapes or carpets.
5. Vibration detectors are a subset of audio monitors that can be used to protect objects such as file cabinets and to prevent entry through walls, floors, or ceilings.
6. Video monitors can be used for gate control or surveillance. Video motion detectors can be used to compare present scenes with a stored reference scene "frozen" when the area was known to be secure.

Quiz for Chapter 9

1. Audio systems can be used either for aural monitoring or:
   a. gate control.
   b. access control.
   c. intrusion alarm.
   d. all of above.

2. An audio monitor can be augmented by a(n) _____ to prevent unauthorized visitors from slipping in with a careless authorized person.
   a. ultrasonic motion detector
   b. photoelectric beam
   c. field disturbance detector
   d. closed-circuit TV

3. A(n) _____ circuit can be used in conjunction with an audio-monitoring system to relieve security personnel of the need to listen constantly to the monitor.
   a. SCR flashtube
   b. trigger
   c. alarm
   d. oscillator

4. _____ can cause frequent false alarms in an audio intrusion detection system.
   a. RF radiation
   b. Air currents
   c. Background noise
   d. EMI

5. _____ can muffle the sound of an intruder and thereby defeat the system.
   a. Heavy carpeting
   b. High ambient noise
   c. Heavy drapes
   d. All of the above

6. _____ techniques using two or more microphones permit reduction of false alarms by detection of outside sounds.
   a. Sound cancellation
   b. Interferometry
   c. Bistatic monitoring
   d. Ratio detection

7. A(n) _____ detector/sensor is sometimes used to augment audio and video detectors.
   a. audio
   b. vibration
   c. low-frequency
   d. laser

8. _____ discourages amateur shoplifters but is (are) considerably less effective against professionals.
   a. Closed-circuit TV
   b. Dummy TV cameras
   c. Audio monitoring
   d. Photoelectric systems

9. Image-intensifier tubes and diode array detectors are used in _____ systems.
   a. closed-circuit TV
   b. audio
   c. TV
   d. low-light TV

10. A _____ can be used with any TV or monitor, without special connection, to form a motion detector.
    a. photoelectric cell
    b. low-light–level cell
    c. frame freezer
    d. laser

Alarm and Signaling Systems

ABOUT THIS CHAPTER

No intruder alarm system is of any use whatsoever if there is no means for sounding the alarm. In other words, it must have an output device or system. Some systems sound a local alarm bell or siren, while others call the police or security authorities. In this chapter, you will learn about the equipment and devices that form the output for intruder alarms.

LOCAL ALARMS

Local alarms are located on the protected premises and generally provide inexpensive protection.

A local alarm is just what the name implies—an alarm located on the premises to be protected. Local alarms in general are not as effective as the more sophisticated systems to be described later, but they definitely have their place in security systems. The local alarm has two functions.

1. It must attract attention—the attention of either the police, the proprietor, or some civic-minded citizen who will call the police.
2. It should frighten or at least unnerve intruders so that they will either abandon their plans or will take so much time that they can be caught.

Typical Circuits

A simple system can be foiled by shorting the wires carrying power to the bell or siren.

Figure 10-1 shows a typical circuit used for operating a local alarm. Normally, the alarm contacts in the intrusion detector are closed. The current through the connecting wires will hold relay K1 closed and the contacts open. When the intrusion detector is actuated, the alarm contacts in the detector circuit open. This deenergizes relay K1, closing the circuit to the alarm. The connecting wires must be well protected with conduit and run inside the protected area. This system could be foiled if the two connecting wires at the bell were shorted together or if one of the wires were cut. In spite of this limitation, this arrangement is often used in installations where the connecting wires cannot be reached without tripping whatever intrusion detector is used.

In installations where the possible gain from burglary is very great, a burglar might think it worth the time and risk to drill through a wall to reach the connecting wires leading to the bell. In a case like this, additional protection can be obtained by using the circuit of *Figure 10-2.* Here, a bias-voltage source is included in the intrusion detector. This system is almost identical to the electromechanical system described in Chapter 4. In this system, cutting the connecting wires will remove the bias on transistor Q1, allowing it to conduct and thus setting off the alarm. Shorting the connecting wires together will also remove the bias and set off the alarm because of the voltage drop across diode X1.

The cabinets or cases containing alarms are usually equipped with a small snap-action switch arranged so that it will set off the alarm if anyone tries to open the case.

**Figure 10-1.
Simple Alarm Circuit**

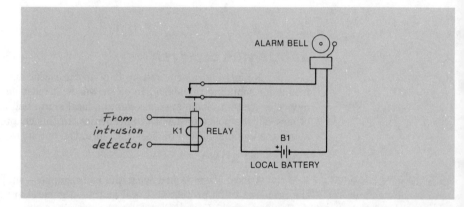

**Figure 10-2.
Alarm Circuit that Trips
on Open or Short
Circuit**

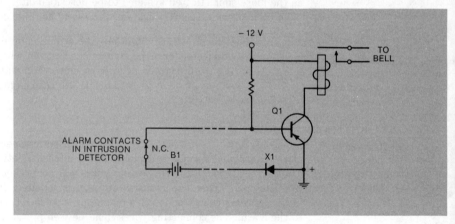

Types of Local Alarms

The simplest local alarm is a loud bell mounted on an outside wall of the premises. Usually a separate battery is supplied for operating the bell so that it cannot be foiled by cutting the power lines.

Another type of local alarm that is gaining popularity is the electronic siren. This circuit produces a wailing sound and is often used as a siren on police cars. The siren has a pronounced psychological effect simply because it sounds like a police car. An already nervous intruder would become even more nervous and less likely to complete the planned theft. Also, since the alarm is a siren, it will tend to mask the sound of approaching police cars, increasing the chance that the intruder will be caught.

Electronic sirens have a pronounced psychological effect, and they mask the sound of approaching police cars.

Figure 10-3 shows the circuit of an electronic siren. In this circuit, unijunction transistor Q1 is a sawtooth generator that generates a voltage having the waveform shown in *Figure 10-4a*. This waveform changes the frequency of an audio oscillator consisting of transistors Q2 and Q3 and their associated circuitry. The result is that the audio-frequency output periodically increases in frequency, then suddenly jumps back to its original frequency. This produces the familiar wailing sound of the electronic sirens used on many police cars. The output from the circuit shown is less than 1 W. This is not loud enough to attract any attention, but the circuit can be followed by an audio power amplifier of the type used in public-address systems to provide an adequate sound level.

**Figure 10-3.
Electronic Siren Circuit**

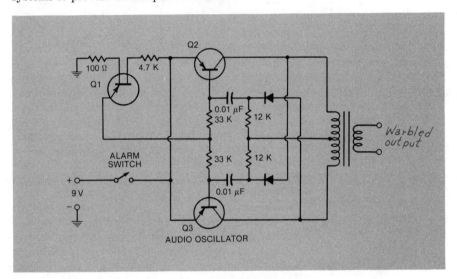

High-powered electronic sirens are among the most effective alarms. They can be made almost invulnerable to foiling if they are mounted in cases that are protected by interlock switches. Of course, there are more components in an electronic siren than in a simple bell and, consequently, more possible things to fail. However, the high reliability of solid-state circuits will minimize the possibility of circuit failure. A test switch should be provided so that the user can be sure that the circuits are working properly before turning on the system for the night.

Correct mounting can make high-powered electronic sirens almost invulnerable to foiling.

Control of Lights

A local alarm is frequently connected to the lights in the protected area. Then, when an intruder trips the alarm, the protected area is flooded with light. This has the double advantage of frightening the burglar and enabling the police to see what is going on when they respond to the alarm.

A variation of this light control is the addition of flashing bright lights that are set off in the protected area by the intrusion detector. These lights have a pronounced psychological effect on the intruder who trips the alarm—while attempting to perform the robbery, blinding lights are flashing.

Light turn-on switches can both frighten the intruder and make it easier for police to see what is going on.

**Figure 10-4.
Waveforms of
Electronic Siren**

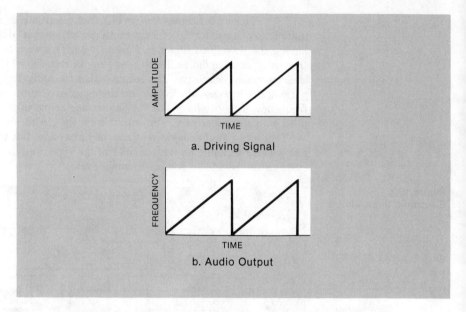

a. Driving Signal

b. Audio Output

Figure 10-5 shows a circuit of the type normally used in flash photography. Under quiescent conditions the silicon-controlled rectifier (SCR) and the flashtube are not conducting. The 2-μF capacitor is charged to the full value of the dc power-supply voltage. When a positive-going pulse is applied to the input circuit, it triggers the SCR into conduction. The sudden surge of current through the SCR induces a high voltage in the secondary of the transformer. The secondary of the transformer is connected to a coil consisting of about six turns wrapped around the flashtube. The high voltage in this coil ionizes the gas in the flashtube, causing it to fire. All of the charge in the 2-μF capacitor then discharges through the flashtube, causing a bright flash.

This circuit may be used in connection with automatic cameras to get a photograph of a burglar in action. This provides evidence for future identification. Another use is to position the flashtube so that it will flash directly in the burglar's face when he or she touches a safe or some other specific object to be protected. In this case, the circuit can be driven by a low-frequency pulse generator such as that shown in *Figure 10-6*. The flash rate may be adjusted by changing the value of capacitor C. A flash rate of 2 to 5 flashes per second is not only blinding, but very disconcerting.

**Figure 10-5.
Photoflash Circuit**

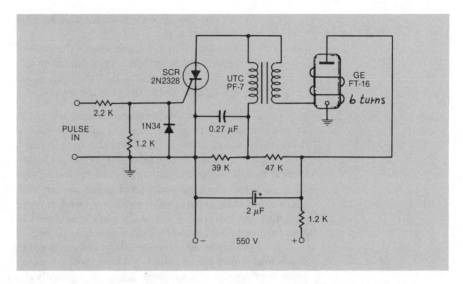

**Figure 10-6.
Pulse Generator to
Drive Photoflash Unit**

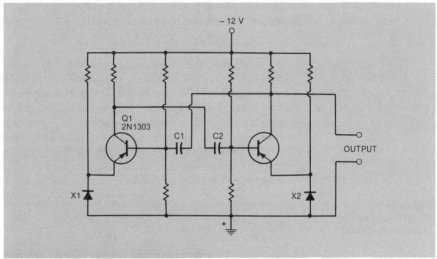

REMOTE MONITORING

In large facilities such as industrial plants, government
installations, and schools, it is usually necessary to monitor the security
status of the entire facility at one central location. This might be either a
central point on the same premises or the headquarters of a private
security company several miles distant. In any case, the following
indications are required at the monitoring point:

1. Normal or Secure. This is an indication that the system is turned on
   and is operating properly.

2. Alarm. This indication shows that an intruder has entered the protected area.
3. Trouble. This indication shows that there is trouble with the system, caused either by component failure or an attempt to foil the system.
4. Access. This indicates that the system has been disabled to allow authorized people to enter the protected area.

Printouts can provide supervisory personnel with the date and time of each event.

In addition to the foregoing indications, many installations provide an automatic printout of the time and date that each of the indicated functions changes. Some installations also have controlled door locks, intercoms, and closed-circuit television systems connected between the central monitoring point and each of the protected areas.

When the monitoring point is not too far from the protected areas, there are usually separate wires run from each intrusion alarm. When large distances are involved, it is usually more economical to use a coded system that transmits information from all detectors through a single pair of wires.

Security monitoring consoles vary in complexity with the security needs and size of the installation where they are used. The monitoring point may consist of a simple indicator in a guard's shack, or it may be an elaborate console in which a security officer can trace the progress of an intruder through a facility while directing police to a point of interception.

Remote Monitoring Circuit

A battery, zener diode, and simple voltmeter can indicate alarm, secure, or access conditions.

Figure 10-7 shows a circuit to remotely monitor the security status of an area. In normal operation, the access switch in the "secure" position and the alarm contacts are closed. Under this condition, there is a 6-V drop across zener diode X1 in the protected area, and the voltage across the voltmeter is 6 V. The voltmeter is shown in *Figure 10-8*. The scale is marked so that at midscale (6 V) it will indicate a secure condition. That is, the intrusion alarm has not been tripped. When the alarm contacts are opened by the presence of an intruder, the circuit will be opened and the voltmeter will show a zero-scale indication that is labeled "alarm."

Figure 10-7.
Simple Remote
Monitoring Circuit

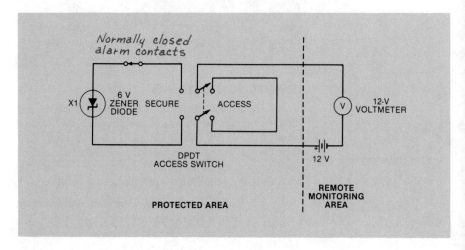

**Figure 10-8.
Indicator Scale for
Security System**

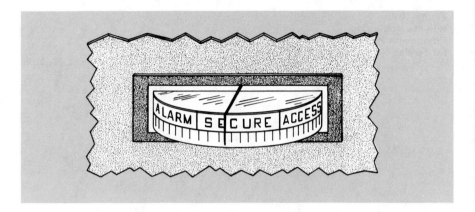

When the access switch is thrown to the "access" position to allow authorized persons to enter the protected area, the switch is shorted, so there will be no voltage drop across it. The voltmeter will then show full-scale deflection, indicating an access condition. The guard monitoring the console will then know that the area in question is no longer protected.

A Disadvantage

One disadvantage of the arrangement as described so far is that a short circuit across the lines from the protected area will cause the same indication as throwing the access switch to the "access" position. This disadvantage is overcome by adding a test switch and a second zener diode connected as shown in *Figure 10-9a*. When the test switch is in the "normal" position, the circuit is identical to that of *Figure 10-7*. The addition of X2 across the "access" position will not affect the operation, since it is backward and there will be little voltage drop across it. This switch merely reverses the polarity of the battery and the voltmeter when in the "test" position. When the polarity is reversed (switch in "test" position), a short circuit across the line will form the circuit shown in *Figure 10-9b*. The voltmeter will still read full scale in the "secure" position. If, however, the access switch is in the "access" position, the circuit will be as shown in *Figure 10-9c*. Zener diode X2 will then be connected in the circuit in such a way as to reduce the voltage across the meter to 6 V, and a "secure" reading will be obtained. Thus, by using the test switch, the guard can distinguish between an actual access condition and a short on the line.

Many variations of this basic remote-monitoring circuit are in common use. One of the most common is the use of voltage-sensitive circuits and indicator lamps instead of meter-type indications.

Local Buzzer or Bell

In addition to the meter or indicator-light monitor, it is desirable to have some kind of audible annunciator such as a buzzer or a bell that will alert the guard to the fact that the status of one of the indicators has changed. It is not necessary to use a separate buzzer for each indicator.

**Figure 10-9.
Remote Monitoring
Circuit with Provision
for Testing**

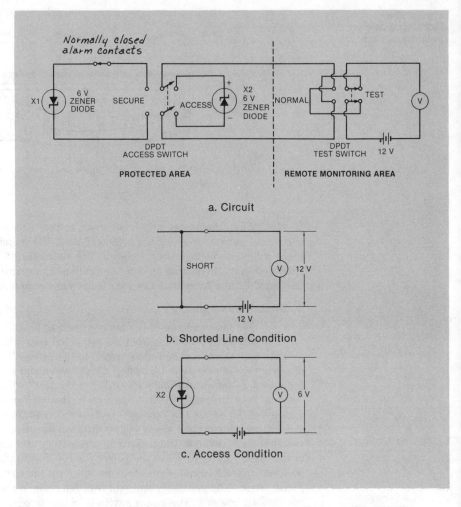

a. Circuit

b. Shorted Line Condition

c. Access Condition

Figure 10-10 shows a simple circuit using silicon-controlled switches (SCS's) that will operate a buzzer whenever any of the channels is activated but will cause only the proper lamp to light. Normally, none of the silicon-controlled switches is conducting. When any of the inputs exceeds a predetermined level, the associated SCS will fire, causing the appropriate indicator to light. When any of the circuits is tripped, the buzzer will sound. A switch is provided to permit the guard to silence the buzzer.

**Figure 10-10.
Circuit Using One
Buzzer with Several
Indicators**

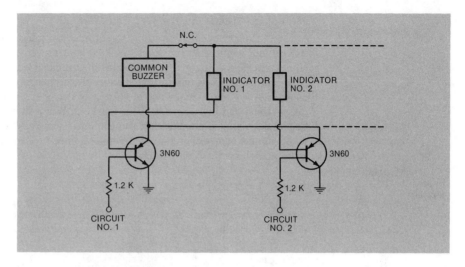

**Figure 10-10.
Circuit Using One
Buzzer with Several
Indicators**

Coded Signaling Systems

Audio tones can be used to signal remote monitoring sites up to several miles from the protected premises.

In many applications, the security monitoring point is located several miles from the protected areas. This is particularly true when a private security organization provides the protection. In such cases, it is usually more economical to use a single pair of wires from several different protected areas to the monitoring point. This is accomplished by using a code system that will identify each protected area and its security status.

A simple system that will accomplish this goal is shown in *Figure 10-11*. Here, at each protected area or at some central point near several protected areas, a coder is located. This consists of a group of oscillators that generate different frequency signals corresponding to the security status of each protected area. These signals are then combined and transmitted to the monitoring point over a single pair of wires. At the monitoring point, the signal is separated into its various components by filters. The output of each filter is then fed to the corresponding indicator.

**Figure 10-11.
System to Transmit
Several Signals over
Telephone Line**

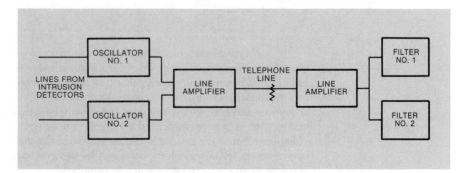

Microcomputer Event Recorders

Modern security systems sometimes use microcomputers for control and monitoring functions. Such computers can communicate alphanumeric data over telephone lines in standardized codes such as the American Standard Code for Information Interchange (ASCII). Such coding allows the system to make use of relatively low-cost equipment developed for personal and business computer markets. When fitted with a modem (modulator/demodulator) device, the computer can receive ASCII-coded audio signals over either regular telephone lines or local audio lines. Such a system is shown in *Figure 10-12*.

Figure 10-12. Modem

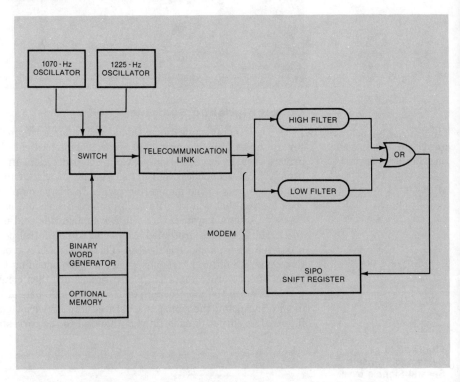

A typical system will represent the two states ("digits") of the binary number system with two separate audio tones (e.g., 1070 Hz and 1225 Hz). When a binary word-generator circuit creates the binary code for any given ASCII word, a switcher selects the appropriate audio tone sequences and transmits them over the telephone link. An advantage of this system is that preformatted messages can be sent and displayed on a video terminal. Such messages can be stored in the alarm system in a read-only memory (ROM). Each message can be designed according to the type of alarm signal received or the action required.

AUTOMATIC TELEPHONE DIALING

Automatic dialers dial the police or security department telephone number when an intruder is detected.

One of the latest and most sophisticated additions to intrusion-alarm systems is a device that will automatically dial the local police department or security organization in the event of an intrusion. To some extent, this arrangement gives the small facility some of the advantages formerly enjoyed only by firms that could afford their own security forces. An automatic dialing system is shown in *Figure 10-13*.

Figure 10-13. Automatic Telephone Dialer

Some automatic dialers can be preprogrammed to respond differently to different types of alarm conditions. For example, the police or security can be called when the intrusion alarm is tripped, the fire department can be called when the smoke detector sends out a signal, and the repair department can be called when a trouble signal is received.

Rotary Dialing

A diagram of a rotary telephone dial is shown in *Figure 10-14*. Switch A connects the phone to the line. It operates when the phone is lifted from the cradle. Switch B opens the circuit to the receiver and shorts out the transmitter. This switch operates when the dial is moved from its normal talking position, and it remains in this position until the dial gets back to its normal position. Switch C is called the "impulse switch." By opening and closing, it generates the dial pulses. Note that the dial pulses are actually circuit interruptions. For example, dialing the number 5 will open the line five times. The slowest dialing rate in use today is about twelve interruptions per second.

Figure 10-14. Telephone Dial Circuit

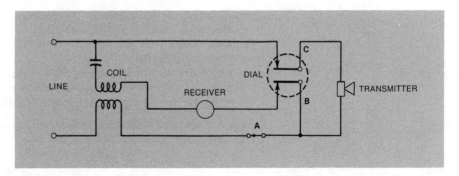

Touch-Tone Dialing

The touch-tone dialing principle is also used in automatic dialers. The touch-tone system operates by transmitting high/low tone pairs in sequence. In order to minimize interference from other signals, two separate tones are combined to represent each number. The frequencies used to represent each number are listed in Table 10-1.

Table 10-1.
Tone Frequencies Used in Touch-Tone System

Digit	Tone Frequencies (Hz)
1	697 and 1209
2	697 and 1336
3	697 and 1477
4	770 and 1209
5	770 and 1336
6	770 and 1477
7	852 and 1209
8	852 and 1336
9	852 and 1477
0	941 and 1336

The following specifications should be met by any device that is used to dial automatically using this system.

1. The frequency of the various tones must be held within 1%.
2. The amplitude of the dialing signal must be held within the limits specified by the telephone company.
3. Each double tone should have a duration of at least 40 milliseconds.
4. The maximum dial rate should not be faster than twelve tone bursts per second.

Sequence of Events

We know the sequence of events involved in dialing a telephone call.

1. The telephone is connected to the line.
2. A short time later, the dial tone comes on the line.
3. The number is dialed.
4. hortly after dialing, one of two things happens. Either the 20-Hz ringing signal appears on the line or a busy signal comes on.
5. After the phone being called is answered, the ringing signal stops.

From the previous sequence of events, we can see the functions that the automatic dialer must perform.

1. When an intrusion alarm is tripped, the dialer must connect itself to the telephone line.
2. There is then a delay until the dial tone appears on the line.
3. After the dial tone comes on the line, the circuit must be interrupted the proper number of times in sequence to dial the desired number. An alternative approach is to apply two-tone signals to the line as is done in the touch-tone dialing system.
4. There is then another delay until the phone is answered or a busy signal appears on the line.
5. Finally, the tape-recorded message must be transmitted and the device must be turned off. In some systems, another number is called and another message is transmitted after the first one. In that way, the first call can be to the police department, and the following calls can be to authorized employees who will go to the scene of the intrusion to investigate.

The extensive use of touch-tone signals in the telephone system makes it easier to provide a range of control or monitoring functions in addition to automatic dialing. For example, security personnel can use the touch-tone buttons on their ordinary desk telephone to query or test the system from remote locations. They can also reset the alarm remotely if it appears to be a false alarm condition. It is also possible to use touch-tone codes to switch sensors or cameras remotely.

Circuit Operation

Figure 10-15 is a block diagram of an automatic dialing system. The sequence of operation is as follows. When the circuit from the intrusion detector is interrupted, relay K1 is deenergized, closing the contacts that start the system in operation. This connects the system to the telephone line but does not start the tape recorder. An amplifier is connected across the line, and when the dial tone comes on the line, the tape transport is started. The tape has a prerecorded number of tones corresponding to the number to be dialed. These tones are amplified and rectified so that each tone will cause the impulse relay to open, thus dialing the number. A prerecorded tone then causes the tape transport to stop, and it connects an amplifier to the line. This amplifier has a sharp response at 20 Hz so that it will pick up the ringing signal. As long as the ringing signal occurs every few seconds, nothing further will happen. When the ringing signal stops, the tape transport will start and will transmit the desired message two or three times, after which a prerecorded tone will cause the system to shut down.

If the called telephone is not answered after about one minute, a timer will cause the tape transport to start until the next recorded message is reached, which it will then transmit in the same way. In this way, two or three messages can be transmitted. Often, the last message is coded to the telephone operator so that if for some reason the police cannot be reached, the operator can continue to call until there is a response.

**Figure 10-15.
Automatic Dialer**

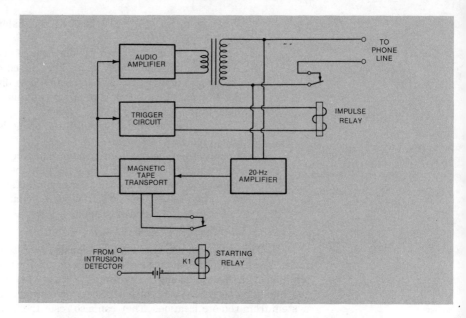

Another feature of the system is an amplifier and filter that will recognize a busy signal. If a busy signal is received after dialing, the tape transport will advance to the next message.

Systems designed for use with touch-tone dialing are somewhat simpler because the impulse relay and its associated amplifier and circuitry are not required. The tones may be recorded directly on the magnetic tape. This is usually done with the telephone set that is also connected directly to the line.

Installation

Connection of an automatic dialer to a telephone is usually accomplished through a coupler furnished by the telephone company. This ensures that the dialer will match the 900-ohm impedance of most telephone lines and that the amplitude will not be great enough to cause cross-talk interference with other telephone lines.

Automatic dialers are often much more complicated than the one shown in *Figure 10-15*. They contain additional recorded messages that can be used for purposes other than reporting a burglary. Dial codes are generated by complex electronic circuitry.

Two-Tone Oscillators

One of the system elements of some automatic dialers is an oscillator that will oscillate at two frequencies simultaneously. This circuit is used to generate the two-tone signals that are used in the touch-tone dialing system. Such oscillators can also be used to generate tone codes for other types of signaling systems.

The operation of a conventional LC oscillator can be explained using the simplified diagram shown in *Figure 10-16a*. The tube or transistor is used to produce an effective negative resistance, R_n. When this resistance is less than the actual resistance, R, of the tuned circuit, the circuit will not oscillate. If the effective negative resistance is larger than the resistance of the tuned circuit, the circuit will oscillate, but the oscillations will continually increase in amplitude. In a practical circuit, the amplitude increases until it is limited by the non-linearity of the tube or transistor. This non-linearity is what keeps the amplitude of the signal from a conventional oscillate or constant. However, because of the non-linearity, the circuit tends to oscillate at a single frequency or to produce spurious signals at several frequencies.

Simplified Circuit

A simplified equivalent circuit of the two-tone oscillator is shown in *Figure 10-16b*. Here, the tube or transistor is again represented by a negative resistance, R_n, but this time the value of the negative resistance is kept constant. In other words, the tube or transistor operates in a linear fashion. As we saw before, this would ordinarily lead to an oscillation that would continually increase in amplitude. In this circuit, however, a diode that acts as a non-linear resistor is connected across the coil of the tuned circuit. As the oscillations increase in amplitude, the current through the diode will increase and its resistance will decrease. This lowers the Q of the coil. Lowering the Q of a tuned circuit is exactly the same as increasing its series resistance. Thus, the oscillations increase in amplitude until the resistance of the tuned circuit is equal to the negative resistance. This limits the amplitude of the oscillations.

Since the limiting is done by the tuned circuit, the tube or transistor will operate in a linear manner. We can now use more than one tuned circuit as shown in *Figure 10-16c*. Because the circuit is linear, it will now oscillate at two frequencies, just as a linear amplifier can amplify two signals simultaneously.

Practical Analog Two-Tone Oscillator

A practical version of the two-tone oscillator is shown in *Figure 10-17*. The two transistors provide a negative resistance in series with the tuned circuits. The diode connected across each coil will limit the signal, and the circuit will oscillate simultaneously at the resonant frequency of both of the tuned circuits. In this circuit, the L/C ratio should be approximately 3,250,000. The values of L and C can then be found from the following equation.

$$L = \sqrt{\frac{3.25 \times 10^6}{2\pi f}}$$

$$C = \frac{1}{\sqrt{(2\pi f)3.25 \times 10^6}}$$

where,

        L is the inductance in henrys,
        C is the capacitance in farads,
        f is the frequency in hertz.

Although the two-tone oscillator has been the method of choice for generating touch-tone codes, and is still used extensively in telephone sets, some systems use any of several digital IC chips now on the market to generate the twelve standard high/low tone pairs representing digits (0—9, #, and *) in response to 4-bit digital word inputs. These chips were originally designed for use in low-cost telephone and computerized modem equipment.

ADVANTAGES AND LIMITATIONS OF AUTOMATIC DIALING

Automatic dialing devices give small business operators some of the advantages that they would gain by having their own security guards. In addition, they may be used for many purposes other than protection against intrusion. One of the most important is their use by heart patients to call a doctor if they have an attack. Other less spectacular, but

**Figure 10-16.
Oscillator Circuits**

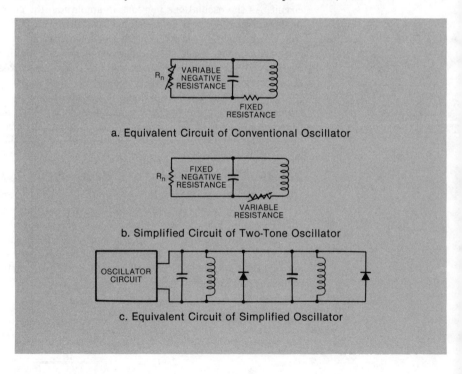

a. Equivalent Circuit of Conventional Oscillator

b. Simplified Circuit of Two-Tone Oscillator

c. Equivalent Circuit of Simplified Oscillator

**Figure 10-17.
Practical Two-Tone
Oscillator Circuit**

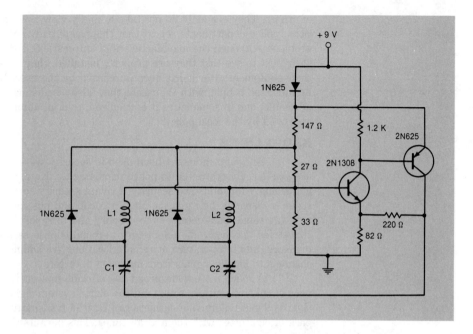

important, uses permit a business executive to monitor important aspects of the business from home. For example, a grocer can connect an automatic dialer to a refrigeration system so that it will call the home if the refrigeration fails.

The automatic telephone dialer has some limitations. For example, it may get a busy signal when dialing the police. Most systems are arranged to call again if they get a busy signal the first time or to place a backup call to someone who will call the police. Nevertheless, there is still a chance that the call will not get through. Unlike systems that use leased lines, it is not practical to equip regular telephone lines with failure-monitoring systems that will cause an alarm if a line is cut. It is thus possible for an intruder to disable the system by cutting the phone lines outside the building. The danger from this can be minimized by providing a backup local alarm. Some firms market radio links to the police department that avoid this possibility.

False Alarms

Automatic dialers make false alarms more serious because they often summon the police needlessly. Some localities have stiff regulations covering these devices.

Perhaps the most serious limitation of the automatic dialer is the seriousness of false alarms. These systems are not necessarily any more susceptible to false alarms than other systems, but false alarms are much more serious in systems that reach the police department than in systems that merely sound a local alarm or summon a security guard who is already on the premises. The latter calls are annoying and lead to distrust of the system, but they cause no danger to human life. On the other hand, when members of the police department receive a call indicating that a crime is in progress, they usually rush to the scene, risking their lives and the lives of others. They certainly do not take a kindly view toward false alarms. Some police departments report that this has already become a serious problem. Although the manufacturers of automatic telephone dialers do their best to see that they are properly installed, they have no control of their equipment after it has been purchased by the user. It can be installed by unskilled people, with the result that false alarms may be frequent. It is advisable, and in some cities it is required, that all automatic systems be approved by the local police.

RADIO LINKS

Although radio has been used in security work for many years, its use was largely restricted to police departments. Now, radio is being used increasingly for industrial security. Private security services use two-way radio to dispatch their guards. Many taxicab and bus companies are using two-way radios as a deterrent to robbery and to report robberies quickly. Industries that use radio telemetery to monitor processes such as flow, pressure, and temperature at remote locations are adding additional channels to handle signals from intrusion detectors.

A much more widespread use of radio in security is the use of very small transmitters to extend the alarm system right to the individual. Guards, bank tellers, and cashiers can carry a transmitter no larger than a pack of cigarettes with them at all times. This permits them to trip an alarm without detection.

A transmitter used with alarm systems is shown in *Figure 10-18*. This circuit consists of a tunnel-diode crystal oscillator operating in the vicinity of 27 MHz, with an audio-frequency (af) tone generator. The transmitter has a range of 50 to 250 feet, depending on local conditions. The receiver is simply a communications-type receiver tuned to the frequency of the transmitter. An audio filter in the output is tuned to the same af tone generator.

This arrangement works well with an automatic telephone-dialing system connected as shown in *Figure 10-19*. Here, the guard, watchman, or bank teller carries the miniature transmitter. When an emergency exists, he or she merely turns on the switch on the transmitter. The tone-modulated rf signal is picked up by the receiver, which produces an output consisting of the audio tone. This tone is used to turn on the automatic dialer which will then automatically dial and transmit a prerecorded message. If the two-tone oscillator described earlier is used as a tone generator in the transmitter, it is possible to transmit two or more different messages. Thus, it is possible for a guard to carry a miniature transmitter with several different switches. The guard discovers an emergency and throws a switch, causing a prerecorded message to call for police, fire department, or an ambulance. The possibilities of this system are almost unlimited.

**Figure 10-18.
Miniature, 27-MHz
Transmitter Circuit**

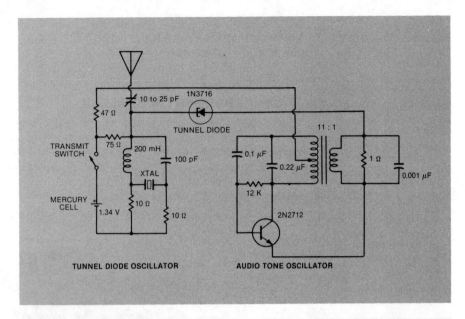

**Figure 10-19.
Radio Link with
Automatic Telephone
Dialer**

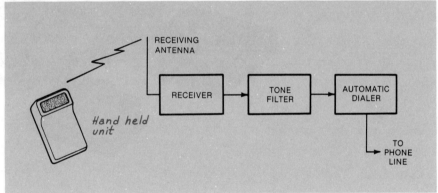

Autodialers and radio
links can be used to pro-
vide protection for ill or
handicapped persons.

A variation of this system is used by individuals in their homes. The device may be coded to serve as a security alarm in the event of an intrusion, or it may be used by a handicapped or ill person to summon medical aid in an emergency.

Operating Frequencies

Modern systems avoid the 27-MHz portion of the spectrum because of the tremendous expansion of citizens band radio. This portion of the spectrum is so crowded in some parts of the country that it is unusable for alarm purposes. Depending upon use, certain frequencies in the 49-MHz and 72-MHz bands are more popular than the crowded 27-MHz band. Some systems also use the guard bands between video and audio carriers in locally unused TV channel assignments.

Regardless of the frequency used, the device is a radio transmitter, albeit a small one, and must comply with the rules of the FCC.

LAW ENFORCEMENT SIGNALLER

Figure 10-20 shows a radio system that is used by law enforcement agencies in addition to their regular two-way radio. The system consists of a small radio transmitter that can be carried on a belt and a receiver that is located in the police car. An officer who gets out of the cruiser to check on someone speaks the location into the unit. This message is recorded.

**Figure 10-20.
Emergency Location
Alerting System**
*(Courtesy Antenna
Specialists Co.)*

If nothing serious happens during the investigation, the message will not be transmitted. If, however, trouble occurs, the officer can press a button on the belt unit. This will transmit a signal to the unit in the car which will, in turn, transmit a distress message, including the recorded message giving the location, over the regular police radio. A special tone that precedes the message indicates that a distress message will follow and the channel will be cleared.

The belt unit also has a position sensor that will sense if the officer should fall. If the officer remains in a prone position for more than fifteen seconds, the distress message will be transmitted.

EVENT RECORDERS

Many thefts from large plants and institutions are carried out with the assistance of guards and other trusted employees. Many security people feel that a means must be provided to check on trusted employees if for no other reason than to remove the temptation to steal or to collaborate with thieves. One important accessory that can help in this function is an event recorder of the type shown in *Figure 10-21*. In a large security system, the event recorder is connected to record as many different security functions as are deemed necessary. For example, it may be arranged to print out a record giving the date and time of every change in a security system. It will make a record every time an access switch is thrown from secure to access, every time an intrusion alarm is tripped, or every time a door or gate is opened outside of normal business hours. A record of this type, shown in *Figure 10-22*, has many functions. It provides an excellent opportunity for checking the cause of false alarms. We noted earlier that one scheme for frustrating the most elaborate intrusion alarms is for a prospective burglar to cause a number of false alarms without being detected. After the number of annoying false alarms has been so great that no one has any faith in the alarm system and will no longer respond to it, the intruder quickly loots the protected area. If a record is kept of all false alarms and their cause is carefully investigated, this practice can be spotted quickly. In this case, the area in question would actually be given additional surveillance, greatly increasing the chance of catching the intruder.

**Figure 10-21.
Event Recorder**

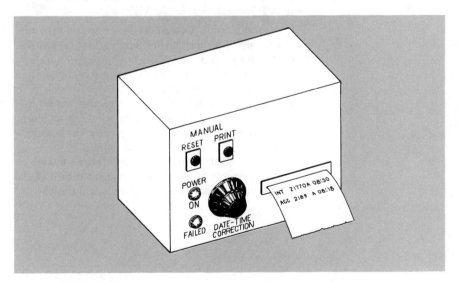

Another valuable function of the event recorder is that it will provide a check on security guards. For example, if a security guard at a central monitoring point intentionally allows a thief to enter a factory gate after hours, a record will be made and the guard can be tracked down.

**Figure 10-22.
Event Recording of
Changes in Status**

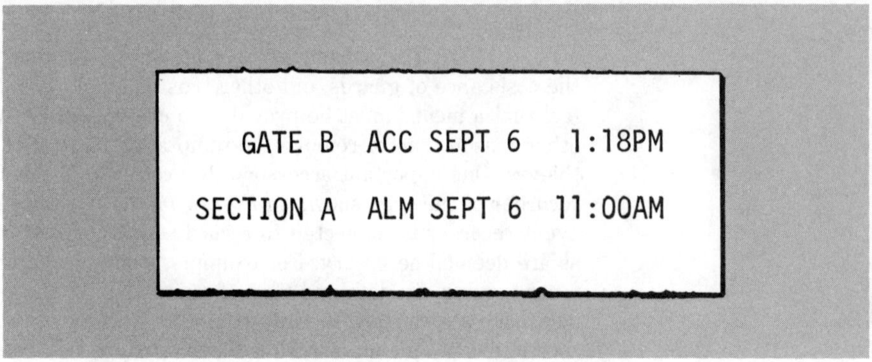

```
GATE B   ACC SEPT 6      1:18PM

SECTION A   ALM SEPT 6   11:00AM
```

Many other supervisory uses can be made of event monitors. They can record the times that guards make their rounds, of fire alarms or other emergencies, and of any other important plant functions that are desirable to monitor.

The microcomputer (or "personal computer," as it is also called) can easily be configured to act as an event recorder. When equipped with a modem and a Real-Time Clock (RTC) or RTC software, the computer can record signals from each remote station. If the signals are properly coded, the computer can log and display authorized access, guard check-ins, tests, intrusions, and any other event that the sensors can detect.

WHAT HAVE WE LEARNED?

1. A local alarm is located on the protected premises and may consist of either a bell, siren, or horn and/or a lights turn-on switch.
2. Remotely monitored alarms use a central location to monitor the status of the protected premises. The following conditions are monitored: normal/secure, alarm, access, and trouble.
3. Both pulsed and touch-tone telephones can be used to dial automatically a preprogrammed telephone number when an alarm condition occurs.
4. Radio links can be used to overcome the possibility of an intruder cutting the telephone lines prior to illegal entry.
5. A local alarm, especially a computerized model, can be used as a flexible event recorder to make a permanent record of the status conditions, including check-in times of guards and the like.

Quiz for Chapter 10

1. A(n) _____ should unnerve intruders, thereby either encouraging them to flee or causing such delay that they can be caught.
   a. ultrasonic alarm
   b. microwave alarm
   c. photoelectric alarm
   d. local alarm

2. Diode X1 in Figure 10-2 prevents disabling the alarm by:
   a. shorting the protection loop.
   b. opening the protection loop.
   c. biasing the protection loop.
   d. electromagnetic interference.

3. A(n) _____ local alarm masks the sound of approaching police cars.
   a. bell
   b. photoflash
   c. siren
   d. ultrasound

4. A flashing phototube with a rate of _____ is both blinding and disconcerting to the intruder.
   a. 1—2 per second
   b. 16 per minute
   c. 30 per second
   d. 2—5 per second

5. List four conditions that should be monitored in a remote system.

6. An "access/secure" remote monitoring system can be provided by a _____ and a voltmeter.
   a. battery
   b. zener diode
   c. power supply
   d. tunnel diode

7. A well-designed security system should have a:
   a. battery back-up.
   b. microwave detector.
   c. window foil loop.
   d. plunger switch actuator.

8. The touch-tone telephone uses _____ for signaling over telephone lines.
   a. low single tones
   b. high single tones
   c. high/low tone pairs
   d. low/low tone pairs

9. An autodialer must _____ when it receives an alarm signal.
   a. turn itself on
   b. turn itself off
   c. connect itself to the line
   d. turn on the siren

10. A(n) _____ can be used to automatically record guard check-in times at standard security points.
   a. clock timer
   b. digitizer
   c. event recorder
   d. key clock

Access Control

ABOUT THIS CHAPTER

One of the most important components of any electronic intrusion alarm system is the access control. Although the intrusion alarm must protect the premises from entry of any kind, it is, of course, necessary for authorized people to enter the protected area without tripping an alarm. This is usually accomplished by some kind of switch that disables the alarm. Of course, the switch must not be so simple that a prospective burglar can operate it.

The devices described in this chapter may also be used to assure that only authorized persons enter a protected area. In this application, the devices can be used to protect sensitive areas such as computer rooms.

ACCESS SWITCHES

An access switch allows authorized persons to enter a protected area without setting off an alarm.

Any intrusion alarm system must have a provision for allowing authorized persons to enter the protected area without setting off the alarm. This is usually accomplished by a switch that will disable the alarm system.

Key-operated Switches

The most common type of access switch is a key-operated switch, shown in *Figure 11-1*, similar to the ignition switch of an automobile. Keys for the switch are issued to authorized personnel only. Additional protection is sometimes provided by using two different access switches that require different keys to operate them. In this way, the keys can be issued to two different employees, so that both employees must be present to shut off the alarm. No one employee may enter the facility alone without setting off the alarm.

The access switch may be connected to remove power from the entire alarm system, or it may disable the alarm only. The exact arrangement depends on the type of detector and alarm system.

Vibration detectors and other means are often used to foil attempts to breech the access key system.

A great deal of sophistication is used in the manufacture of keys for access switches to prevent their being counterfeited or the lock being picked. Sometimes a vibration detector is included with the lock. Its sensitivity is set so that it will not be tripped by normal operation of the lock, but it will trip an alarm if the lock is treated roughly as it might be if someone were trying to pick it. Additional protection is often provided by using a more complex arrangement than a simple single-pole, single-throw switch. In the circuit shown in *Figure 11-2*, one set of contacts must be closed and the other opened to disable the alarm system. Intruders cannot foil the alarm by jumping or opening wires unless they get the right combination.

The chief disadvantage of key-operated access switches is that the keys may be lost or stolen. Anytime a key is missing even for a short time, the lock should be changed, because a clever intruder can have a duplicate key made very quickly.

Figure 11-1.
Key-operated Switch

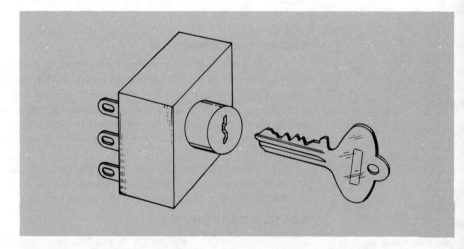

Figure 11-2.
Complex Circuit for
Key-operated Switch

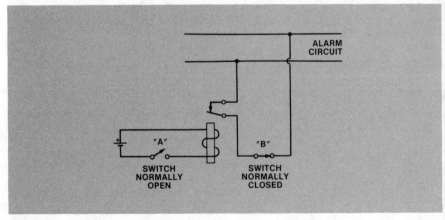

Timing Circuits

There are many ways in which simple timing circuits can control access to a protected area. The first is an arming or exit delay. This arrangement allows one to turn the alarm system on, but allows a short time for the person to leave the premises before the system will respond to anything, such as opening and closing the door. With this arrangement, the system starts protecting the premises shortly after the last authorized person has left.

Entrance-delay features allow an authorized person a short time to enter the premises and cancel the alarm.

The limitation of the arrangement previously described is that it has no provision for an authorized person to enter the premises once the alarm is actuated. This is handled by another time-delay circuit that is called an entrance delay. The alarm system is operative and will respond to an intrusion, but the actual sounding of the alarm is delayed for a few seconds to allow an authorized person to enter and shut off the alarm.

Time Switches

A thief can kidnap a holder of an access key and thus gain easy entrance to the protected premises.

One of the limitations of an access switch that can be operated only by a particular person is that a serious intruder with a lot to gain by the burglary may kidnap the person or a family member, forcing the person to open the premises and disable the alarm. Many burglaries have been performed this way, and employees who have resisted have been seriously injured.

A system that will eliminate this possibility is shown in *Figure 11-3*. Here, a time switch is connected in parallel with the access switch. For the alarm system to be made inoperative, both the key-operated access switch and time switch must be opened. The time switch is set to open during normal business hours. Thus, if someone is forced to open the key switch, the alarm system will still be active. Time switches are available with omitting devices which can be set to prevent them from operating on days the protected establishment is not normally open. This is an important feature; otherwise, a burglar might force a store manager to open the store during normal business hours on a day when it is closed.

Figure 11-3.
Access Switch Disables Alarm at Specified Times

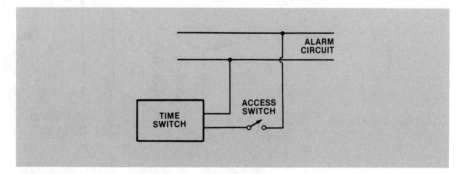

Computerized Access Switches

Again, we find that computers can perform a function that has traditionally been performed by mechanical or electromechanical devices. Computers can keep track of time of day and date, so they can be programmed to open the lock only at authorized times and on authorized days. Care must be taken in selecting these systems, however, to ensure that they are "fail secure." Power line transients, or power loss, can leave the system unprotected for that period of time.

At least one system uses a back-up monitoring system in which microcomputers built into door locks, and other microcomputers that operate alarm systems, report periodically to a central monitoring computer. If any one computer fails to report, or reports what programmers call "garbage," an alarm is sounded.

ELECTRICAL COMBINATION SWITCHES

Electrical combination switches such as those shown in *Figure 11-4* are becoming increasingly popular as access switches for secure areas. The circuit is arranged so that when the push-button switches are depressed in the correct sequence, the alarm-disabling relay will operate. Any other sequence of switch operation will not operate the relay. Thus, the switch can be operated only by one who knows the proper combination. There may be up to 30,000 wrong combinations in a system with several push buttons.

**Figure 11-4.
Push-Button
Combination Switch**

The principle of operation of combination switching systems may be understood by first considering the latching relay shown in *Figure 11-5*. In this circuit, the relay is energized by momentarily closing switch S, which may be a simple push button. Once the relay is energized, contacts A will close, holding the relay in the energized state after switch S is opened. The other contacts, 1, 2, and 3, may be used for logic functions.

**Figure 11-5.
Latching Relay Circuit**

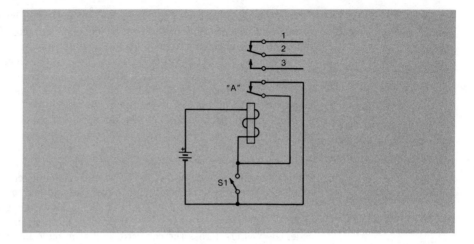

In the circuit of *Figure 11-6*, the latching relays are arranged so that the contacts of relay No. 2 supply power to the coil of relay No. 1, and the contacts of this relay in turn furnish power to the circuit of relay No. 3. Thus, the push-button switches must be pressed in the order 2, 1, 3. Pressing the buttons in any other sequence will have no effect. An additional refinement that may be added will de-energize all of the relays if a button is pressed out of sequence. When the buttons are pressed in the proper order, the last relay in the chain will disable the alarm system.

**Figure 11-6.
Combination Access
Switch Principle**

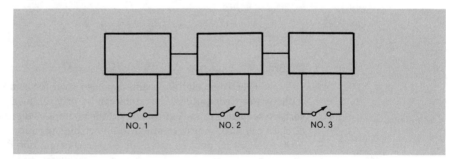

Digital Logic Devices

Traditionally, relays have been used in these systems because they are both reliable and easy to use in designs. Recently designed systems, however, may use digital IC logic elements to simulate relays. These devices are flexible and inexpensive, but they are subject to some of the same problems as computers (which are built from digital logic elements). In some systems, the entire circuit will be digital IC logic elements, except the output switch, which is a relay. This permits the relay to fail to an alarm condition if power is lost.

Simple combination locks can be foiled by an intruder with the patience to try many different combinations.

A disadvantage of this arrangement is that an intruder may keep experimenting until finding the proper sequence, although if several different circuits are used, the odds are against this. A simple addition that will overcome this limitation is shown in *Figure 11-7*. Here, a line from each of the buttons is connected to an OR circuit. This circuit will provide an output whenever any one of the buttons is pressed. This output drives a trigger circuit that applies a small pulse to capacitor C1, which discharges slowly through resistor R1. The discharge rate of the RC circuit is set so that if all of the push-button switches are pressed only a few times in a ten-minute period, no substantial voltage will develop across the capacitor, and the second trigger circuit will not operate. Thus, if a person operates the switches in the proper sequence, the second trigger circuit will not do anything. Even if the person makes a mistake and has to try again, the voltage across the capacitor will still be small. However, if an intruder should start pressing the switches at random in an attempt to break the code, the voltage across the capacitor will soon build up enough to operate the second trigger circuit, which will then either initiate the intrusion alarm or activate a signal at a central location.

**Figure 11-7.
OR Circuit Alerts to
Tampering**

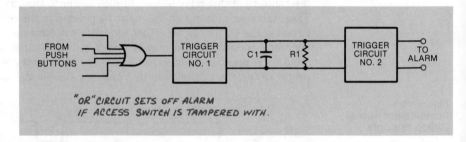

"OR" CIRCUIT SETS OFF ALARM
IF ACCESS SWITCH IS TAMPERED WITH.

Digital Electronic Combination Locks

Electronic digital circuits are also used for combinations switches. Although any computerized system can be programmed to recognize only a correct sequence of switch closures, other (simpler) digital electronic circuits can also be programmed to allow this operation. If complementary MOS (CMOS) IC devices are used, power consumption drops to approximately that of a calculator or digital watch—making battery power in a door lock feasible. This type of application is a natural for special-purpose medium-scale (MSI) or large-scale (LSI) integrated circuits.

Combination locks can be designed with two "legal" combinations: one unlocks the door normally while the other unlocks the door but also transmits an alarm to police.

Combination access switches can be equipped with an ingenious device to foil the burglar who forces an employee to operate the access switch. An arrangement can be made whereby if one digit in the correct combination is changed, an automatic telephone dialer will transmit a prerecorded message describing the situation to the police. For example, if the correct code is 7819, the number 7818 may be arranged to dial the police. Thus, if a burglar forces an employee to use the combination, a message will go to the police that someone is being forced to open the facility. The message may include the warning that the employee or family may be in danger if the police appear openly. In this way, the police can act accordingly and apprehend the burglar at the opportune time. A custom integrated circuit that will operate an electronic combination lock is described in Chapter 13.

CARD-LOCK SYSTEMS

Card locks can be designed to admit personnel selectively according to date/time, area, or other factors. Card keys can be used for personnel ID as well as to permit access.

Another type of access control system used frequently in connection with intrusion alarms is the card lock shown in *Figure 11-8*. In this arrangement, a coded card is inserted into the lock to throw the switch. Any card that is not properly coded will have no effect.

Cards can be coded in many different ways. One effective way to code cards is to deposit small amounts of magnetic material in the card in such a way that they cannot be seen. A magnetic detector in the lock will throw the switch only when a card having the proper magnetic pattern is inserted in the lock.

**Figure 11-8.
Coded-Card Switch**

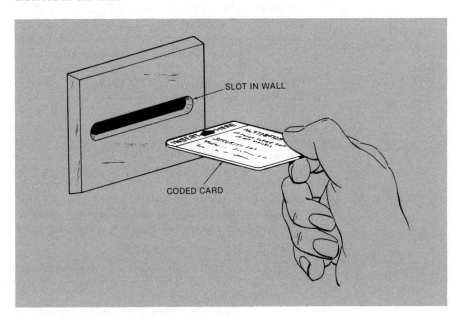

SLOT IN WALL

CODED CARD

Punched-Hole Cards

In other cards, a series of holes is punched with a special pattern or binary code. These holes can be read in the lock either by mechanical or electronic means. In mechanical systems, pins fall through the holes to unlock the system. If one or more of the pins is pushed up, indicating that no hole is present, the lock remains secure. Another system uses LEDs and phototransistors positioned so that the LED shines on the transistor only when a hole in the key card is present. A blinded phototransistor prevents the system from unlocking.

Bar Code Cards

Another form of card system is the laser-read variety. A printed code, such as the Uniform Pricing Code ("bar code") seen on consumer products in stores, is placed on the card. A laser optical scanner or light pen reads the code and determines whether or not it is authorized.

Applications

Card locks are used in a variety of ways to provide security. In the simplest system, the card lock is arranged to open a door lock whenever the proper card is inserted in the lock. This provides a moderate degree of security in allowing only authorized persons to enter an area.

Key Card Advantages and Limitations

The principal advantage of the card lock is that it is simple and inexpensive. When properly used in connection with other measures, it will contribute substantially to the security of an installation. Its principal limitation is that cards may be lost or stolen and used illegally before the combination can be changed and new cards can be issued.

Key cards also have several applications that are not ordinarily possible with other forms of access control. We can, for example, encode the card with a means of identifying the card holder. The security system can then be programmed to record who comes and goes and at what hours. In addition to detecting illegal activity, this type of system also permits management to monitor employees who habitually come in late or leave early or take long lunch hours. Although such use must be balanced against the probable strain in employee relations, it is available to management when abuse becomes a pattern rather than an exception.

The key card can also function as an employee identification badge. In some installations, the normal security badge containing the employee's photograph and signature is also encoded for use as a key to areas of the plant to which the employee has legitimate access.

WHAT HAVE WE LEARNED?

1. The access feature allows authorized personnel to enter the protected area. Entrance- and exit-delay timer circuits permit access and egress without creating a false alarm.
2. Several types of access control devices are used: mechanical keys, electrical and mechanical combination door locks, and key cards.
3. Time switches on door locks and safe locks are used to prevent the premises from being used except during normal business hours. These switches prevent a thief from gaining entry in league with a dishonest employee or by kidnapping an honest employee.
4. Combination locks are available that disable themselves (or set off an alarm) if an incorrect combination is attempted. Two or three "grace" attempts by clumsy employees who fumble the combination prevent false alarms.
5. Key cards can be either very simple or very sophisticated. They can do double duty as an employee identification card, and be encoded to record who comes and goes—and when.

Quiz for Chapter 11

1. A _____ strip on an entrance card key can be encoded with data.
   a. colored
   b. paramagnetic
   c. magnetic
   d. plastic

2. List three forms of data encoding system used on key cards.

3. Sometimes a _____ is incorporated into a lock or access switch to prevent successful tampering.
   a. vibration detector
   b. jimmying detector
   c. proximity detector
   d. combination lock

4. A(n) _____ allows a certain period of time after opening a door so that authorized personnel can turn off the alarm.
   a. combination lock
   b. exit-delay feature
   c. entrance-delay feature
   d. time-out circuit

5. We can connect a(n) _____ into the circuit with an access control switch to prevent entry except during normal working or business hours.
   a. combination lock
   b. entrance-delay circuit
   c. key card system
   d. time lock

6. Relays and digital logic elements can be connected so that a series of push buttons or access keys has to be pressed _____ before entrance is permitted.
   a. in sequence
   b. for a fixed period of time
   c. in parallel
   d. with the correct pressure

7. A "bar pattern" on a key card is read by a(n):
   a. magnetic detector.
   b. audio pick-up.
   c. laser scanner.
   d. LED.

Holdup and Assault Alarms

ABOUT THIS CHAPTER

Holdups are all too commonplace and are among the most dangerous forms of theft. Usually armed, holdup bandits are typically more aggressive than burglars and are more likely to harm their victims. In this chapter, you will learn about the types of alarms available for holdup protection and how these devices should be implemented for best effect.

PLANNING AN ALARM SYSTEM

Unlike an intrusion alarm which is tripped by an intruder, a holdup or assault alarm must be tripped by the victim or by a witness. In fact, although a holdup or assault alarm can use circuits that are very similar to those used in an intrusion alarm, the actual arrangement is quite different. Intrusion alarms are designed to protect unoccupied premises. Holdup alarms are designed to protect people.

Armed robbers are more confrontational and more prone to commit violent acts than other types of criminal.

When planning this type of alarm, it must be remembered that a robber or assailant is usually a much more violent person than a burglar. A burglar usually strives not to encounter anyone. A robber or assailant plans confrontation and often physical violence. In any holdup, there is always danger of bodily harm or even death.

Type of Response Required

A holdup or assault alarm must be planned around the type of response that can logically be expected in a given location. The most desirable response from an alarm is anything that will frighten a robber or assailant away before any harm is done. This isn't easy to accomplish in many situations. Sometimes a very loud alarm that is sure to attract attention and will mask the sound of an approaching police car will frighten a robber away. In other instances, it will only make the robber more nervous and, hence, more dangerous.

The next best response is to have help arrive on the scene as rapidly as possible. Ideally, the police should respond. If it isn't practical for the police to respond rapidly, a security guard will be almost as good. Finally, anyone at all responding is usually better than no one.

A system that has been used with success is a hidden switch that turns on a tape player in a back room. The recorder plays voice sounds for a short time creating the illusion that there are more people in the area. The recorder than shuts off. The thief investigates and finds no one, which can be very unnerving.

ALARM DEVICES

Holdup alarms can be local or remote, although the remote type is preferred.

Any of the alarm devices described in Chapter 10 can be used with a holdup alarm. The automatic telephone dialer is often used. The device is hidden where its presence will not be noticed. By using a hidden switch the victim can automatically dial the police or a security guard service. It is possible to combine the dialer with an intercom so that the police or guard service can actually listen to the robbery. Of course, no arrangement of this type should be installed without the knowledge and cooperation of the police department.

HOLDUP SWITCHES

The holdup switch should be unobtrusive to prevent the robber from seeing an employee trip the alarm.

One of the most important requirements of a holdup alarm is that it be capable of being actuated without attracting the robber's attention. Most security people feel that the danger of irritating a criminal to the point of harming a person is very great if it is apparent who set off the holdup alarm. In banks or ticket offices, where the lower part of the cashier's body is hidden from view, an alarm can be tripped secretly by the use of a foot-bar switch such as that shown in *Figure 12-1*. In stores where the employees can be watched by the robber, this is not advisable.

**Figure 12-1.
Foot-operated Switch**

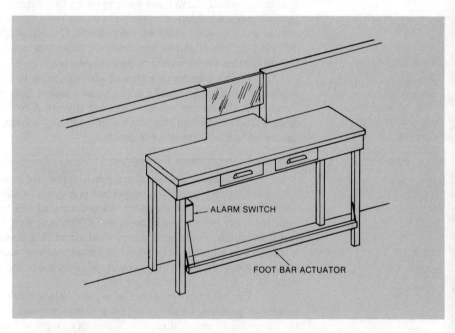

ALARM SWITCH

FOOT BAR ACTUATOR

The money clip shown in *Figure 12-2* is an ingenious holdup switch that may also be used in a regular intrusion alarm as a detector. This switch is actuated whenever anyone removes the money from the clip. The switch can be arranged so that it is cut out of the circuit by a hidden push button. Thus, whenever an authorized person takes money from the clip, he or she will first disable the alarm by means of the hidden push button. A thief, however, not realizing the way the system operates, may simply remove the money and unwittingly trip an alarm.

**Figure 12-2.
Money Clip**

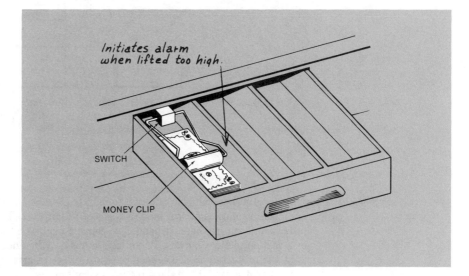

Many other types of holdup switches will suggest themselves for particular applications. The principal consideration is that the switch be located so that it can either be actuated without attracting any attention or so that the robber will unwittingly actuate it.

TIMING ARRANGEMENTS

One thing that can be done with any holdup alarm to both prevent false alarms and not let the robber know that the victim tripped the alarm is to use time-delay circuits. Suppose, for example, that a victim could trip an alarm by the switch arrangement of *Figure 12-2*. If while the robber was taking money, an alarm sounded, it would be immediately apparent that the victim could have tripped the alarm, and the robber might become violent. However, if the alarm didn't sound until sometime later when the victim was perfectly still, the robber would have trouble correlating the events. It might even be possible to convince the robber that someone elsewhere in the building tripped the alarm.

A timing device can be used to prevent false alarms. *Figure 12-3* shows a typical arrangement. Here the first timer starts timing when the holdup switch is tripped. Nothing visible or audible happens. After a short time interval, a local annunciator will sound or a light will flash. This starts the second timer. If the system is not reset before this stage times out, the main alarm, telephone dialer, or whatever else is used to summon help will be tripped.

Figure 12-3.
Timing Arrangement to
Prevent False Alarms

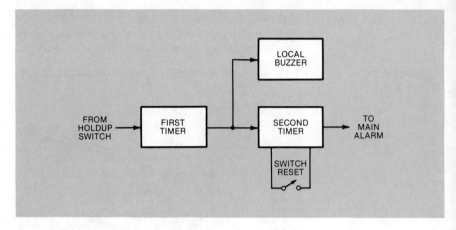

CAMERA SYSTEMS

Cameras aid in identifying
the criminal later and provide evidence for a trial.

Another valuable addition to an intrusion or holdup alarm is an
automatic camera that will take pictures of the protected area after the
intrusion alarm has been tripped. The camera may be either a still camera
or a motion picture camera. Photoflash lamps may be added to adequately
light the protected area. Perhaps the most effective arrangement is a
camera that is timed to take a picture every few seconds after the intrusion
alarm has been tripped.

The camera system adds to the security of an installation in three
ways. First, the fact that their actions are being photographed will often
frighten intruders into fleeing without stealing anything. Secondly, the
photographic record will aid in identifying the criminal. Finally, the
photographic record of a completed crime points the way to changes to
make the area more secure.

PERSONNEL TRAINING

An important part of protection is thorough training of all
employees on proper behavior in case of a robbery or assault attempt. No
system will be very effective if the victim is unprepared. A robbery or
assault attempt is very traumatic experience; one cannot count on the
spontaneity of the victim for proper behavior. The proper routine must be
thoroughly explained. The local police department is usually helpful in this
type of training.

In general, police and FBI recommend that the victim submit to
the robber's demands and not resist. Although there is always the
possibility that a particular robber intends to harm the victims regardless
of their actions, most will not harm the victim who obeys. If the victim
resists, it is more likely that the robber will become violent.

Armed robbers are more assertive, more confrontational, and more
prone to violence than other types of thief. We should not, however,
assume that other types of criminal are somehow non-violent. The general
wisdom regarding burglars, for example, is that the amateur burglar is

likely to commit violent acts while the professional is less dangerous. A physician in Washington, DC, died from gunshot wounds inflicted by a professional burglar with a long criminal history. When authorities searched the burglar's $300,000 home they found hundreds of thousands of dollars worth of loot. Professionals aren't dangerous? Don't count on it.

WHAT HAVE WE LEARNED?

1. When planning a holdup alarm, assume that the holdup person is inherently more violent and confrontational than other types of crook. The type of response created by the alarm should be calculated with this in mind.
2. Alarm devices can be local alarms, such as bells, horns, or sirens, or silent devices designed to summon help.
3. Holdup alarm switches should be designed to be actuated in an unobtrusive manner. Robbers who see a teller or clerk trip the switch may take violent reprisals.
4. Timing switches can be used to create a delay between pressing the alarm switch and its actuation. This delay keeps the robber from associating the two events.
5. Camera systems can help in identifying the robber later and aid in obtaining a conviction.

Quiz for Chapter 12

1. Holdup alarms are similar to intruder alarms, except that they must be tripped by:
  a. the intruder.
  b. violent actions.
  c. breaking a light beam.
  d. the victim.

2. A robber is typically more oriented towards violence than burglars. True or false?

3. Holdup alarm actuator switches should be:
  a. hidden.
  b. slow operating.
  c. fast operating.
  d. easily observed.

4. In some cases, the _____ will trip the holdup alarm.
  a. police
  b. robber
  c. robber's gun
  d. witnesses

5. A(n) _____ can help prevent false alarms.
  a. photoelectric beam
  b. entrance delay
  c. timer device
  d. exit delay

6. A(n) _____ can be used to record the holdup and provide evidence in a trial later.
  a. tape recorder
  b. photoflash
  c. event recorder
  d. camera

7. _____ is perhaps the most important aspect of any holdup alarm system.
  a. Auto dialing of telephone
  b. Employee training
  c. A loud alarm
  d. A recording camera

Digital Electronics

ABOUT THIS CHAPTER

Digital electronics moved to the forefront of electronics technology almost two decades ago with the introduction of inexpensive digital integrated circuit logic elements. In this chapter, you will learn the basics of digital electronics with special emphasis on the custom chips used in electronic security systems.

LOGIC ELEMENTS

All digital circuits are built from just a few basic elements.

Digital electronic circuits are constructed from certain basic elements: gates (NOT, OR, AND, NAND, NOR) and flip-flops (Type-D, R-S, J-K). We define these devices in the sections below.

The logic elements can be combined in discrete form as individual integrated circuits or in the form of medium-scale integration (MSI) and large-scale integration (LSI) chips. They can be formed into universal circuits, custom digital IC circuits, and microprocessor chips.

LOGIC FAMILIES

A logic family is a group of interrelated devices that are easily interfaced.

A logic family is a series of interrelated devices which share certain common properties that allow direct interfacing among elements of the family without external circuitry other than electrical conductors.

The members of each logic family operate from a common dc supply voltage, and they have nearly identical input and output circuits to ease the interfacing chore. The two most common logic families are transistor-transistor-logic (TTL) and complementary metal-oxide semiconductor (CMOS).

TTL Family

The TTL logic family uses bipolar npn and pnp transistor technology. The standard power supply for TTL is +5 V dc (regulated). The standard logic levels are 0 to 0.8 V for low, and +2.4 to +5 V for high. A TTL output is a current sink, while a TTL input is a 1.8 mA current source.

CMOS Family

The CMOS logic family is based on metal-oxide semiconductor field effect transistors (MOSFET). CMOS logic elements typically draw very low current levels compared with TTL elements. A CMOS output is a voltage source, while CMOS inputs have a very high input impedance (measured in megohms). CMOS devices typically operate at slower frequencies than TTL devices.

CMOS devices are sensitive to electrostatic discharge and can be destroyed by such voltages. Special handling procedures are needed when dealing with CMOS devices in the workspace. In general, high dc impedance paths to ground are provided on the work bench.

GATES

Only three basic elements form all other digital logic elements: NOT, AND, and OR gates.

The most basic digital electronic circuit elements are the gates. All other digital elements can be formed from a combination of only three types of logic gate: NOT, OR, and AND. Although some multiple input gates are available, we will base our discussion on the basic two-input gate. *Figure 13-1* shows the circuit schematic symbols for five forms of gate.

Figure 13-1. Gate Schematic Symbols

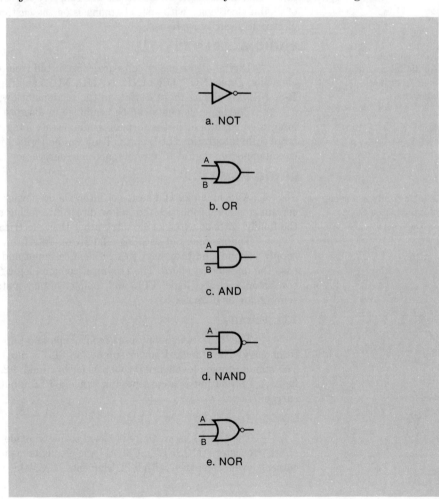

a. NOT

b. OR

c. AND

d. NAND

e. NOR

NOT Gates

The NOT gate shown in *Figure 13-1a*, is also called an "inverter," or "complementer," because it produces an output that is the opposite of the input. In other words, a low input produces a high output and vice versa. The truth table of the NOT gate is shown in *Table 13-1*.

**Table 13-1.
NOT Gate Truth Table**

Input	Output
0	1
1	0

Among available inverters there is a special class that has application in security systems. The open-collector device has a special output circuit that consists of an npn transistor in a common-emitter configuration with only its collector tied to the output terminal. When the output is low, the terminal is grounded, and when the output is high, it is ungrounded.

OR Gates

The OR gate produces an output if either input is high. Its symbol is shown in *Figure 13-1b*, and the truth table is shown in *Table 13-2*.

**Table 13-2.
OR Gate Truth Table**

Input A	Input B	Output
0	0	0
0	1	1
1	0	1
1	1	1

AND Gates

The AND gate, shown in *Figure 13-1c*, produces an output only when both inputs are high. In some technologies, therefore, AND gates are called "coincidence gates." That is, they produce an output only when the signals at the inputs are coincident. The truth table for the AND gate is shown in *Table 13-3*.

Input A	Input B	Output
0	0	0
0	1	0
1	0	0
1	1	1

Combination Gates

The three basic gates are NOT, OR, and AND. The NOT gate can be combined with the other two forms to make two additional gates that are now considered basic because of wide use: NOR (NOT-OR) and NAND (NOT-AND). In this case, NOT means that the output produces a signal that is opposite the OR and AND equivalents.

NAND Gates

The NAND gate is an AND gate with an inverter at the output. In *Figure 13-1d*, this is indicated by the circle on the output of the NAND gate symbol. The NAND gate produces a high output if either input is low, and a low output only when both inputs are high, as shown in *Table 13-4*.

Input A	Input B	Output
0	0	1
0	1	1
1	0	1
1	1	0

NOR Gates

The NOR gate is an OR gate with an inverter at the output. In *Figure 13-1e*, this circuit situation is indicated by the circle on the output of the OR gate symbol. The NOR gate produces a low output if either input is high, and a high output only when both inputs are low, as shown in *Table 13-5*.

Table 13-5.
NOR Gate Truth Table

Input A	Input B	Output
0	0	1
0	1	0
1	0	0
1	1	0

FLIP-FLOPS

Flip-flops are 1-bit memory elements formed from combinations of the three basic gates.

Flip-flops are one-bit digital memory elements. In other words, they will "remember" a logic level, either 1 or 0, and store it for future use. There are several types of flip-flop that are in common use: Type-D, R-S, and J-K.

All flip-flops can be made from combinations of NOT, OR, and AND gates. In modern usage, however, these elements have become standard in their own right because they are available as individual units in IC form.

Type-D Flip-Flops

A Type-D flip-flop, shown in *Figure 13-2*, also called a "data latch," will transfer the logic level on the D-input to the Q output whenever the clock goes active (most commercial types use active-high clock lines). The Q output will remain in that new state after the clock goes inactive again.

Figure 13-2.
Flip-Flop Schematic Symbols

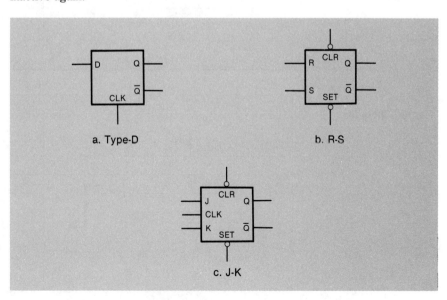

a. Type-D

b. R-S

c. J-K

Most flip-flops have a second output that is the complement of the Q output. This NOT-Q output will be low when the Q output is high, and it will be high when the Q output is low. On circuit diagrams, the NOT-Q output is indicated by the letter Q with a bar over it.

R-S Flip-Flops

The R-S flip-flop as shown in *Figure 13-2b*, uses two inputs: set (S) and reset (R). When the set input is active, the Q output goes high and NOT-Q goes low. On the other hand, when the reset input is active, the Q output is forced low.

The version shown in *Figure 13-2b* also has clear and preset inputs. Holding these inputs low will force the operant condition regardless of activity on the other inputs. Preset makes Q go high and preclear makes Q go low.

J-K Flip-Flops

The J-K flip-flop is a dual-mode, complex flip-flop that forms the basis of many digital circuits. It has two modes: clocked and unclocked. These modes are defined in *Tables 13-6* and *13-7*.

**Table 13-6
Direct Mode
(Unclocked) Operation**

Input		Clock	Output	
J	K		Q	$\overline{Q}$
0	0		Disallowed	
0	1	Doesn't	1	0
1	0	Care	0	1
1	1		Clocked Operation	

**Table 13-7.
Clocked Operation**

Input		Clock	Output	
J	K		Q	$\overline{Q}$
0	0		No Change	
0	1		0	1
1	0		1	0
1	1		Binary Division	

In the clocked mode, with inputs J and K high, the J-K flip-flop acts as a binary divider. The outputs change state once for every negative-going transition of the input line. Thus, a new pulse is formed for every two input pulses; the output frequency is one-half the input frequency.

CUSTOM INTEGRATED CIRCUITS

LSI chips can be custom built for almost any purpose.

Solid-state technology has reached the point where it is possible to develop a large-scale integrated circuit for almost any purpose. Many different functions can be provided on the same chip, such as in electric watch circuits, function generators, and calculators. It is also possible for a complete intrusion alarm to be incorporated in a single integrated circuit.

Although large-scale integrated circuits can be produced very economically in large quantities, the initial cost, including development and tooling up for production, is very high. Thus, there must be a very great demand for such a circuit to justify its development. In the security field, there are many different manufacturers with many different products. Consequently, there hasn't been enough demand for any one special integrated circuit to justify the development costs. However, the manufacturers of integrated circuits have perceived that they would be justified to develop a few circuits that would have very wide application.

Digital Lock Circuit

One of the first large-scale integrated circuits for security systems that appeared on the market was the Type LS7220 Digital Lock Circuit made by LSI Computer Systems, Inc. It is a 14-pin integrated circuit manufactured using PMOS technology. The device can be used to make a push-button lock with the addition of a very few components. *Figure 13-3* shows the pinout of the device and *Figure 13-4* shows a push-button automobile ignition switch using it.

Figure 13-3.
Type LS7220 Digital Lock Circuit
(Courtesy LSI Computer Systems, Inc.)

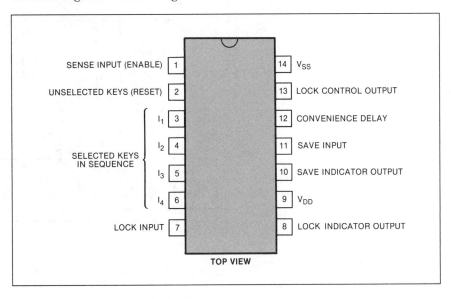

Figure 13-4.
Push-Button Ignition
Switch *(Courtesy LSI*
Computer Systems, Inc.)

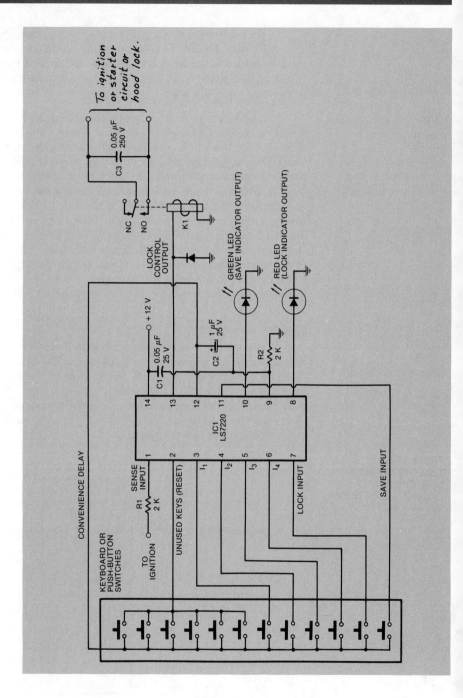

Another version of this device which has tamper protection is the Type LS7225. *Figure 13-5* shows the pinout and *Figure 13-6* shows a functional block diagram. As can be seen, many different functional units are included inside the integrated circuit.

**Figure 13-5.
Type LS7225 Digital
Lock Circuit Pinout**
*(Courtesy LSI Computer
Systems, Inc.)*

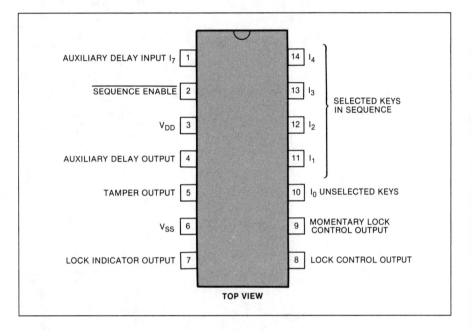

Probably the best way to describe the circuit of *Figure 13-6* is in terms of what happens at its pins. The power supply is connected to pins 3 and 6 with pin 6 positive and pin 3 grounded. When a series of logical high signals is applied to pins 11 through 14 (Inputs 11, 12, 13, and 14) the internal sequential memory is set. This causes the lock control output (pin 8) and the momentary lock control output (pin 9) to go high and the lock indicator output (pin 7) to go low. An external capacitor connected to pin 11 sets the amount of time available for pressing the selected keys in the proper sequence.

Thus, if the selected keys are pressed in the proper sequence, the circuit will provide an output that can be used for access control, ignition control of an automobile, or any other desired function. The circuit operates from a minimum of four push buttons. More than four push buttons can be used to provide greater security. The unused push buttons are connected to the unselected keys input (pin 10). If any one of these unselected keys is pressed, the sequential memory will reset and a positive pulse will appear at the tamper output (pin 5). This pulse can be used to sound an alarm to attract attention to the fact that someone is tampering with the system.

**Figure 13-6.
Type LS7225 Digital
Lock Circuit Block
Diagram** *(Courtesy LSI
Computer Systems, Inc.)*

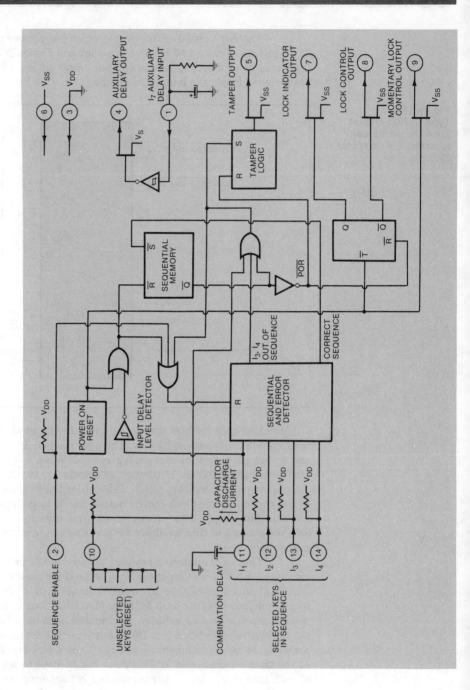

Use for Access Control

When the device is used for access control, the alarm can be connected to the lock control output (pin 8). This pin changes state in response to the proper combination. The momentary lock control output (pin 9) also goes high in response to the proper sequence of input signals, but it doesn't stay high. It will revert to a low state after the capacitor connected to pin 11 discharges. This output can be used to control an electric door lock. It will unlock the door long enough for an authorized person to enter, but the door will revert to its locked condition immediately.

Figure 13-7 shows a push-button access control circuit using the Type LS7225. In this particular arrangement, the push buttons must be pressed in the sequence 4, 7, 2, 0, but the combination can be changed easily.

**Figure 13-7.
Push-Button Access
Control Circuit**

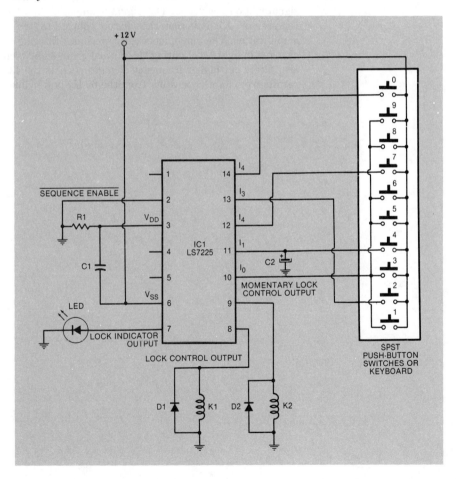

AN INTEGRATED INTRUSION ALARM

The complete intrusion alarm on a single integrated circuit described in the following paragraphs was developed by the Sprague Electric Company. The development was justified because the basic technology has a broad base of applications. The project began as a motion sensor and sound generator for use in toys whose production quantities were very high. It was later modified for use as an intrusion alarm.

The circuit itself is very complex and involves the use of npn and pnp amplifiers, 1^2L logic, a photodiode, and power transistors all on the same chip.

The original design included a sound generator and a photoelectric motion detector. A functional diagram is shown in *Figure 13-8*. The device senses motion by detecting small changes in the amount of light reaching the photodiode. When the amount of light reaching diode D1 changes, a signal will be developed. This signal is amplified in a logarithmic compressor, A1. It is then capacitively coupled to two additional stages of amplification. The amplifier circuitry includes filtering to avoid the slow changes in light level during the normal change between day and night. It also filters out higher frequency changes such as the 120-Hz flicker that results from lights operating from the 60-Hz power line.

**Figure 13-8.
Integrated Motion
Detector Block Diagram**
*(Courtesy Sprague
Electric Co.)*

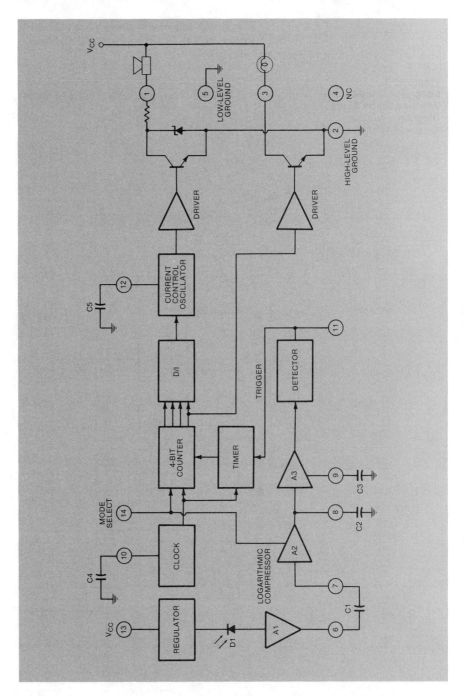

This circuit was modified as shown in *Figure 13-9* to operate as a motion detector for use in a security system. Entrance- and exit-delay functions were added.

Figure 13-9. Integrated Circuit Intrusion Alarm Block Diagram *(Courtesy Sprague Electric Co.)*

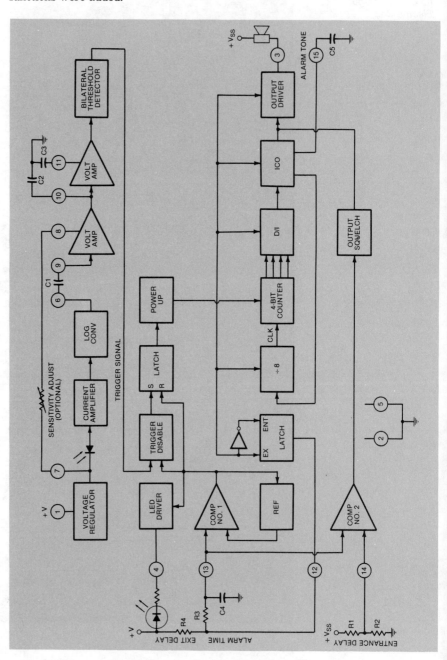

Capacitor C4 together with resistors R3 and R4 set the exit delay and the time that the alarm will operate. When the system is energized, the LED connected to pin 4 will light and the triggering signal from the photodiode will be blocked; the device will not respond to motion. After the voltage at pin 13 reaches a reference value of 8.4 V, comparator 1 will change state. The LED will go out, indicating that the system is armed and the comparator reference will be changed to 1 V.

When the light level reaching the photodiode changes by more than 5%, a triggering signal will be developed by the appropriate circuitry. The trigger will enable the latch which would allow the alarm to sound except that it is squelched by a signal from comparator 2. This comparator holds the alarm off until capacitor C4 discharges to the 1-V reference level on comparator 1. This allows an entrance time for an authorized person to enter the protected area and disable the alarm. The time that the alarm will sound is determined by resistor R3.

The time delays in the system may be adjusted by changing the values of the external resistors. The entrance time may be adjusted from 0 to 100 seconds; the exit time can be from 50 to 100 seconds; and the alarm time can be adjusted up to 10 minutes.

Figure 13-10 shows a diagram of a complete intrusion alarm system using only the integrated circuit and twelve additional components. Most of the complexity of the system is inside the integrated circuit.

**Figure 13-10.
Complete Intrusion
Alarm** *(Courtesy Sprague
Electric Co.)*

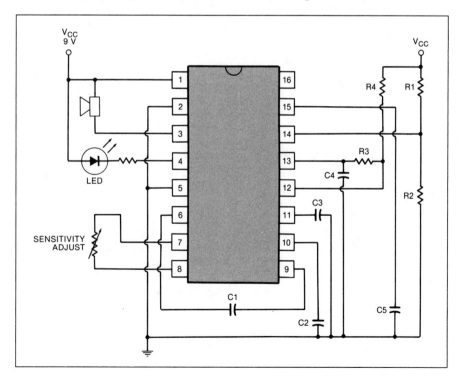

THE FUTURE OF SECURITY INTEGRATED CIRCUITS

As we noted at the beginning of this chapter, the only thing holding up the development of special integrated circuits for security systems is that the usage is not great enough to justify the development costs. Two factors will change this situation. One is standardization of security systems. If this occurs, more systems from different manufacturers will contain the same functions so the possible usage of special circuits will increase. The other factor is that integrated circuits developed for completely different applications may be useful in security systems. The Sprague system is an example of this.

WHAT HAVE WE LEARNED?

1. All digital circuits can be built from combinations of three basic gates: NOT, AND, and OR.
2. Inverse function gates (NAND and NOR) are formed by adding an inverter to AND and OR gates, respectively.
3. Three basic forms of flip-flop are used as 1-bit memory elements: R-S, Type-D, and J-K.
4. Electronic security systems can be built from either discrete digital logic elements or from special purpose large-scale integration (LSI) chips.

Quiz for Chapter 13

1. List the two modes of the J-K flip-flop.

2. On a Type-D flip-flop the D-input is high when the CLK line goes active and remains high thereafter. The Q output after the clock pulse passes will be:
   a. high.
   b. low.
   c. unaffected.
   d. changed to opposite state.

3. An R-S flip-flop has active low inputs. What is the state of the Q output after the R input drops low?
   a. High.
   b. Low.
   c. Uaffected.
   d. Changed to opposite state.

4. The J and K inputs of a J-K flip-flop are high. What mode is it operating in?
   a. Clocked.
   b. Unclocked.
   c. Direct mode.
   d. Inoperative.

5. A(n) _____ flip-flop acts as a binary divider under certain circumstances.
   a. R-S
   b. Type-D
   c. J-K

6. What is the relationship of the output frequency to the input frequency of the J-K flip-flop in the clocked mode?
   a. One-third.
   b. One-to-one.
   c. One-half.
   d. One-fourth.

7. The LSI type LS7220 device is a(n):
   a. digital lock.
   b. intruder detector.
   c. J-K flip-flop.
   d. R-S flip-flop array.

8. List the three basic forms of gate circuit.

9. What other digital logic element is used with the AND and OR gates to form NAND and NOR gates?
   a. J-K FF.
   b. Type-D FF.
   c. R-S FF.
   d. NOT gate.

10. A high output occurs whenever either input of a particular gate sees a high. What kind of gate is it?
    a. AND.
    b. NAND.
    c. OR.
    d. NOR.

Computers in Security Systems

ABOUT THIS CHAPTER

The modern digital computer has been pressed into service in the design of electronic security systems. Only a few years ago, programmable digital computers were too large and too expensive to be used in all but the most sophisticated and important security systems. Today, small personal computers and single-board computers are showing up as components in more and more systems. In this chapter, you will find an overview of the use of these machines in electronic security systems.

COMPUTERS AND CRIME FIGHTING

The use of computers in the fight against crime is not new. For many years computers have been used by law enforcement agencies to trace stoeln cars, keep track of arrest warrants, and maintain criminal records. Computers have also been used in security systems, but for the most part this use has been restricted to very large industrial and military installations. Large computers were so expensive that they were not economically viable in small and medium-sized installations.

The rapid development of the microprocessor and other large-scale integrated circuits completely changed this situation. The cost of a computer is now so low that it is practical to use computers in all but the smallest security systems.

Computerized systems can be changed almost at will by changing software.

The computer offers many advantages over the more conventional security systems. One of the principal advantages of a computer-based system is that it is programmable; its functions and wiring can be changed by means of a stored program. It can be thought of as a system in which the wiring diagram can be changed at will without ever touching a soldering iron.

UNIVERSAL COMPUTER-BASED SYSTEM

Figure 14-1 shows a block diagram of a typical industrial security system. The inputs come from intrusion detectors, guard stations, and access controls. The outputs may be local alarms, remote alarms, and recorders. No two installations will be exactly alike. One may have several doors and windows and few guard stations. Others will have a different number of each type of input. A signal from an intrusion detector may trip a remote alarm in one installation, whereas it will only activate a local annunciator at the security guard headquarters in another installation. A signal from a guard station might merely operate a printing recorder to show the time that a guard passed by a particular station.

**Figure 14-1.
Typical Industrial
Protection System**

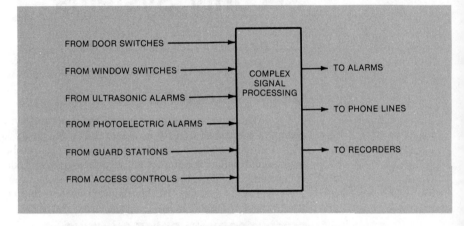

FROM DOOR SWITCHES ⟶

FROM WINDOW SWITCHES ⟶

FROM ULTRASONIC ALARMS ⟶

FROM PHOTOELECTRIC ALARMS ⟶

FROM GUARD STATIONS ⟶

FROM ACCESS CONTROLS ⟶

COMPLEX SIGNAL PROCESSING

⟶ TO ALARMS

⟶ TO PHONE LINES

⟶ TO RECORDERS

Each installation will be somewhat different from others and customizing each installation increases the cost of the system. Futhermore, when it becomes necessary to change a system, much of the actual wiring must be changed.

Figure 14-2 shows a block diagram of a computer-based system. Note that all of the inputs are merely labeled inputs without regard as to where the input signal might come from. The function of each of the inputs is determined by the program inside the system, rather than by a wiring arrangement. Thus, a given input may be programmed to handle signals from intrusion detectors, access controls, guard stations, or any other devices.

Multiple sensors can be accommodated because internal computer programming determines the function of each input.

**Figure 14-2.
Universal Computer-
based System**

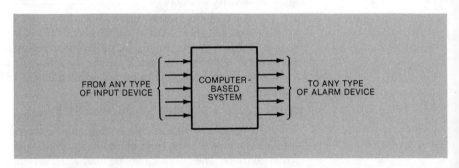

FROM ANY TYPE OF INPUT DEVICE

COMPUTER-BASED SYSTEM

TO ANY TYPE OF ALARM DEVICE

Output terminals are similar in versatility. Any given output terminal can be connected to any type of device. The program will handle the change in functions between devices.

FLEXIBILITY

A computer-based security system can make decisions based on combinations of inputs or even on the time of day. For example, it is easy to program a computer-based system to turn on in phases with changes in time. During the night, it might be programmed to initiate an alarm if an entry occurred anywhere in the building. Shortly before time for the office force to begin work it would shut off the alarm function for the office doors, but it would continue to protect the rest of the plant, including the shipping doors at the back of the building where no employees had yet started work. As time passed, the system could permit access to various parts of the plant. The system could also be programmed to provide a completely different type of protection on weekends, when the plant was closed or only a part of the plant was used.

Flexibility is the key word for computerized systems. Only the designer's imagination limits the design.

The number of different types of protection that can be provided by a computer-based system is limited only by the imagination of the user. It is possible, for example, for the system to respond to an access card of a particular employee and disable the security sensors over the route through the plant that he or she is authorized to take. If the employee should attempt to enter an unauthorized area, the alarm would be initiated.

Anti-kidnapping Feature

The kidnapping of a manager in order to burglarize the office or store is difficult to protect against. However, a computer-based system can be programmed so that the manager can enter the facility at any time, but if it is after normal business hours the manager must take an indirect route to the office or the safe in order to avoid tripping a remote alarm. When forced by a burglar, the manager can trip the remote alarm merely by taking a direct route.

It is possible to program as many security traps as seem necessary. Some of these can be kept secret from all but the most trusted employees. Employees who think they understand how the system works can easily walk into security traps they never dreamed existed.

MULTIPLEXING

A computer-based security system is well suited to multiplexing where one set of leads can be used for all inputs to the system. In a large system, this can result in a considerable saving in installation costs. *Figure 14-3* shows such a system. Each of the individual intrusion detectors, access controls, guard stations, and so on, generates a unique serial digital signal. All of these signals are applied to the same pair of wires leading to the central control. At the central control, when a signal arrives, the computer decodes and identifies it. There is no need to run separate wires from each input device.

**Figure 14-3.
Multiplexed System**

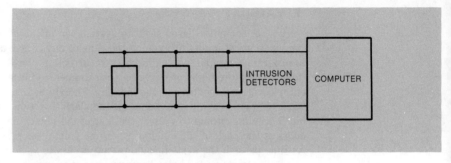

CITY-WIDE PROTECTION SYSTEM

Figure 14-4 shows a block diagram of a city-wide system for security protection. The area to be protected, which might be anything from an industrial complex or an apartment building to a single home, is equipped with intrusion detectors. Each terminal contains a semiconductor memory that identifies the building or home by its full address and even identifies each entrance. When an intrusion occurs, the device will automatically dial a predetermined number at police headquarters or at a security company and will then initiate a printout giving the address of the facility where the alarm originated and the nature of the alarm.

**Figure 14-4.
City-Wide Protection
System**

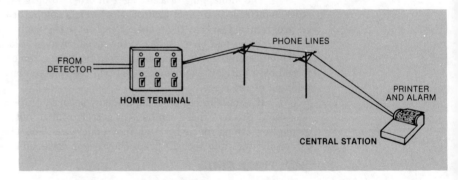

Highly sophisticated systems can be designed using computers.

Because of the flexibility of the digital techniques, some data processing can be performed before the alarm is initiated. For example, if the alarm system guarding the outer perimeter of the premises is tripped, the system will transmit a signal that lets the police know exactly what has happened—the outer perimeter has been penetrated. Other alarms inside the perimeter, such as pressure pads, will be tripped when the burglar reaches this point and another, more urgent, alarm will be transmitted.

With proper design and installation, the probability of false alarms is minimized. When the receiving facility at police headquarters receives several alarms that trace the progress of an intruder through the premises, the police can be virtually certain that an intrusion is taking place and that it is not a false alarm.

Using modern integrated circuits, the amount of equipment needed to implement this system is very little, and the cost is well within the reach of the average homeowner. *Figure 14-5* shows the printed-circuit board containing the system.

**Figure 14-5.
Home Terminal Printed-
Circuit Board** *(Courtesy
Pan-X Corp.)*

Additional Functions

Because of the tremendous data-handling capability of the system, it can also perform many functions in the home other than security monitoring. The details of these are beyond the scope of this book. One function that is related to security, however, is the holdup alarm.

When a home is occupied during the daytime, the security system would usually be turned off to minimize false alarms. Under these circumstances, an intruder could force an entry into the house without tripping an alarm. To combat this possibility, the system is equipped with a holdup alarm: a small radio transmitter, no larger than a pack of cirgarettes, that has a panic button. When the button is pressed, a signal is sent to a local receiver which then directs the system to transmit a holdup alarm to police headquarters. Again, the message contains the address as well as a code indicating that the emergency is a holdup.

Apartment and Office Complexes

Traditionally, large apartment and office complexes have been protected by guards patrolling the facilities. This system is limited because guards cannot be at all parts of the facility at the same time. By using computer-based systems, a tremendous number of intrusion detectors can be monitored and the information relayed to a central facility from which guards can be dispatched.

Very large systems are possible with computers ...systems may recognize up to 1000 inputs.

Many hotels and office buildings are now using computers in their security systems. A typical system may have as many as 1000 intrusion detectors of various types connected to the computer. One of the advantages of the system is that detectors of different types can be used in the same system. When cash drawers are unattended, they can be protected by simple switches that will alert the system if the drawer is opened. Holdup alarms can be provided for cash positions that are in use. Motion detectors can be installed on the roof and in areas that are not normally occupied.

Automated Systems

Because of the decision-making capacity of the computer, many functions can be performed automatically. For example, the system can arm the protective circuits in offices thirty minutes after normal office hours are over. When this occurs, the location of any unlocked doors or occupied offices will be automatically typed out on the printer at guard headquarters. If a person intends to work late, the guard headquarters must be notified in advance. Thus, a detailed record is provided of all activities in the facility after normal business hours. Periodic inspection of this record will improve overall security.

The rapid decrease in the costs of microprocessors and associated equipment may soon bring computer-based systems into almost every home. Systems of this type will be exceptionally hard to foil and will constitute a signficant deterrent to burglary.

"SMART" DETECTORS

The low cost of the microprocessor is leading to the development of what are often called "smart" intrusion detectors. The smart detector is based on the ability of a computer to look at a large amount of data, compare it with data in memory, and decide whether the two groups of data agree.

The principle of a smart detector can be illustrated by the electronic line-scan camera shown in *Figure 14-6*. This camera is similar to an ordinary camera except that the space where the film would be in an ordinary camera is occupied by an array of tiny photodiodes. The photodiodes are scanned linearly, producing an analog signal that is a function of the amount of light at the various points in the array. This signal is compared with preset signal levels to form a digital signal corresponding to the difference in the actual light level at each point on the scene and the preset level. A logical 0 is produced for light levels that are below the preset level and a logical 1 for light levels that exceed the preset level.

**Figure 14-6.
Electronic Line-Scan
Camera** *(Courtesy
Recticon Corp.)*

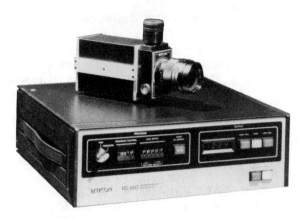

By programming the light levels corresponding to a given scene, the device cannot only detect a change in the scene, but it can also tell something about the nature of a change. For example, the signal could tell if an object moved to the right or to the left and by how much. Since the output is a digital signal, memories can be programmed to print out the nature of the change.

Multimode Sensors

Computers allow multimode sensors that permit collection of large amounts of data about the intruder.

This general concept of using the data-handling capabilities of a microprocessor need not be limited to visual images, although this is a fruitful field of application. It is possible to construct multimode sensors that will establish the nature of an intruder. Infrared sensors can be combined with pressure pads to compute whether or not the intruder is a human being and how many intruders are in an area.

MICROCOMPUTERS IN SECURITY SYSTEMS

The microcomputer, also called the personal computer, can be used in a security system. The addition of the correct interfacing hardware, and the writing of appropriate software, can make ordinary home computers useful in security systems work. Correct interfacing to the computer is most important.

INTERFACING

Interfacing describes the connection of devices from the outside world to the computer.

Interfacing is the art of connecting other devices to the computer. For this chapter, we will assume that the computer has an 8-bit parallel input/output port available. These ports are not the same as parallel printer output ports, but, rather, are ports that make the data on the internal data bus available to the outside world or will accept data from the outside world and pass it to the internal world over the data bus.

Interfacing Sensors

The particulars of an interfacing job depend somewhat on the nature of the sensor being connected to the computer. In general, we can assume that the computer wants to see a signal that is TTL-compatible. That is, the logical 0 (low condition) will be a voltage level from 0 to 0.8 V, while the logical 1 (high condition) is represented by a voltage from +2.4 to +5 V. We must ensure that each form of sensor produces a correct signal when alarm situations exist. This signal we will call "ALM" in our discussion.

Interfacing a Protection Loop

Figure 14-7 shows two examples of interface circuits to create the ALM signal that will be input to the computer. In *Figure 14-7a*, we see a method for making the closed-loop protection circuit compatible with the computer. In this circuit, a CMOS inverter circuit is used. In Chapter 13 we saw that an inverter produces an output that is the complement of the input signal. In other words, a low input produces a high output, and a high input produces a low output. The protection loop shorts the input of the inverter to ground. When the loop is opened by an intruder, the short is removed and the pull-up resistor (R1) forces the inverter input high. Thus, an intrusion situation forces ALM into its active low state. Using a non-inverting buffer in place of the inverter produces an active high ALM signal.

An Electro-Optical Door/Window Switch

Figure 14-7b shows an alternate sensor to the magnetic switches used on doors and windows. The device depicted is a special optoisolator device in which a phototransistor and light-emitting diode (LED) face each other across an open slit. As long as the blinder is not inserted into the slit, the transistor sees the LED and so will be saturated. Under this condition, the output signal ALM is high. But when the blinder is inserted, then the transistor is no longer illuminated and the output drops low. We can mount the optoisolator on the fixed structure of the door or window and the blinder on the movable part.

Direct I/O Port Interfacing

Figure 14-8a shows how assorted sensors can be interfaced directly to a microcomputer input port. For the sake of simplicity only two forms of sensor are shown. Bit B1 is connected to a protection loop with a pull-up resistor, as was true in the earlier case.

At bit B8, on the other hand, we see the method used to interface a mechanical switch such as a plunger switch or magnetic door or window switch. Again, a pull-up resistor is used to force the input bit high when the switch is open and low when the switch is closed. Under the latter condition, the switch shorts both the input connection and the pull-up resistor to ground.

**Figure 14-7.
Interface Circuits**

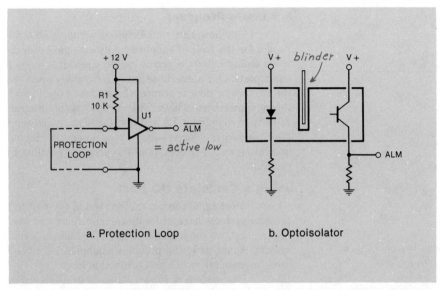

a. Protection Loop   b. Optoisolator

**Figure 14-8.
I/O Port Interface**

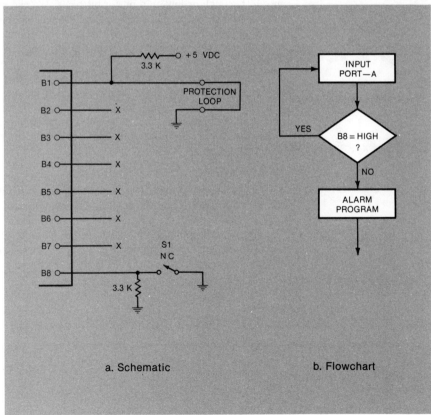

a. Schematic   b. Flowchart

A Sample Program

The flowchart to a simple program is shown in *Figure 14-8b*. Again, for the sake of simplicity only a single bit is discussed even though more sophisticated programs can accommodate many bits from numerous input ports. Our scenario assumes a normally open switch at bit B8. When the window or door is secure, the switch is open and the input to bit B8 of the computer port is high. The purpose of the program shown in *Figure 14-8b* is to sample bit B8 and test for high or low condition. If B8 is high, then the program loops back to pick up another input, but if it is low (indicating an alarm condition) the program continues to the main alarm program.

Using a Complete I/O Port

Most small computers that would be used to form computerized security systems have at least one input port and one output port. In *Figure 14-9*, we see a simple system for making a sophisticated alarm system. Again, as in the previous examples, only two forms of sensor are used: mechanical switch and protection loop.

The system of *Figure 14-9* allows us to program the output port lines either high or low on a bit-for-bit basis. We can also make the system more secure by outputing a unique (and changeable) binary code over each unique active output bit. If the code stops, or if the incorrect code is received, an alarm sounds. This technique provides protection against those crooks who would either short or open the loop to gain entry.

A significant advantage of this method is that a pseudorandom sequence generator (in either hardware or software) can create the binary code and therefore change it on a periodic basis. For example, the computer would be able to output, say, eighty different codes per second while scanning the sensor inputs. This coding scheme would be almost impossible to mimic.

INTERFACING OUTPUT DEVICES

No alarm system is of any use whatsoever if it does not provide an output indicating that an alarm situation has occurred. For computers that have a video display, the output can be a video display indication and the sounding of the computer's internal beeper. On other computers, and where the video display is not appropriate, we must provide another solution.

**Figure 14-9.
Single I/O Port System**

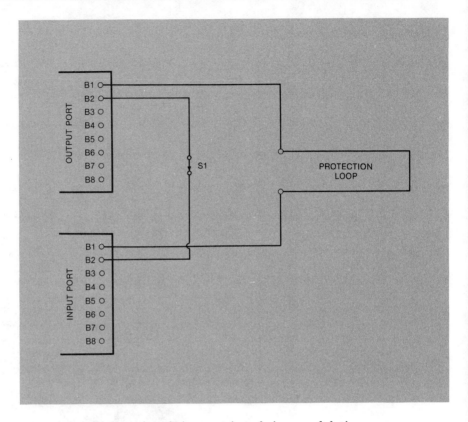

As with input interfacing, certain techniques and devices are combined to connect the various output devices to the computer. *Figure 14-10* shows a single output port connected to several different devices. The purpose in this illustration is to show several possible interfacing methods, not a particular system.

TTL Direct Interfacing

Most microcomputers have TTL-compatible output ports. Typically, such ports are limited to loads of one or two TTL inputs (i.e., either 1.8 or 3.6 milliamperes (mA) at +5 V). If the alarm device has a single-input TTL-compatible trigger line, then we can simply connect it to the computer port.

Two situations can cause us to look for a higher drive capacity. First, if the alarm device requires more input drive current than can be provided by the computer, the interface will have to provide the extra drive. Second, if the connecting cable is long, its internal capacitance may require a larger drive current. In both cases, we can use a non-inverting buffer (as at bit B1 in *Figure 14-10*). While computer outputs drive two TTL loads, regular TTL devices drive ten TTL loads and some special high output bus driver devices can drive thirty to a hundred loads (depending upon design).

Figure 14-10.
Single Output Port

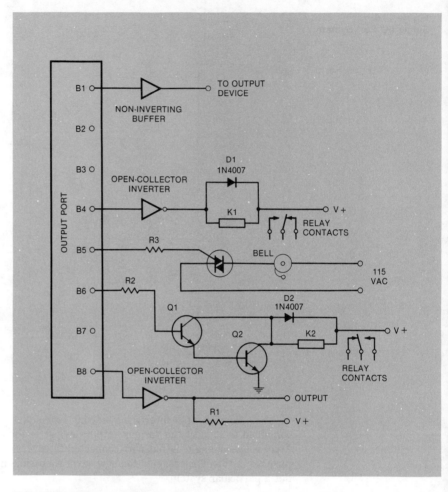

Non-TTL Direct Interfacing

The assumption of the preceding section is that the alarm device input line is a TTL-compatible current source. In some cases, however, we must drive non-TTL devices.

Figure 14-10 shows such an interface circuit at bit B8. The active device is an open-collector TTL inverter or a CMOS equivalent. The output of the device is connected to the V+voltage (which is other than +5 V in most non-TTL devices) through a pull-up resistor, R1. The value of R1 is set to produce a current of 2 to 20 mA.

Relay Interfacing

Some devices should be interfaced to the computer through an old-fashioned electromechanical relay. Two of several possible relay interfacing methods are shown at bits B4 and B8 in *Figure 14-10*. At bit B4 we see the method for interfacing a small, low-current relay, K1. The interface to the computer is an open collector TTL inverter, with the relay coil resistance forming the collector output pull-up to V+. When the inverter input is low, the inverter output is high and therefore, the relay is not energized. But when the computer forces bit B4 high, the inverter output is low and the relay coil is essentially grounded. Thus, the relay is energized when bit B4 is high and deenergized when bit B4 is low.

One of several alternate methods is shown at bit B7. In this case, we use either a superbeta transistor, or a pair of npn transistors connected in the Darlington configuration. This method provides a beta gain equal to the product of the gains of Q1 and Q2, and it can drive a relay at high current if Q2 has sufficient collector current rating. Because of the superbeta nature of this circuit, relays to 25 amperes or so can be driven from the 3.6-mA output from the computer (provided Q2 can handle the high current).

In both examples (B4 and B7), there is a diode connected across the relay coil. This diode is rated at 1000-V PIV, and is included to prevent counter-EMF when the relay is de-energized. The CEMF can reach several kilovolts in a large relay and can damage the other electronic components—or disable the computer program.

Interfacing AC-Line Powered Devices

Several methods are available for interfacing ac-line powered devices. In all of them, however, the idea is to isolate the 115-V ac line from the computer in order to prevent damage. The first method is the electromechanical relay. In fact, ac-powered devices are a principal use of relays in computerized security systems. Second, we can use either half-wave SCR or full-wave triac devices. At bit B5 in *Figure 14-10*, we see the use of a triac (SCR interfacing is almost identical). If the triac gate current requirement is low enough, then we can use the direct method shown. Otherwise, we will need a high-power non-inverting buffer (as at B1), an open-collector inverter (as at B8), or a transistor (as at B7).

Some authorities prefer to further isolate the computer by driving the triac through an optoisolator. Older single-transistor optoisolators are useful, although today there are special purpose optoisolators available that are designed especially for triac driving.

WHAT HAVE WE LEARNED?

1. Computers can be used in two ways to fight crime. First, as a database to trace stolen property, keep track of arrest warrants, maintain criminal records, and so forth. Second, computers can be used to directly control electronic security systems.

2. Computers allow an array of multiple sensors of several types in the same system. They also allow custom design of the system through correct selection of software.

3. Computers make it relatively easy to design plant-wide and city-wide security systems.

4. Smart detectors can be accommodated by a computer. Large amounts of data can be input and processed and sophisticated decisions made.

5. Personal computers can be used in electronic security systems by proper interfacing of sensors and output devices and appropriate programming.

Quiz for Chapter 14

1. A computer can be programmed to be used as a time lock. True or false?

2. A _____ system connects several intrusion detectors to one computer.

3. To force a digital input high when it is not shorted to ground, we use a(n):
   a. inverter.
   b. NOR-gate.
   c. pull-up resistor.
   d. optoisolator switch.

4. An advantage of computers in security systems is that they allow:
   a. multimode sensors.
   b. low cost.
   c. IR sensors.
   d. city-wide sensors.

5. An advantage of using a computer with a complete I/O port is that _____ can be used to prevent foiling the system by shorting or opening the loop.
   a. software
   b. optoisolators
   c. digital codes
   d. diodes

6. _____ can be accommodated by computers to input large amounts of data to make sophisticated security decisions.
   a. Fire detectors
   b. Smart sensors
   c. Photoelectric sensors
   d. Ultrasonic sensors

7. A principal advantage of computerized systems is that their functions can be changed by changing:
   a. software.
   b. wiring.
   c. digital logic.
   d. memory.

8. With proper design, computerized security systems can be built that produce a minimum of false alarms. True or false?

Practical Applications

ABOUT THIS CHAPTER

In this chapter, we will discuss the general principles of security system design and the application of electronic security systems and we will examine examples of specific installations.

PLANNING A SYSTEM

The combined talents of electronics and security experts are required to create an optimal system.

The wide variety of electronic intrusion detectors that are available makes it possible to provide a high degree of security for almost any type of building. At the same time, this variety complicates the problem of determining just which system is best suited for a particular application. This is not an easy problem to solve. It requires not only a thorough knowledge of the advantages and limitations of the various systems, but a good knowledge of security principles in general and the methods that a burglar might use to enter a particular building. Many firms have found that it is advantageous to use the combined talents of electronics and security people to provide the best system for a particular building area.

COST

The first factor to be considered in any application of security electronics is the economics of the situation. Until the property owner or manager feels that the cost of a system is justified, little can be done. In assessing the cost of providing electronic protection, two major factors must be considered—the risk involved and the effect on insurance rates.

Evaluation of Risk

What a business stands to lose by a burglary is often much more than the cash value of any goods that might be stolen. Frequently, a great deal of property is damaged when burglars break into a place. Where doors and windows are protected, the burglars might cut through the floors, walls, or ceiling. Although the value of the stolen goods and the damaged property may be covered by insurance, other losses may not be. A firm might lose business as a result of not having the stolen items in stock. Another possible loss from a burglary is the careless or malicious destruction of the records of a firm. In the long run, such a loss might be much more costly than the loss of merchandise.

Insurance Rates

Favorable insurance rates are often available to businesses who install approved alarm systems. Insurers will sometimes help in system design.

Most businesses carry at least some insurance protection against burglary and theft. When an electronic security system is installed or an existing system is improved, it is a good idea to check with the insurance company to see if a more favorable insurance rate can be obtained. Underwriters Laboratories have issued standards covering various types of electronic security systems. Usually, a system must meet these standards if it is to qualify a property for more favorable insurance rates.

The insurance company can often provide valuable guidance in selecting a security system for a particular type of business. Insurance companies usually employ experts who are familiar with all types of systems and have had a great deal of practical experience with burglaries.

GENERAL SECURITY MEASURES

Electronic security systems are most effective when combined with other general security precautions—such as effective door and window locks.

When planning the details of an electronic security system, one must not forget that an electronic system will not eliminate the need for other commonsense security measures. An electronic system will be most effective in preventing intrusions, or in leading to the apprehension of an intruder, if other factors combine to maximize the time required to enter the premises and steal anything. Even the most advanced security system will be ineffective if a burglar can break into a place, trip the alarm, and escape before anyone has time to respond to the alarm.

The first line of defense against intrusion is good fences, walls, gates, and doors with locks that are not easily picked or broken. All of these will increase the time required to commit a burglary. Along these same lines, cash and small items of merchandise that may be readily converted to cash must be secured as well as possible. Cash should be kept in a good safe that cannot be cracked or carried away easily. Larger items that can be quickly converted to cash, such as automobile tires, should be secured, in this case by a chain and padlock.

Another deterrent to burglary is good lighting. A burglar is less apt to spend a lot of time opening a well-lighted safe that is clearly visible from a front window, than one that is hidden from view.

One commonsense security measure is often ignored: nothing should be left lying around that a burglar could use to break into a building. There are many cases on record where burglars have used heavy boxes that they found on the premises to break a window, or have used ladders that they found behind a building to climb to the second story, where they could gain access to the interior.

Finally, it should be realized that there is no electronic substitute for a security guard on the premises. For complete effectiveness, all larger industries should have security guards as well as electronic systems. There is no substitute for the human judgment of a guard in recognizing false alarms and deciding on the most effective course of action in the event of an actual intrusion.

Although security guards are very effective, they are also very expensive. A proper blend of electronic security measures and guards can greatly improve the security system in installation by reducing the burden on the guards. For example, an installation that might require six or eight guards to patrol effectively often can be covered by a single guard and closed-circuit monitoring. In one installation, effective security was provided by two guards and extensive electronics. One guard remained at the front desk (which doubled as a remote monitoring location), while the other guard patrolled.

SELECTING AN ALARM AND SIGNALING SYSTEM

The proper alarm system for any given premises depends upon economics, location, and other factors.

The particular type or types of alarm and signaling systems that should be used in a given application depend on many different factors, such as whether the buildings are located in an area patrolled by police, in a remote area, or somewhere in between. In general, the purpose of an alarm is to obtain a response that will stop the crime or lead to the apprehension of the burglar. It is important that the response come in the shortest possible period of time. There are four types of alarm and signaling systems that can be used:

1. A private security company
2. A centralized alarm
3. A wired or automatic dialer system
4. A local alarm.

Private Security Company

A private security firm assumes the whole problem of security for a firm. It selects the intrusion detectors necessary to provide the particular type of protection called for in the contract. This can range from perimeter protection to protection of a specific object, such as a safe. The degree of protection required should be carefully explained in the contract; the cost of the service depends on the degree of protection required.

The use of a private security company has certain advantages. In addition to alarm systems, the company maintains patrols that may spot a burglar who manages to foil an alarm system in the protected area. The intrusion detectors installed by the company are connected by telephone wires to its headquarters so that it can exercise some judgment before calling the police. The cost of private security services varies widely. The types of service rendered by private security companies are rated by Underwriters Laboratories.

Centralized Alarm System

When a security force is available, it is customary to connect all intrusion detectors to a central location, usually the guard headquarters. This system makes it possible for a smaller number of guards to provide a greater degree of security. A further advantage is that the use of time clocks and event recorders provides a check on the guards themselves.

Automatic Telephone Dialer

Autodialers are less effective when they transmit frequent false alarms to police—who soon assume a "boy who cried 'wolf'" attitude towards the system.

The automatic telephone dialer is very popular because it provides the small firm with a system that will summon the police the minute an intrusion occurs. On the surface, it appears as an ideal solution to most security problems. The wide use of such systems, however, detracts from their effectiveness because false alarms become a problem. In some large cities, the police are receiving so many false alarms from automatic dialers that they are assigning a low priority to such calls. In some cities, ordinances prohibit direct dialing of the police department by automatic dialers. Perhaps the primary reason for this is the large number of false alarms. For example, in one city, over 90% of the calls received from automatic dialers proved to be false alarms. At the very best, a police car rushing to the scene of a crime in progress jeopardizes the lives of the officers and other motorists. When such calls are false alarms, this represents a needless and careless risk.

In spite of this limitation, the automatic dialer definitely has its place, and it is probably the best type of signaling system for many industries. Perhaps the best type of automatic dialing system consists of two intrusion detectors that are arranged to transmit messages of different priorities. The first could be connected to some type of perimeter protection system so that when the alarm is tripped, it would dial the police to report that there is an indication that someone is trying to enter the premises. The police could then dispatch a car to the scene at safe and reasonable speeds. The second message would be sent when the burglar had progressed to some other area and would be of higher priority. The police would be reasonably sure that a real intrusion was taking place if, for example, they were to receive three successive messages indicating that a burglar had first entered the grounds, had then entered an inner area, and finally was tampering with a safe. On the other hand, if only one of these alarms were tripped, they would recognize the possibility of a false alarm.

In any event, an automatic dialer should not be installed without a conference with the police department that will be expected to respond to it.

Local Alarm

In most applications, a local alarm is not considered very effective unless it happens to be an area that is patrolled regularly by police. In this day of non-involvement, it is not likely that a public-spirited neighbor will respond to an alarm.

There are, however, cases where the local alarm is the only practical type to use. These include homes and businesses that are so remote that neither the police nor a private security service could reach the scene in a reasonable period of time. The local alarm has a definite psychological effect on all but the most intrepid intruder. When combined with other devices, such as flashing lights, it can be made very effective in scaring burglars away before they have completed their burglary.

Another good place for a local alarm is in a private home where the resident feels fully capable of defending the home against intruders but needs a system to provide the alert.

SELECTING AN INTRUSION DETECTOR

The problem of selecting intrusion detectors is complicated simply because there are so many different types from which to choose. Checking over the advantages and limitations of the various types described in earlier chapters will show that there are some obvious applications where one or more types would not be acceptable, but usually this will still leave a choice of two or three different detectors for each application.

Perhaps the best way to determine which detector is best suited to a particular application is to prepare a survey similar to that shown in Table 15-1. This survey will first determine whether perimeter, area, or spot protection is required. Next, the conditions that prevail in the area to be protected will be determined. These can be checked against the advantages and limitations of each of the detectors described in earlier chapters. In this way, a system, or combination of systems, can be selected that will provide optimal protection.

**Table 15-1.
Intrusion-Detector
Installation Survey**

1. Type of Protection Required	
Perimeter	_____
Area	_____
Object	_____
2. Number of Entrances in Area	
Doors	_____
Windows	_____
Emergency exits	_____
3. Environmental Conditions	
Temperature range	_____ to _____ degrees
Humidity range	_____ to _____ percent
Ambient sound sources (outside)	
trains	_____
bells or whistles	_____
Ambient sound sources (inside)	
radiator, heater, etc.	_____
fans, air conditioner	_____
machinery	_____
Moving objects in protected area	
fans, machinery	_____
loose doors, windows, etc.	_____
Radio-frequency conditions	
nearby radio or TV stations	_____
machinery that will generate rfi	_____
equipment susceptible to rfi	_____

TESTING AN INSTALLATION

After an installation is completed, it must be thoroughly tested. The best test is to act like an intruder and try to foil the system. Cut the power to the system and cut any exposed wires. If the system can be foiled, it is only a matter of time until an experienced burglar will foil it. Many systems that respond to rapid motion will not be affected by very slow motion. Try to walk through the protected area very slowly. Do not neglect the fact that the "stay-behind" can usually find a place to hide and will not trip the perimiter system until leaving the premises.

ESTABLISHING PROPER PROCEDURES

No system will work as intended if employees habitually ignore either procedures or routine maintenance of the system.

The effectiveness of any alarm system depends on how well it is used. Definite procedures must be established and responsibilities must be assigned. The number of people who know the details of the security system, including how it works and where the wiring is located, should be kept to an absolute minimum. To make maximum use of an electronic system as a deterrent, tell as many people as possible that it is installed and as few as possible how it works. The wiring must not be shown on any building plans that might fall into the hands of a potential intruder. Therefore, an alarm system should only be installed after a building is erected. Most banks set a good example in that respect. Everyone knows that the bank has an alarm system, but very few people know just how it works or where the various parts of the system are located. Another consideration in this respect is to control the number of persons who can operate the access switches. For a system to be effective, access must be limited to a minimum number of persons.

A security system must be operated in such a way that it provides adequate security at all times. In many installations, it is the usual practice to shut off the entire system as soon as the first authorized employee arrives at work in the morning. This means that the back door and emergency exits are no longer protected. In many cases, merchandise has been taken out through an unprotected back door soon after the first employee arrived at work and disabled the security system. If the system had been properly installed, the back doors would have remained protected until later, when more supervisors were at work. Some firms have found it advisable to keep emergency exits, which are not normally used, protected at all times.

One important procedure that should be established and rigidly enforced is the investigation of every false alarm. There are several reasons for this practice. First, false alarms indicate that the system is not reliable and should be improved. Secondly, and equally important, is the fact that many false alarms are caused by potential intruders trying to learn about the intrusion detection system or trying to determine faith in the system.

If an intrusion protection system is worth installing, it is worth keeping in operation, and in good operating condition. A casual inspection of the protective foil of many business establishments would show the system to be inoperative and probably unused for months. This is an open invitation to skilled burglars.

EXAMPLES OF ACTUAL INSTALLATIONS

It is good to study the basics of the hardware used in electronic security systems. After all, knowledge of one's tools is primary to any profession. But it is also advisable to use the "case study" method and examine both successful and unsuccessful systems.

Example of Small-Store Protection

The following is one example of a protection system successfully used in a small store. A variety store contained many items of value, including a large amount of cash. Its location was so remote that the quickest response that could be counted on was about twenty minutes. For this reason, management decided that a local alarm that would upset a potential burglar was the best protection that could be provided. Most of the items in the store were bulky, and the smaller items could be put in the safe at night, so it was felt that any burglary attempt would be aimed at the safe. The safe was located where it was plainly visible from the front window of the store, and a vibration detector was installed in the store. In order to prevent burglars from kidnapping the manager of the store and forcing him to disable the system, a time switch was installed. This prevented anyone, even authorized employees, from disturbing the safe except during business hours. The alarm was connected to a loud KLAXON® horn aimed at the protected area. The sound level from this horn was so loud that it was actually painful, as well as being audible for several blocks. Combined with the horn were photoflash lamps that flashed blinding light into the protected area. Since installation of the system, the store has not had a successful burglary.

Example of Office Protection System

In this case, the protection system was installed in an office located in a public office building. There was some control over the people entering the building after hours, but it certainly was not rigid. Furthermore, the cleaning people employed by the building had keys to the offices so that they could clean after regular office hours. The valuables to be protected included a small amount of cash, valuable records, office furnishings, and files containing proprietary information that could result in the loss of competitive bids if it were to fall into the hands of competitors.

The system design was turned over to a private security company, which put a switch on the door and protective foil on the windows. These were wired to an alarm at the headquarters of the security agency. Of course, the alarm was tripped every time the cleaning people entered the area, but an arrangement was made that none of the cleaning people would enter the area after 10 P.M. If any of the employees had reason to enter the area after this hour, they had to call the security company and make arrangements, including giving a secret code word. To provide additional protection, the valuable records and cash were kept in a heavy safe protected by a vibration detector which was wired to the headquarters of the security agency. If this detector were jarred by the cleaning people, the alarm would be ignored, but if it were disturbed continually, the police would be called. The arrangement has proven highly satisfactory for a long time.

An Unsuccessful System

Electronics can be either misapplied or incorrectly installed and thus can be foiled by the enterprising crook. Consider the case of an automotive sound dealer in a large midwestern city, selling expensive stereo equipment for automobiles and vans. Typical systems cost $500 and up. Being in the electronics business, the owners thought they could adequately design a protection system without regard for expertise.

Their first step was perimeter protection of windows and doors. Metal tape was installed on the plate-glass windows, and magnetic switches were installed on the two main entrance doors, a window to the boss' office and the garage door in the shop area. Inside the store was a storage room where new merchandise still in boxes was stored. Normally, a clerk worked in the room and handed merchandise to installation mechanics through a "dutch door" window. Both upper and lower halves of the dutch door were protected with a magnetic switch.

One night just before Christmas an owner was notified by police that a burglary had taken place. Inventory showed that thieves had stolen more than $50,000 worth of merchandise. How had they managed to foil the system?

First, entry into the establishment was gained through an unprotected ventilator shaft in the roof. Considered too small for human passage, the shaft was overlooked—or ignored—by the system planners. Second, the room was of crude construction and wires were left exposed. Entry into the storage room was obtained by shorting together wires to the magnet switches. Finally, the thieves disabled the crude, homemade alarm system so that they could use the garage door to load merchandise into their truck.

Another Unsuccessful System

A stereo store in an eastern seaport town was robbed on the Sunday immediately prior to Memorial Day. An alarm system was in use at the store. Burglars rented a 24-foot truck from a national rental chain and backed it up to the rear door of the store. One of them called the alarm company, whose name was printed on a sticker affixed to the local alarm bell, and said that "employees" would be working on Sunday and to ignore any alarms. When the alarm was set off, the security people ignored it and the thieves were able to disable the bell.

The local police noticed the truck in the alley and investigated. One of the thieves, holding a clipboard and posing as a supervisor checking off merchandise as it was "delivered," told the police officer that the store was receiving an off-hours delivery because of the advertised special sale for the next day (Memorial Day). The officer accepted the story and drove off.

Two critical mistakes were made in this case. First, the security company failed to follow proper procedures by allowing the caller to identify himself without the required code words. Second, the police officer failed to follow procedures as well. The local police department keeps a file system of business owners, and policy required officers to call the owner of record when an unusual situation was noted. This last case study demonstrates the necessity of following proper procedures all of the time.

WHAT HAVE WE LEARNED?

1. There are many different options regarding security systems. The best solutions to problems are realized through collaboration of security and electronics personnel. There are few general solutions; each installation must be planned according to the situation.
2. In addition to the cash value of goods stolen, possible business losses include important records, damage to property, lost business opportunities, and compromise of proprietary information. These peripheral losses are often more serious than cash losses.
3. Insurance companies often provide owners of approved systems more favorable rates, and some companies will also make professional security personnel available to asssess the needs of policy holders.
4. Four types of alarm system can be considered: local, automatic dialer, centralized alarm, and private security service.
5. All new or reworked installations should be tested under realistic conditions.

Quiz for Chapter 15

1. A well-lighted _____ is the most effective means of protecting cash and other portable valuables.
   a. entrance
   b. premises
   c. safe
   d. protection zone

2. Police are receiving so many false alarms from _____ that they place a low priority on such calls.
   a. automatic dialers
   b. security firms
   c. electronic alarms
   d. private guards

3. _____ standards must usually be met if a security system is to qualify for a reduced insurance rate.
   a. National Bureau of Standards (NBS)
   b. Fire Protection Association (FPA)
   c. Underwriter's Laboratories (UL)
   d. American National Standards Institute (ANSI)

4. List four types of security system that can be designed.

5. A method used to reduce the number of false alarms from autodialer systems is to use:
   a. battery backup.
   b. spot protection.
   c. double or multiple detectors.
   d. local alarms.

6. Some systems are not tripped by _____, so a good test would be to attempt walking through the area very slowly.
   a. fast movement
   b. animals
   c. small objects
   d. slow movement

Detection of Objects

ABOUT THIS CHAPTER

Most of the alarms we have considered elsewhere have been intruder-detection systems. In this chapter, however, we will examine alarms that detect objects. Applications range from airport weapons detectors to department store anti-shoplifting systems.

WHY IS OBJECT DETECTION NEEDED?

Object detectors alert against crime committed by persons passing through a protected area, e.g., shoplifters and terrorists.

There are many situations where security depends, not on detecting a person entering or leaving a facility, but on detecting the presence of an object that the person may be carrying. For example, it is perfectly normal for employees to pass through the gates of an industrial plant, but as they pass through it is desirable to know whether they are carrying stolen items of value concealed within their clothing. Similarly, it is normal for passengers to pass through the gates at an air terminal, but the security of the flight could be endangered if one of the passengers is actually a highjacker carrying a concealed weapon.

In most cases it is impractical, and it is often illegal, to search people entering or leaving a facility. For this reason, electronic systems are being used increasingly to detect concealed objects.

The increase of terrorism in recent years has led to the development of many different object-detection systems that will detect the presence of weapons or explosives.

Shoplifting

As many as 1 in 12 visitors to department stores may be shoplifters.

The detection of shoplifting is another area in which object-detection systems are being widely used. A report issued by the National Retail Merchants Association states that, out of a group of 500 shoppers who were monitored in a large store, 42 were found to be shoplifting, a ratio of about 1 shoplifter for every 12 customers. The exact extent of shoplifting is not known because many shoplifters are not apprehended; but merchants agree that the problem is severe and is becoming worse.

There is a basic difference between the problem of detecting a concealed weapon or explosive and the problem of detecting hidden merchandise carried by a shoplifter. The shoplifter steals merchandise that the security people have had an opportunity to tag. The terrorist, on the other hand, carries a weapon that security people do not have access to until the person has been apprehended. To an extent, then, shoplifted merchandise is easier to detect.

METAL LOCATORS

Many security systems that are used to detect concealed objects operate on the same principle as the treasure locators widely used by hobbyists and land mine detectors used by military agencies.

Inductive balance circuits are a sensitive form of metal detector.

The basic principle of an inductive-balance metal locator is shown in *Figure 16-1*. Here, an ac source is connected to one of two coils that are mounted at right angles to each other. The coils are constructed so that there is no magnetic coupling between them. That is, their mutual inductance is zero and no voltage is induced in the secondary coil. If a metallic object is placed in the field of the coil, as shown in *Figure 16-2*, a voltage will be induced in it by the field of the primary coil. This causes eddy currents to flow, which, in turn, sets up a comparatively weak magnetic field. This weak field will induce a small voltage in the secondary coil. The voltage induced in the secondary coil is usually very small, so devices of this type are not very sensitive and large amounts of amplification are required.

Figure 16-1.
Metal Locator

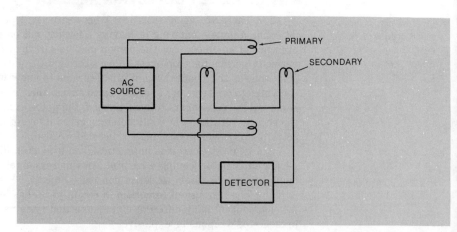

Figure 16-2.
Metal Object Field

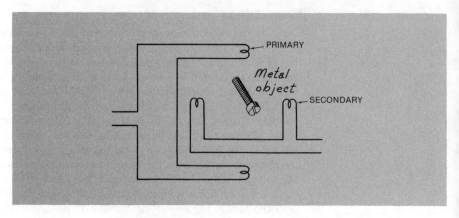

Methods of Detection

There are three basic methods that can be used to detect the change in the circuit of *Figure 16-2* that is caused by the presence of the metallic object in the field of the coil.

1. Measurement of the impedance of the primary coil
2. Measurement of the mutual inductance between the primary and secondary coils
3. Measurement of the voltage induced in the secondary coil.

All three methods have been used in practical metal-locator systems. The measurement of mutual inductance is the most popular method because changes in the geometry of the coils caused by temperature changes can be canceled out easily and the resistive and reactive components of the induced signal can be easily separated. This method will discriminate between magnetic and non-magnetic objects, which is often important.

The voltage induced in the metal object that is to be detected is proportional to the square of the frequency used. This would indicate that a higher-frequency system would be more sensitive, an indication borne out in fact. However, high-frequency systems are easily influenced by such non-metallic objects as human bodies and moisture in the air. High-frequency systems are also influenced by stray fields, with the result that they often have shielding problems.

Although metal-locator systems have been made using frequencies all the way from about 15 Hz to the radio frequencies, the low audio frequencies are the most popular.

A Practical Metal Locator

Figure 16-3 shows the circuit of a practical metal locator that can be used for detecting the presence of concealed metal objects. The signal source in this case is actually a full-wave rectifier that develops a 120-Hz signal from the 60-Hz power line. This arrangement is more economical than using an oscillator, and it has the added advantage that its frequency stability is good. A voltage-regulating transformer in the primary circuit provides the necessary amplitude stability.

Sensitivity

Ordinary metal detectors are too insensitive to be used where people must walk through them.

Metal locators are inherently insensitive devices. Usually about 100 watts (W) of power must be delivered to the primary coil if metal objects are to be detected in any space large enough for a person to walk through unhindered.

The detector is a mutual-inductance bridge, such as is shown in *Figure 16-4*. The signal is amplified and detected by a phase detector that can be switched to distinguish between non-magnetic conducting objects and magnetic objects. The output of the phase detector is fed to a trigger circuit that initiates an alarm whenever a metal object is detected. The sensitivity of the circuit can be adjusted so that it will not trigger on such small metallic objects as watches and cigarette lighters, which anyone is apt to be carrying, but will initiate an alarm if a larger object such as a stolen tool or a concealed gun passes through the area.

**Figure 16-3.
A Practical Metal
Locator**

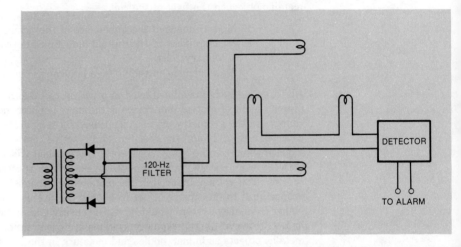

**Figure 16-4.
Mutual-Inductance
Bridge**

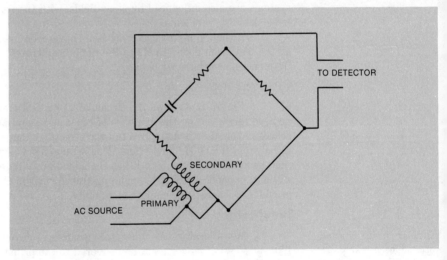

Effectiveness

The effectiveness of the metal detector as a security measure depends not so much on its technology as on the limitations in its use. In prisons, where the inmates have few rights, this device is very effective. A prisoner returning from a work area to the cell has no right to carry any metal objects. A metal detector that will be used with no restrictions can be made very sensitive to detect the presence of even very small metal objects. If the alarm is initiated, the prisoner can be challenged and searched, if necessary. In some national defense establishments, metal locators can be made almost as effective. Because of the much more important consideration of national security, employees give up many of their rights and consent to being challenged and searched, if necessary. In most situations, however, people do not give up their rights, and, furthermore, in business it is essential to preserve their good will.

The metal detector will detect the presence of metal objects over a predetermined size with no trouble. The trouble lies in deciding what action should be taken after the alarm goes off. If the person passing the protected area is a customer, there is the question of incurring ill will by a challenge. If the person is an employee, he or she may become sufficiently embarrassed to resign. Many industrial security officers feel that a metal locator is best used to get an idea of who is carrying concealed metal objects. When the alarm is initiated, no specific action is taken toward the employee, but the situation is noted and that employee is watched in the future.

Object detectors are not as widely used as intrusion detectors, but with the high rate of shoplifting from stores and pilferage from industrial plants, we can expect to see new developments in this area.

PORTABLE MAGNETIC-OBJECT DETECTOR

Figure 16-5 shows an object detector that is being used by police departments to search suspects when they are arrested. The device consists of a flux-gate magnetometer mounted in a police nightstick. When the end of the nightstick comes close to magnetic material, it causes an indication on the meter in the handle. The device has the obvious advantage that it permits its user to keep at a safe distance while searching a person for weapons.

**Figure 16-5.
Portable Metal Locator**

MAGNETIC-GRADIENT DETECTOR

Magnetic-gradient detectors are used especially for locating hidden bombs.

The magnetic-gradient detector was invented many years ago by the military for locating unexploded bombs. Recently, it has found its way into security systems. The device consists essentially of three collinear coils as shown in *Figure 16-6*. One of the coils is a transmitting coil and the other two are receiving coils. The transmitting coil is connected through an impedance-matching network to an oscillator that produces a 100-kHz signal.

Figure 16-6. Magnetic-Gradient Detector

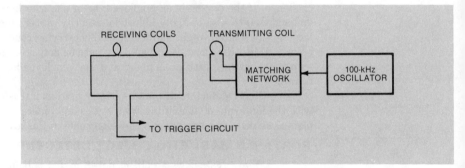

The magnetic field from the 100-kHz transmitting coil induces nearly equal voltages in the two receiving coils. These coils are connected in phase opposition, so the net voltage across the two coils is zero.

When a connecting object is brought close to the assembly, eddy currents are induced in it by the magnetic field from the transmitting coil These eddy currents in turn produce magnetic fields of their own that either add to or cancel part of the field from the transmitting coil. As a result of this variation or gradient in the magnetic field, the voltages induced in the receiving coils are no longer equal, so they no longer cancel. The resulting voltage across the receiving coils is fed to a sensitive trigger circuit that sounds an alarm.

Magnetic-gradient detectors are used to detect weapons and explosives. They are also buried in the ground to detect the presence of passing vehicles.

DETECTING EXPLOSIVES

Explosives are among the objects that must be detected by object detectors ...but, to date, it has proven difficult to accurately identify explosive materials.

With the increase of terrorism, one of the most important applications of object detectors is the detection of hidden explosives. Terrorists can carry explosives aboard aircraft or into buildings. Detectors located at the entrances of these facilities permit early detection of suspect objects. Bombs and explosives ranging from fairly large devices in packages to small letter bombs are sent through the mail. Object detectors can be arranged to screen packages and letters to detect such objects.

The principal consideration in the detection of explosives is that the object must not radiate or induce a great amount of energy into the suspected package. Whereas, a firearm will withstand a rather large magnetic or electric field without firing, many bombs and explosives are critical in this respect, and there is a possibility that the device that is intended to detect them will actually detonate them.

Systems designed to detect explosives should induce no more energy into the area being searched than is absolutely necessary. Thus, the detection circuits must be very sensitive. Since sensitive circuits are subject to triggering by external influences, the design is usually a compromise.

The problem of explosives detection has become even more difficult in recent years. Explosives are available that can be molded like tar paper into the bottom of a suitcase, while detonators with tiny batteries can be built into the X-ray-opaque locks of the luggage. Some authorities use specially trained dogs to sniff out the explosives, with only marginal success, while others are working on electronic sniffers. Unfortunately, good prior intelligence still seems to be the best defense against determined terrorists...but the engineers are still working.

DETECTING TAGGED OBJECTS

Merchandise in a store can be tagged to make its presence easier to detect. *Figure 16-7* shows the principle of a system designed to detect tagged objects. The detection circuit consists of an oscillator that is swept in frequency across a considerable portion of the spectrum—say over a range of 2 MHz in the high-frequency portion of the spectrum. A circuit is provided to detect the amount that the oscillator is loaded by an external circuit. A sensing coil connected to the oscillator provides an induction field that covers a large area.

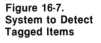

**Figure 16-7.
System to Detect
Tagged Items**

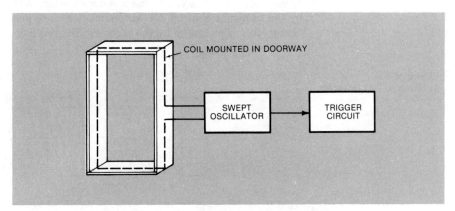

COIL MOUNTED IN DOORWAY

SWEPT
OSCILLATOR

TRIGGER
CIRCUIT

The merchandise that is to be protected carries a tag containing a small resonant circuit. As the frequency of the oscillator sweeps through the resonant frequency of the tag, the oscillator will be loaded and a signal will be delivered to the trigger circuit that initiates an alarm. The entire arrangement works in much the same way as the old-fashioned dip oscillator.

These tags are usually fastened to the object to be protected by means of a strong nylon link which is difficult to break. When an item is purchased, the salesperson cuts the tag free when the item is paid for. If a shoplifter carries a tagged item through the door of the store, an alarm will sound. Similar tags are fitted into the bindings of books to prevent the books being taken out of the store or library without being paid for or properly checked out.

Disadvantages

This system has some disadvantages. A shoplifter may remove the tags from several items of clothing, place the clothing under his or her street clothes, and then leave the store without paying. This type of action can be frustrated to some extent by locating detectors in the fitting rooms. If a tag is found in the fitting room after a customer has finished trying on a garment, it can be assumed that the customer has removed the tag from the garment. The detector in the fitting room will alert the store's security personnel.

Another disadvantage of the tagging system is that it can be thwarted if a cashier in a store cooperates with a shoplifter. This action can be checked by arranging a detector so that the cashier must insert a tag in an opening each time an item is rung up on a cash register.

Microwave Tag Detector

A variation of the tagging system is shown in *Figure 16-8*. Here the detection systems consist of a microwave transmitter with a receiver tuned to the second harmonic of the transmitter frequency. The tag is a small resonant device containing a semiconductor. When the tag is radiated by the transmitter signal, the semiconductor diode generates harmonic energy that is picked up by the receiver. The receiver then triggers an alarm.

**Figure 16-8.
Microwave Tag Detector**

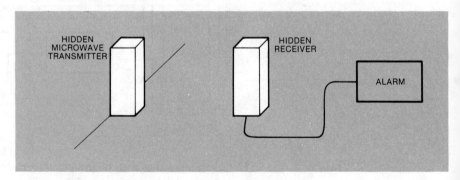

HIDDEN
MICROWAVE
TRANSMITTER

HIDDEN
RECEIVER

ALARM

Because the potential for interference exists in any rf device, some manufacturers transmit the microwave energy in the form of binary coded digits. If the modulating digital signal is not received at the second harmonic frequency, the receiver ignores the signal. Only properly coded signals cause a response. This type of arrangement is especially useful where several systems are operated on multiple entrances or exits in close proximity. If a different binary code is assigned to each, then it is possible to differentiate which signal is received and act accordingly.

> **WARNING** *When any radiation device is used, its effect on persons in the vicinity wearing electronic cardiac pacemakers must be considered. The U.S. Food and Drug Administration has investigated this matter, and it requires new pacers to demonstrate low electromagnetic interference (EMI) susceptibility. There are two particularly bad situations for pacemaker wearers. First, any microwave source that generates a low-frequency modulation in the range of normal heart rhythms (i.e., 0.5 to 2 Hz) can mimic physiological signals. Microwave ovens with mechanical energy "stirrers" sometimes show this effect. Second, those digitally encoded microwave systems whose frequencies and binary coding approximate those of the externally programmable pacemakers must be regarded as dangerous.*

WHAT HAVE WE LEARNED?

1. Object detectors are used when it is inconvenient or illegal to search visitors.
2. Object detectors must be easy to operate, give few false alarms, and pose no danger to people examined by them.
3. Inductive-balance metal detectors use four mutually interconnected inductors to form a bridge balance. A metallic object will upset the balance and provide an output.
4. A mutual inductance bridge can be used to distinguish between magnetic and non-magnetic materials.
5. Portable flux-gate magnetometers are used as handheld metal detectors.
6. Two popular forms of merchandise detector are used. One type requires that LC resonant circuits placed on or in the protected merchandise absorb energy from the merchandise in a manner similar to old-fashioned radio dip oscillators. The other type uses a merchandise tag that contains a diode and antenna that is resonant to the second harmonic of the transmitter frequency. When the diode is irradiated, it (being non-linear) generates the second harmonic. A receiver looks for the harmonic and sounds an alarm when it is received.

Quiz for Chapter 16

1. A National Retail Merchants
   Association report states that 1
   out of every _____ visitors to
   department stores may be a
   shoplifter.
   a. 100
   b. 20
   c. 12
   d. 4

2. Protecting against shoplifters is
   essentially the same problem as
   protecting against terrorists.
   True or false?

3. List three methods for detecting
   a presence in the field of the coils
   in an inductive balance system.

4. Non-metallic objects, such as the
   human body, sometimes affect
   _____ object-detection systems.
   a. low-frequency
   b. high-frequency
   c. inductive
   d. flux-gate

5. A _____ circuit is used in some
   inductive bridge systems to
   distinguish conducting and non-
   magnetic materials.
   a. null
   b. permeability
   c. phase-detector
   d. high-frequency

6. Metal detectors' circuits can be
   adjusted to not respond to small
   objects such as cigarette lighters,
   but to alert to the presence of
   larger objects, such as handguns,
   by:
   a. high-pass filtering.
   b. increasing sensitivity.
   c. low-pass filtering.
   d. reduce sensitivity.

7. A microwave anti-shoplifting
   system uses a diode and antenna
   hidden in the protected
   merchandise. What is detected
   by the microwave receiver?
   a. Second harmonic.
   b. Binary coding.
   c. Fundamental loss.
   d. Reflected energy.

8. Microwave detector schemes
   depend upon:
   a. diode non-linearity.
   b. high-power rf energy.
   c. standing waves.
   d. non-resonant antennas.

9. A merchandise protection scheme
   uses a swept rf oscillator, and
   operates like a dip oscillator.
   What is embedded in the
   merchandise tags?
   a. Diode.
   b. LC tuned circuit.
   c. Diode/antenna.
   d. Magnetic strip.

10. A(n) _____ detector uses three
    coils and an excitation frequency
    of about 100 kHz.
    a. inductive-balance
    b. flux-gate magnetometer
    c. magnetic-gradient
    d. inductive-bridge

Automobile Protection

ABOUT THIS CHAPTER

Americans have indulged in a love affair with their automobiles for more than three-quarters of a century. Some of us own luxury or sports cars loaded with expensive (and enticing) accessories such as CB radios, fancy stereo equipment, and even television receivers. In this chapter, you will learn how security electronics can protect that investment from those who would rip off the expensive "bolt-ons" or the car itself.

CARS NEED PROTECTION

One of the most common types of thefts in the country today is car theft. Cars are stolen for resale, for the value of the parts and accessories, and for use in committing other crimes. It is unfortunate that so few cars are equipped with electronic security systems because it is easy to provide a lot of protection at a reasonable cost.

One of the reasons the automobile is so vulnerable to theft is that it not only provides a built-in means of escape for the thief, but it also deprives the owner of a means of pursuit.

Many, perhaps most, car thefts are accomplished by professionals. Ordinary burglars run the gamut from bungling amateurs to skilled professionals, but car thieves seem to number more highly skilled operators in their ranks. This may be so because one car is similar to another, and a skill learned on one type of car can readily be adapted to another.

Theft by a professional is by far most likely to cause permanent loss of the vehicle. Amateurs often bungle the job and are caught. When the theft is perpetrated by a youth for a joy ride, the car is most often abandoned shortly after theft. Unfortunately, many thefts in this category result in accidents.

Professional car thieves can drive away an unprotected car in less than one minute!

A professional car thief can gain access to a car, hot-wire it, and drive away in less than a minute. In fact, much of the success of the crime depends on executing it rapidly. Therefore, the protection that will be most effective is anything that will increase the amount of time required to steal the car.

Police departments have efficient reporting systems for tracking stolen cars. As soon as a car theft is reported, the information is introduced into a nationwide computer network. Once the information is in the computer, it is just a matter of time before the car will be recognized as stolen. Thus, the car thief needs to gain as much time as possible before the theft of the car is discovered. If stealing a particular car proves to be a time-consuming or unfamiliar process, the thief might readily abandon it and look for one that is easier to steal.

The second deterrent, after making the job difficult, is to provide an attention-getting alarm that is difficult to foil. The last thing a thief wants is attention.

IGNITION PROTECTION (ELECTRICAL)

Hot fuse circuits on older cars make it difficult for thieves to hot-wire.

The problem with most ignition-protection systems on older cars is that they can be jumped rather easily by a professional. The best protection against jumping is to make the situation unfamiliar. *Figure 17-1* shows the "hot fuse" circuit, a deceptively simple, but quite effective, system of ignition protection. A concealed wire is run from where the ignition hot lead attaches to the coil through a concealed switch to the automobile ground. The hot wire is broken at some inconspicuous place, and a fuse is inserted. The fuse must be rated high enough to handle the normal ignition current.

**Figure 17-1.
Electrical Ignition-
Protection System**

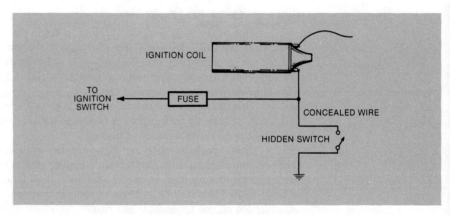

When the car is parked, the hidden switch is closed, thus connecting the hot wire of the ignition to ground. If the ignition is turned on, or the ignition key is jumped, the fuse will blow, interrupting the ignition current. The thief will not realize that a fuse has blown but will think either that the car won't start, or that this is an unfamiliar situation which he or she is not competent to handle. If the thief attempts to connect a hot wire directly to the terminal of the coil, in effect connecting a wire between the battery supply and ground, the wire will become red hot very quickly. This alone is often enough to discourage even a professional.

Modern cars are more difficult to hot-wire in the traditional way because they use modern electronic ignition systems. These systems are not foolproof, but they do require more expertise of the thief.

Electronic Combination Locks

The digital electronic combination lock opens the line from the ignition switch to the electronic ignition system. A control set on or near the dashboard contains a series of pushbuttons, and perhaps a digital readout or some indicator LEDs. The driver is required to punch in a three- or four-digit code before the lock frees the ignition system. In some models, three attempts to enter a wrong code shuts the ignition system down for a period of ten to thirty minutes (depending upon design). The latter type of electronic combination lock is useful for both protecting against theft and preventing the owner from drunk driving. Supposedly, an inebriated person will enter incorrect codes and therefore inactivate the auto ignition system.

IGNITION PROTECTION (MECHANICAL)

Most newer cars provide a degree of mechanical protection to the ignition system. The most elementary systems bury the key inside the steering column and place armor around the wiring. These techniques make it very difficult, and time-consuming, for the thief to gain access to the electrical circuitry for the purpose of hot-wiring.

HOOD AND TRUNK LOCKS

Probably the most effective step that can be taken to prevent car theft is to install good hood and trunk locks, such as those shown in *Figure 17-2*. The ordinary trunk lock can be punched out so quickly that it is usually quicker to open a trunk in this way than to use a key. Most hoods have no protection. The use of a hood lock is inconvenient when checking the oil level, but the amount of protection it provides is worth the inconvenience.

**Figure 17-2.
Hood or Trunk Lock**

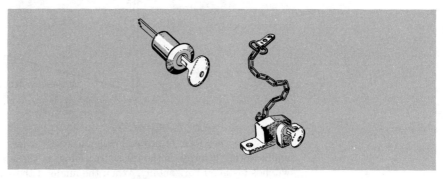

Any lock, even a heavy one with a strong chain, can be broken, but it takes time. As a further deterrent, both the hood and trunk should have tamper switches that will initiate an alarm when an attempt is made to open them.

The usual approach to stealing a car that might be equipped with an intrusion alarm is to open the hood and disconnect the battery cable in less than a minute. The alarm will of course be triggered, but it will stop as soon as the battery cable is disconnected. The thief can then find the alarm wires, disable the alarm, jump the ignition, and drive away with impunity. Finding that it will take more than a few seconds to get the hood open after tripping the alarm, the thief may well give up. Some backup systems use a trunk-mounted alarm battery to foil the thief who pries open the hood.

ACCESSORY PROTECTION

Theft of tires, radios, stereos, and CB radios is probably more common than theft of the car itself. Here again, it is important to make the job time-consuming. Special bolts and nuts are available that cannot be easily removed without special tools. Everything of value in the car should be made hard to remove. Even tires can be protected by special lug nuts.

Once the job has been made time-consuming, the next step is to provide a good alarm. If all the alarm circuitry is mounted under the locked hood, there is less likelihood that it can be foiled. With proper alarms, door switches are usually adequate to protect accessories inside the car.

Stealing a car should be time-consuming and attention-getting.

To protect the tires, transmission, and other undercar parts, an alarm is needed that will trip when the car is vibrated, such as when it is jacked up. The shaker switch shown in *Figure 17-3* is made specifically for this purpose. It will trip the alarm as soon as the car is vibrated or moved. Naturally the shaker switch should be mounted where it cannot easily be detected until it is too late.

**Figure 17-3.
Shaker Alarm Switch**

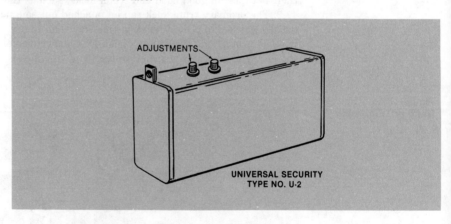

Another form of protection against a thief jacking the car up, or simply towing it away, is the tilt switch. Most of these are mercury switches installed horizontally. When the angle of the switch is changed drastically, the mercury inside the switch rolls to one end and shorts the contacts to set off the alarm. A limitation of tilt switches is that they must be rebalanced if the car is parked on a hill.

COMPLETE PROTECTION

The measures described in the preceding paragraphs are usually sufficient to provide a great deal of protection for an automobile. They cannot totally prevent theft, but, by making it difficult, they will make it time-consuming and will therefore constitute an effective deterrent.

Solenoid fuel valves can cause a stolen car to run out of gas a few blocks from where it was stolen.

Where it is thought necessary, additional measures may be taken. A feature that is commercially available but not commonly used, is a solenoid valve in the fuel line. The solenoid valve is controlled by a hidden switch or electric combination lock. The car can be started without defeating the valve, but it cannot be driven very far before it will appear to have run out of gas and will almost always be abandoned.

Figure 17-4 shows a very complete automobile protection system. In this arrangement, an electromechanical alarm system is connected to door, trunk, hood, and shaker switches. If anyone tampers with the car, the alarm will be initiated. A time delay is provided so that the alarm will shut off soon after the tampering has stopped. This will prevent the battery from running down. An emergency battery is provided in the trunk so that even if the thief manages to open the hood and disconnect the battery cable, the alarm will still sound.

**Figure 17-4.
Complete Automobile-
Protection System**

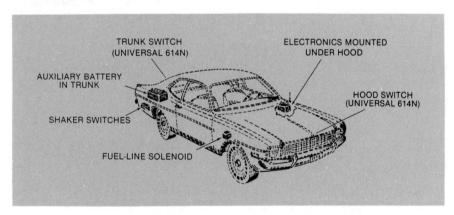

A fuel-line protection system is installed so that even if the thief detects all of the other protective measures, the car will seem to have run out of gas.

Two-way radios have long been a popular theft item. This crime probably hit its peak when Citizen's Band (CB) radio was at its peak, but has dropped off now that CB sets are both inexpensive and less popular. Recently, however, there has been an upsurge in theft of non-CB two-way radios from boats and cars. Some of these radios are expensive cellular radio sets, while others are amateur radio rigs or marine VHF-FM equipments. A protection scheme used on some radios is to build in a module that transmits the call sign of the owner in either Morse code or ASCII digital code. It becomes apparent to legitimate owners when a stolen radio is being used on the frequency. Such a modification is inexpensive, not obvious, and requires a technically competent person to detect and disengage.

WHAT HAVE WE LEARNED?

1. Auto theft and theft from autos is a major category of crime in the US. Some cars are stolen by young joyriders, but the thefts that result in total loss to the owner are usually committed by professionals. Amateurs more often steal from unprotected vehicles.
2. The motive for car theft can be resale of the stolen vehicle, or resale of the expensive parts. Most resold parts cannot be traced to the original vehicle.
3. The goals of the protection system should be (a) making theft more difficult, and (b) attracting attention to the thief's activities.
4. Auto thieves can be deterred, or stopped, by protecting the ignition switch. Electrical circuit schemes and mechanical schemes are both used.
5. Hood and trunk locks are used to prevent the thief from gaining access to those areas. The hood lock prevents an underhood hot-wire.
6. The most complete protection of a vehicle and its contents involves (a) secure locks on doors, trunk, and hood, (b) mechanically and electrically secure ignition systems, and (c) properly designed and installed alarms that squawk at attempts to enter, start, tow, or lift the vehicle.

Quiz for Chapter 17

1. List two types of ignition protection scheme.

2. List two factors that encourage thieves to abandon a theft attempt.

3. List two forms of electrical ignition protection.

4. A proper backup to a hood lock is a(n):
   a. double latch.
   b. hot fuse.
   c. hood alarm.
   d. electronic combination lock.

5. Name the two items we might provide to guard against the daring thief who, after setting off the alarm, pries open the hood to disconnect the battery.

6. Underdash accessories are probably stolen more often than the car itself. Thieves can be foiled by alarm systems and _____.

7. Protection of the tires and other undercar parts can be accomplished by:
   a. plunger switches.
   b. hood locks.
   c. combination switches.
   d. shaker, tilt, or vibration switches.

8. A means for preventing car thieves from being successful after they foil the alarm and lock systems might be to use a(n):
   a. radio beacon.
   b. tilt switch.
   c. fuel line shut-off valve.
   d. hot-wire fuse short circuit.

9. Most tilt switches are actually _____ switches.
   a. SPDT
   b. mercury
   c. plunger
   d. spring-loaded

10. _____ serve not only to foil thieves, but also discourage drunk drivers.
    a. Tilt switches
    b. Electronic combination locks
    c. Security alarms
    d. Vibration switches

Computer Crime

ABOUT THIS CHAPTER

We have seen in an earlier chapter that the computer is a powerful weapon in the war against crime. Unfortunately, the computer has also opened up an entire new field of criminal activity known as computer crime. As computers rapidly proliferate, this field of criminal activity also grows. The situation is aggravated by the fact that many computers are being installed in high-risk environments.

Computer crime has given rise to a new group of criminals. The people who commit computer crimes come from the ranks of computer programmers, computer operators, magnetic tape librarians, and electronics engineers.

Virtually all persons or organizations who use computers are potential victims of computer crime.

The potential victims of computer crime are all organizations and persons who use or are affected by computers—nearly everyone. Unlike most other crimes, there are practically no geographical limitations on crimes involving computers. Although many such crimes take place at the computer, many others are committed by telephone from remote locations.

TYPES OF COMPUTER CRIME

The field has led to the development of a completely new vocabulary of crimes known by such names as data diddling, Trojan horse, and salami techniques.

Data Diddling

Data diddlers alter computer input documents before or as they are entered into the computer.

This is the safest, simplest, and most common form of computer crime. It consists of changing data either before it is entered into a computer or while it is being entered. The crime can be accomplished by almost anyone involved in entering, handling, or transforming data. Typical examples include forging or counterfeiting documents, exchanging data storage devices such as tapes or disks, making improper data entries, and neutralizing or avoiding manual controls.

An Example

A typical crime of this type involved a clerk who filled out time records of some 300 employees of a railroad. He noticed that all data forms that were used to enter data into the computer required both the employee's name and payroll number, but that the computer used only the number. The computer used the number not only for figuring the payroll, but even for looking up each employee's name and address. The clerk also noted that all recordkeeping, except that done by the computer, was done by the employees' names and that nobody identified employees by number.

The clerk capitalized on this situation by filling out forms for overtime using the names of employees who frequently worked overtime and using his own payroll number. His income increased by several thousands dollars a year. The scheme was not discovered for years until, quite by accident, an auditor checking W-2 income tax forms questioned why a payroll clerk should make such a high salary.

Trojan Horse

A Trojan horse program performs an unauthorized function as the computer does its legitimate work.

This name is given to the technique of inserting hidden instructions in a regular program so that it will perform certain unauthorized functions while it is accurately performing its regular function. This is the method most commonly used in computer-based frauds and sabotage. It is very hard to detect and when it is found it is very hard to trace to the criminal.

Business computers often have millions of instructions in their operating systems and programs. A Trojan horse of as much as 100,000 instructions might not be noticed. The Trojan horse sits in the middle of a program and waits until it is called up. Then it executes its instructions for a few milliseconds.

One such Trojan horse, in a system that mailed out checks regularly, interpreted a death notice as a change of address for three months, then automatically entered the death notice, and erased the temporary address. Of course, the temporary address was one that was accessible to the perpetrator. Thus, each recipient was "kept alive" for three months after death while the criminal received the checks. The system so cleverly changed records back to their original form that the scheme was very difficult to detect.

Variations on Trojan Horse

Some Trojan horse programs, called "phantom glitches," can be humorous or annoying, but they do not destroy data. In one eastern university, there was a phantom glitch in the IBM 370 used by students and administration alike. Some impish student built a Trojan horse that examined certain values in registers, and when certain number combinations appeared, printed out, I AM THE PHANTOM GLITCH— CATCH ME IF YOU CAN HEE HEE HEE! Most students found the printout amusing. Other Trojan horse programs are less than amusing.

Another variation is the "Arf-Arf" program, which is usually embedded in an otherwise useful utility program that is circulated free either on disk or on computer bulletin boards. The utility works properly most of the time, but it soon blows up and destroys all data in the computer's main hard disk drive. A typical arf-arf program allows the user to run the utility several times before it blows up.

Salami Technique

Salami techniques can be used to shave tiny amounts off every account and deposit the money into a bogus account owned by the criminal.

The salami technique involves the theft of very small amounts of money or inventory from a large number of sources. For example, the theft might involve taking ten or twelve cents from each of a few thousand accounts. This amount could then be transferred to a checking account where it could be drawn out. This type of action may shortcut many security controls because at the time of the crime nothing is taken out of the institution. A small amount is merely transferred from one account to another.

The theory behind the salami technique is that the individual losses are so small that they might not even be noticed and if they are noticed, they are so small that it is hardly worth complaining about. Many salami crimes go undiscovered because of this. The skilled operator avoids using any identifiable pattern, frequently changing the small amount taken and avoiding hitting the same accounts regularly.

Superzapping

Computers occasionally get into endless loops. Legitimate Superzap programs help the programmer break that loop...but also can be used illegally.

This technique is named after a program that computer centers use as an operating tool. Any computer that can operate in a secure, controlled mode needs a program that can be used to override all of the controls in case of emergency. Computers occasionally get caught in a loop and cannot be started and stopped by the regular means. In a case like this, a superzap can be used to gain access to all of the data in much the same way that a master key is used to open a lock in an emergency.

In the hands of a prospective computer criminal a superzap is a powerful tool. It enables the shortcutting of all of the safeguards that are normally built into a system to avoid unauthorized operations.

One example of superzapping occurred in a bank in New Jersey and cost the bank $180,000. A manager of a computer operation was using a superzap at a time when some of the regular computer programs were not working. He was making changes to accounts under the direction of his management. He soon realized what a powerful tool the superzap really was and began transferring money into the accounts of three of his friends. The fraud was continued for some time. Finally, it was detected when the bank responded to a customer's complaint of an irregularity.

A superzap can be used not only to effect a theft, but also to erase all traces of it. Thus, a clever criminal having access to such a program can occasionally use it, erase all traces, and then not use it for some time. A crime of this type is very hard to detect.

Trap Doors

Trap doors allow the programmer to enter the program at will and make changes.

It is common for a programmer to insert breaks in a program while the program is being developed. These breaks, called trap doors, are later used in the debugging process to insert additional instructions. Normally, trap doors are eliminated during the final editing of a program. Occasionally, though, a few trap doors are left for use later in debugging future problems.

An unethical programmer can leave trap doors in a program to put them to use later. Furthermore, operators often find trap doors that were left in a program. In either case, unauthorized instructions can be inserted.

Trap doors are often a problem in time-sharing services because they may permit one of the users to gain access to the programs and data of another user. In one instance, a trap door permitted some engineers that were using a time-sharing service to search for secret passwords. They found one and used the password to gain access to secret programs and data. The crime was discovered, but, as is often the case, quite by accident.

Logic Bomb

A logic bomb is an unauthorized program activated when an event does or does not occur. The event may be a time or date or an entry in the computer.

One computer operator installed a logic bomb that would operate if his own payroll number was ever omitted from the company payroll, as it would be if he were dismissed. The bomb erased all of the payroll information on all employees.

Datanapping

A new form of computer crime is datanapping. Datanappers access a computer via a modem to enter the program illicitly. They download all data from the disk and then command the computer to erase the disk. The criminal then leaves a ransom note on the computer for the owner to find. The idea is to extort money from the computer owner to retrieve the data.

Scavenging

Scavenging is the unauthorized gathering of data used by a computer in any way. One company managed to scavenge data from a time-sharing service also used by competitors by always requesting that a "scratch tape," which is used for temporary storage, be installed before they ran their programs. These tapes have usually been used before, but they are erased while being used the next time. An operator at the time-sharing service noticed that the "read" light always came on before the "write" light whenever this company ran a program. They were reading whatever data happened to be on the scratch tape before they used it and thereby gaining a lot of information on their competitors.

Bugging, Eavesdropping, Wire Tapping

One of the earliest recorded cases of bugging a computer occurred during the Viet Nam war when a miniature radio transmitter was found inside one of the computers used in the war effort.

Inasmuch as many computers are linked together by telephone lines, it is possible to steal data from the computer by simple wire tapping. The information can be recorded and later decoded. Some computers use microwave and satellite links; their data is available to anyone who wishes to pick it up.

Piggybacking and Impersonation

In a large restricted computer operation, entry may be gained by walking through the door with someone who is authorized to enter. The usual trick is to approach the door with both arms full of paper and tapes at about the same time as an authorized person. Often the authorized person will courteously hold the door for the prospective computer criminal.

Hacking

Computer hackers are hobbyists who use personal computers for their own amusement. Although most hackers are honest users of personal computers, some of them cannot resist the challenge of breaking into other peoples' computers. Almost all industries have hacker break-in stories. Hackers even broke into super-secret computers at plants that design nuclear weapons!

Some hackers obtain the telephone number of computers by using a sequencing autodialer program (as in the movie "War Games"). Others obtain the telephone number through careless employees of the company that owns the computer. Still others obtain them over computer bulletin boards where other hackers have listed the number.

Using Computer Time Illegally

Using a large mainframe computer system for personal use is almost irresistible. When a major military base computer was systematically searched it was loaded with personal programs ranging from recipes to check-balancing programs. While this practice seems harmless on the surface, it locks up resources that the company may need, and it costs the company computer time. Therefore, it is a form of petty—or not so petty—larceny.

The best protection against this form of theft is to maintain a strict control system over user account numbers and periodically inspect user account files to see if the computer is being used for anything unauthorized.

PROTECTION OF THE COMPUTER

There are many commonsense measures that can be taken to reduce the opportunities for computer crime. A problem to overcome is that most computer users and owners feel that "it can't happen here," and they fail to take necessary protective steps.

Once commonsense security measures have been taken, there are several ways that electronic devices can be used to afford further protection. Probably the most obvious is access control as described in Chapter 11. A good access control system can keep the number of persons that might make unauthorized use of the computer to a minimum. This also increases the risk that the criminal may be caught and so acts as a deterrent.

Of course, the computer itself can also be used for security. It can check and record any access to sensitive areas, allowing only authorized persons and allowing nobody to enter during unauthorized hours. Simple annunciators that call the attention of someone in authority whenever a terminal is used are also deterrents.

Some of the personal identification schemes described in Chapter 20 are also helpful.

Encoding data transmitted over telephone or microwave links helps protect against eavesdroppers.

Much security can be gained by encoding all data that is transmitted over telephone lines or microwave links. In fact, the problem of eavesdropping can be well controlled by this means.

The biggest problem in getting good security in a computer operation is convincing whoever must approve the cost of a security system that one is really needed. In spite of the number and variety of computer crimes, they do not account for a very large percentage of the total losses that a business incurs. Often a bank will lose much more through genuine mistakes than from fraud.

There will always be a few highly skilled computer criminals who will tackle the most secure system, sometimes successfully. However, most of the computer crime on record occurred in facilities that used few if any security measures.

A computer terminal should be treated as securely as a cash register that contains a large amount of cash. Any security system that might be used to protect such a cash register can be used to protect the computer terminal. A room containing the circuits of a computer and its wiring should be treated at least as securely as a warehouse containing valuable merchandise.

NON-COMPUTER PROTECTIVE SYSTEMS

Although in most security systems it is advantageous to use computers, the computer itself can often be better protected by adding devices that cannot be controlled by the computer. The reason is simple. In computer crime, the criminal is often a computer expert—frequently a software expert—but not necessarily an electronics expert. The criminal can often detect and defeat security measures that involve the computer itself, but he or she may not be aware of the electronic systems that do not involve the computer.

Figure 18-1 shows an access recording system. Each person who is authorized to use the computer has a method of accessing the system. It may be a key or an access control card. In a very secure installation, it might be a device that will recognize a fingerprint. Each time the computer is used, the system records the time and who used it and for how long.

**Figure 18-1.
System for Recording
Computer Access**

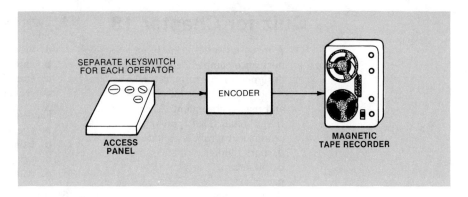

This record cannot prevent crime, but it may act as a deterrent. It may also be helpful in apprehending a criminal after a crime has occurred.

WHAT HAVE WE LEARNED?

1. Computer crime has increased along with the increased use of computers in business and other organizations. Two problems in detecting such crime are that (a) it is often perpetrated by skilled programmers whose knowledge is more sophisticated than other employees, and (b) it can be committed from remote locations via telephone lines.
2. Data diddling consists of altering computer data documents prior to their being input to the computer.
3. Trojan horse programs are nestled in legitimate programs, and will execute for only a few milliseconds at a time. Such programs often change data to the benefit of the criminal.
4. Salami techniques consist of shaving small amounts, sometimes less than one cent, and then depositing them to a holding account. Some salami programs take advantage of rounding, while others simply shave tiny amounts from each regular account, hoping to go undetected because of the small amounts.
5. A superzap program is used legitimately to unhang a computer gone awry. But such a program can also be used by computer criminals to enter the computer and manipulate data.
6. Trap doors are break points in the program that a programmer can use legitimately to fix glitches or to alter the program illegally at a future date.
7. A logic bomb is a program that will do some damage to the program when activated by certain occurrences in the normal execution of the program. An arf-arf program is a type of logic bomb that destroys data when activated.

Quiz for Chapter 18

1. A program sub-routine in an insurance company computer is designed to interpret death notices as a change of address, and mails subsequent checks to the criminal. This type of criminal program is called a(n):
   a. data diddler.
   b. superzap.
   c. arf-arf.
   d. Trojan horse.

2. A(n) _____ program is used legitimately to unlock an erroneous endless loop. It can also be used by criminals.
   a. superzap
   b. Trojan horse
   c. arf-arf
   d. logic door

3. A programmer installed a program that looked for his payroll number when running the company payroll program. It was designed to erase much of the company payroll data if his own payroll number was ever deleted from the company rolls. This type of program is called a _____ program.
   a. trap door
   b. superzap
   c. logic bomb
   d. trap door

4. Logic bomb programs are also called:
   a. arf-arfs.
   b. superzaps.
   c. trap doors.
   d. scavenger programs.

5. Eavesdropping can be foiled by:
   a. encrypting data.
   b. using microwave.
   c. using telephone lines.
   d. using ASCII codes.

6. A(n) _____ can help foil computer thieves by recording who uses the machine.
   a. data logger
   b. access recording system
   c. encoder
   d. magnetic logger

7. _____ techniques can help prevent computer crime by restricting physical access to the computer.
   a. Trap door
   b. Write-protect
   c. Access recorder
   d. Physical access control

Electronic Eavesdropping and Secure Communications

ABOUT THIS CHAPTER

One of the first and most pervasive forms of security electronics is electronic eavesdropping, which consists of monitoring radio communications, placing wired or wireless microphones, or tapping telephones. In this chapter, you will learn about electronic eavesdropping, both measures and countermeasures.

SCOPE OF THE PROBLEM

All of the electronic security systems described in the preceding chapters are used to provide security against vandalism, personal injury, or theft of property. There is another aspect of security in which electronics is playing an increasingly important role. This is the area of electronic eavesdropping or "bugging," as it is commmonly called.

Legitimate bugs are used by law enforcement agencies to help capture criminals. Some private investigators also use them, but that use is often illegal.

Eavesdropping is being carried on by electronic means for reasons both legitimate and illegitimate. Law enforcement agencies use bugs to help in the capture of criminals, and private investigators use them to obtain information for their clients. However, the most significant application of electronic eavesdropping devices is their use by criminals for stealing business or personal secrets or for listening to police broadcasts to avoid apprehension.

LEGAL AND ILLEGAL EAVESDROPPING

There is no way of telling how much illicit eavesdropping is being carried on. Several companies are engaged in the manufacture of these devices, but much of their output goes to legitimate law enforcement agencies. In addition, modern scanner receivers, and certain other devices, have legitimate uses. It is difficult to determine intent at the time of purchase.

We do know, however, that anyone with even a rudimentary knowledge of electronics can build a miniature bug that can be easily concealed. In fact, with the advent of microminiature circuitry and compact batteries, the state of the art seems to be on the side of the eavesdropper, rather than on the side of the law-abiding citizen. The availability and ease of construction of electronic eavesdropping devices make it safe to assume that any given location may be bugged if someone considers it worth the risk and effort. For this reason, wherever business secrets are considered worth stealing, it is advisable to take adequate countermeasures against eavesdropping. Several management consultants now specialize in the "debugging" of business facilities.

Eavesdropping on Computers

Another area in which secure communications are needed is in the computer field. The computer has proven to be such a valuable aid to business that it is being used to handle all kinds of information, much of it proprietary. In some firms, all of the records are kept in computer memory. Their theft by a competitor might well destroy a company.

In addition to stealing information from a computer, a competitor with access might change the information stored in the computer. Many crimes against business consist of juggling the records in the computer in such a way that the criminal benefits financially from the change.

Mainframe computers store data entered through terminals. The terminals are connected to the mainframe of the computer either through direct dedicated wires or through a communication system such as the telephone company. In the latter case, unless security precautions are taken, it is possible for anyone to dial the proper number and gain access to the computer. We'll examine techniques to improve the security of data communications later in this chapter.

BUGGING OR EAVESDROPPING DEVICES

Law enforcement agencies need information on eavesdropping techniques that they can use in the detection of crimes and the apprehension of criminals. Law-abiding citizens and security personnel need information on the subject so that they can protect themselves against the eavesdropper.

Fortunately for our purposes, the same information is required for bugging and for countermeasures. We must know how the bugs work if we are to use them intelligently or to find and disable them. So, we will briefly review the principles of operation of some common eavesdropping devices.

Most of the eavesdropping devices that are in use today fall into one of the following categories.

1. Hidden microphones connected by wires to a listening or recording point
2. Hidden radio transmitters
3. Telephone wiretaps.

Hidden Microphones

The hidden microphone is a miniature microphone that is connected by concealed wiring through a sensitive amplifier to headphones or a tape recorder. Microphones may be made very small, particularly where high amplification is available to recover the signals. The use of integrated-circuit amplifiers makes large amounts of amplification available in a very small space. The power required to operate these miniature amplifiers is extremely small. They can operate continuously for weeks or months on power from a small battery.

The Spike Microphone

The spike mike, shown in *Figure 19-1*, consists of a small microphone element, similar to a phonograph pickup mounted on a hollow spike, together with a miniature amplifier. The spike can be driven into a door or wall of the area to be monitored, as shown in *Figure 19-2*. The spike carries the sound vibrations to the microphone in much the same way that a phonograph needle carries sound to the pickup element. Although the sound picked up by a spike mike is not as clear as that from a regular microphone, it can produce remarkable results. Most modern spike mikes use integrated-circuit amplifiers.

**Figure 19-1.
Spike Mike**

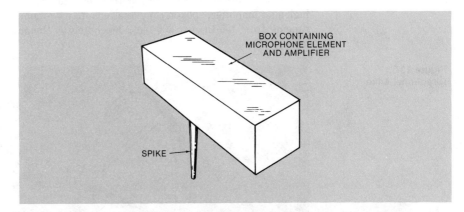

**Figure 19-2.
Spike Mike Driven in
Wall**

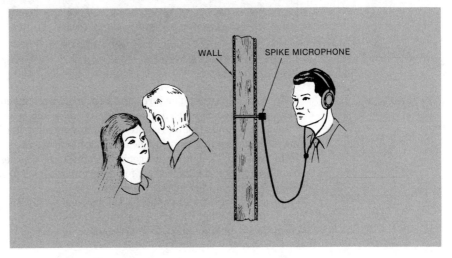

The ability to plant and conceal a microphone is limited only by the ingenuity of the eavesdropper. The wiring is usually more difficult to hide. When low-impedance microphone elements are used, very fine wires may be run around the walls or under carpets, or they may be imbedded in the carpets.

Directional Microphones

A variation on the hidden microphone is a high-gain directional microphone that may be used to pick up conversations up to 300 feet away. In order to use a microphone to pick up a conversation many feet away from its location, the microphone must have a very narrow beam. Otherwise, the extraneous sound reaching the microphone will completely mask the conversation. *Figure 19-3* shows an arrangement that has a sound pickup confined to a narrow beam. Here, an ordinary microphone element is mounted at the focal point of a parabolic reflector. The reflector focuses the sound waves arriving from a single direction on the microphone, just as a parabolic mirror focuses light. With a reflector diameter of 3 feet and a high-gain amplifier, spoken conversations may be monitored at distances ranging from 150 to over 300 feet, depending on the amount of background noise.

**Figure 19-3.
Directional Mike**

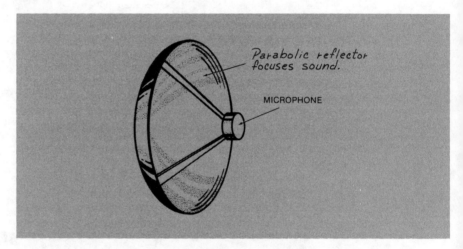

Parabolic reflector focuses sound.

MICROPHONE

Another popular form of directional microphone is the shotgun microphone, which is used extensively in radio and television broadcasting to pick up sounds from a remote location. An example of such use is the microphone used on the sidelines during football games to pick up sounds from the field. A shotgun microphone consists of a series of parallel tubes of differing lengths (to account for different resonant frequencies) that all drive a common microphone element.

Directional microphones are large and may be spotted easily if used during daylight hours. Therefore, they are most often used at night or concealed behind an open door or window.

Hidden Radio Transmitters

The miniature radio transmitter is a popular bug because it sends signals to a distant location. The eavesdropper need not be too close to the monitored site.

By far the most popular type of bug in use today is a miniature radio transmitter concealed in the area to be monitored. It picks up conversations in the monitored area and transmits them to a remote monitoring area. The range of these devices is a matter of compromise and is usually limited by the permissible size and available power. The usual range of such a transmitter is about 300 feet, but if the transmitter can be hidden in a radio, television set, or lamp, where ac power is available and size is not a serious limitation, it can operate continuously and may have enough power to transmit a mile or more.

Operating Frequency

Theoretically, the eavesdropper can use any frequency for the clandestine transmitter. For practical reasons, however, only a few frequencies are suitable. The eavesdropper must keep the power low and choose a frequency that is not apt to be intercepted accidentally. In one case, a bug was discovered because it interfered with commercial aircraft transmissions. For this reason, bugs seldom operate in the standard am and fm broadcast bands.

The feedback phenomenon, the effect often experienced in public address systems, can be used to help detect bugs. A radio receiver is slowly tuned across the radio spectrum. When a bug frequency is located, the radio's speaker output is acoustically coupled to the bug's microphone input, and in a few seconds a howling will be heard from the speaker.

When bugs are operated in the broadcast (usually fm) band, this effect is sometimes experienced accidentally when no one is actually looking for a bug. It should always be considered suspicious. Normal fm radio receivers do not produce feedback howls, so we must assume the cause is a clandestine bug.

Other factors influencing the choice of an operating frequency are the required length of the antenna and the availability of commercial receivers for monitoring. The requirement that the antenna be as short as possible so that it can be concealed dictates the use of very high frequencies (VHF). The availability of economically priced sensitive receivers has led to the use of many bugs either in or just outside the standard fm band of 88 to 108 MHz. Police departments use the 30- to 50-MHz bands and the 150- to 174-MHz bands, making this an inadvisable frequency range for illegal transmitters. In actual practice, almost all bugs operate somewhere between 60 and 200 MHz. Usually, commercially available fm receivers can be modified to cover a frequency in this range with a minimum of trouble. The use of fm helps greatly to combat radio noise.

Figure 19-4 shows the circuit diagram of a bug that is commonly used. It consists of an emitter-coupled oscillator that is frequency-modulated by a single audio amplifier. More elaborate devices use more stages, but the principle is the same. These devices can be made very small. Several commercially available units are shown in *Figure 19-5.*

**Figure 19-4.
FM Bug**

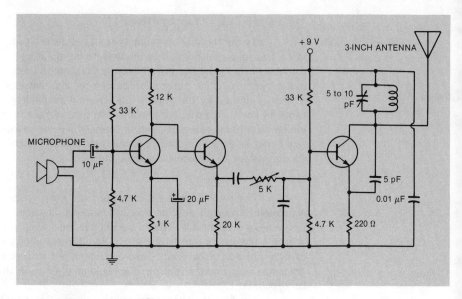

**Figure 19-5.
Commercially Available
Bugging Transmitters**

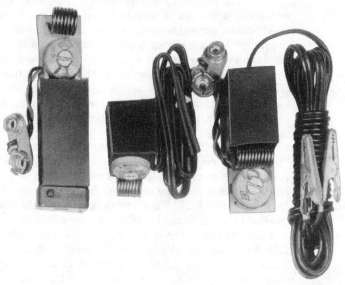

Most law enforcement agencies engaged in bugging use transmitters that operate in one of the following frequency ranges: 25–50 MHz, 88–120 MHz, 150–174 MHz, 400–570 MHz.

Reasons for Frequency Selection

Radio antennas for bugs should be as short as possible...which means the higher frequencies should be used where possible.

In general, the trend is toward higher frequencies because small antennas radiate better at higher frequencies. The requirements for the antenna of a bugging device are conflicting. On one hand, the antenna should be as short as possible so that it can be concealed easily. On the other hand, it should be long enough to radiate efficiently, minimizing the power requirement for the bug.

An antenna shorter than about a quarter wavelength usually will not radiate efficiently because its losses will be high. The higher the frequency, the shorter the wavelength, so the easier it is to build an efficient antenna. *Figure 19-6* shows a plot of the length of a quarter wavelength as a function of frequency. Note that at 30 MHz a quarter-wave antenna would be about 8 feet (250 cm) long, whereas at 500 MHz it would be only about 6 inches (15 cm) long. This explains the trend toward higher frequencies.

Figure 19-6.
Length of Quarter
Wavelength for Various
Frequencies

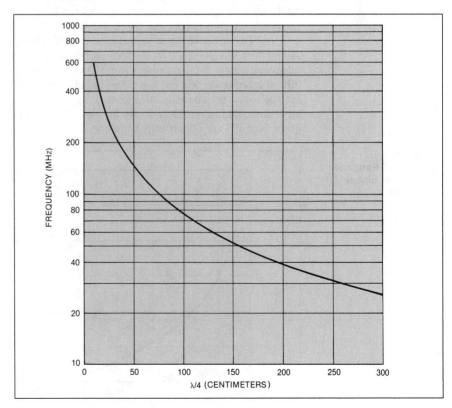

Another consideration in the selection of a frequency for operation of a bug is interference. Bugs used by police sometimes operate on police frequencies under a regular license. In such a case, the frequency can be kept clear of interference. Surreptitious bugs are used on any frequency the eavesdropper can use without either detection or interference.

Operating Range

Operating range of small bugs is limited mostly by their low output power.

In general, the signal from a bug should be receivable at a distance great enough that the eavesdropper is out of sight and cannot be easily detected. This is true whether the eavesdropper is a law enforcement officer or a criminal. The range that can be obtained by using a small bug depends on many factors. One such factor is the power output. This means the actual power output at the fundamental frequency. Since bugs must necessarily be small, the transmitter often is merely a modulated oscillator.

Most modulated oscillators have a very high harmonic content in their outputs. A broad-band power measurement that measures both the fundamental frequency and the harmonics can be very deceptive. It is only the power at the fundamental frequency that is effective.

The effect of signal attenuation on range is plotted in *Figure 19-7*. In this plot, the point 1.0 on the axis corresponds to the maximum range, whatever it may happen to be. From the plot, it can be seen that 6 decibels (dB) of attenuation will cut the range in half and 20 dB of attenuation will cut the range to one-tenth. Attenuation may be introduced by buildings, structures, and so on. Thus, it can be seen that the range obtained from a given bug will vary drastically from one situation to another.

**Figure 19-7.
Normalized Range as
Function of Signal
Attenuation**

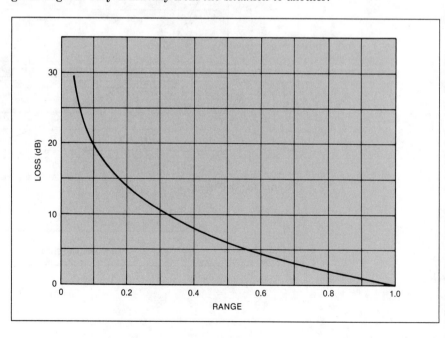

Sound-Operated Relay

The lives of electronic eavesdropping devices are limited by the small batteries usually used with them. When operated continuously, bugging devices have a fairly short life. Continuous operation of a tape recorder at a monitoring point is equally wasteful. If a recorder is operated so that it continuously monitors an area, it may run for twenty-four hours and record only a few hours, or even a few minutes, of conversation.

Sound-operated relays turn the bug on and off according to sound levels in the monitored areas. These circuits increase the operating time of the bug by reducing power consumption.

This limitation may be overcome by the use of a sound-operated relay. This is a small device having a very low power drain that will actuate a relay only when sound is picked up by a microphone connected to it. When it is connected to a transmitter, the transmitter will normally be turned off. When a sound is picked up in the monitored area, the relay will turn on the transmitter. A time-delay circuit will keep it on until a few seconds after the sound has died out. This has the dual advantages of conserving battery life and keeping the transmitter on the air only when it is transmitting something. This greatly reduces the chances of its being accidentally discovered by someone idly tuning through the frequency of operation.

A sound-operated relay can also be used at the monitoring point so that a tape recorder will run only when there is something to be recorded.

A circuit of a sound-operated relay that uses a miniature integrated-circuit amplifier is shown in *Figure 19-8*. The amplifier, which uses very little power, is in operation at all times.

**Figure 19-8.
Sound-operated Turn-on Relay**

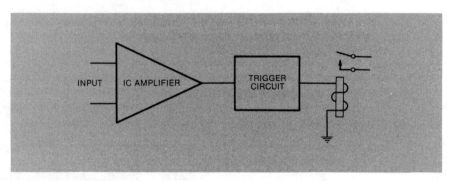

Telephone Taps

Miniature fm transmitters that fit inside the telephone handset are often used in bugging.

Telephone wiretapping is by far the oldest form of electronic eavesdropping. In its simplest form, the telephone tap consists of simply bridging a headset or a tape recorder across the line. Usually, a high-impedance amplifier is used to prevent disturbance of the telephone circuits. In recent years, telephone bugging has become much more sophisticated. Miniature fm transmitters are available that can be concealed within the telephone set to broadcast not only telephone calls but also any conversation that can be picked up by the telephone transmitter. *Figure 19-9* shows a complete fm transmitter circuit that can be constructed around the carbon microphone element of a telephone. This unit can be installed in a telephone in a few seconds. The cover need only be unscrewed from the phone and the regular microphone element replaced by the new one containing the transmitter.

**Figure 19-9.
FM Transmitter for
Telephone Tap**

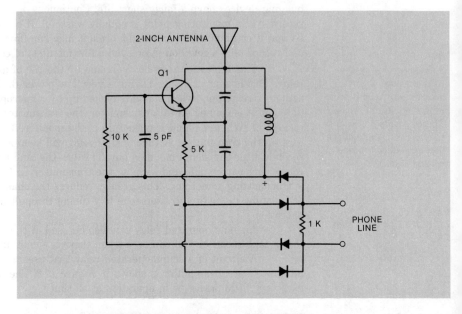

An elaborate room bug that uses the victim's telephone is shown in the block diagram in *Figure 19-10*.

**Figure 19-10.
Bug Using Victim's
Telephone**

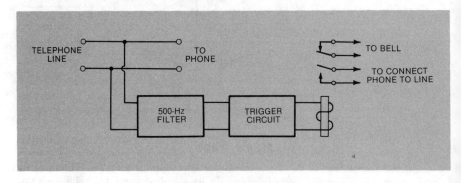

When the unit of *Figure 19-10* is installed in a victim's phone, the eavesdropper may listen to conversations in the room from any location having telephone service. The eavesdropper first dials the number of the bugged phone, then before the bell starts to ring, puts a 500-Hz signal on the line, usually by blowing a small whistle. The 500-Hz signal passes through the 500-Hz filter in the bug and operates a sound-operated relay similar to the one described earlier. This relay effectively answers the phone and disconnects the ringing circuit. The bugged phone is now connected to the eavesdropper's, who can listen to any conversations that reach the telephone transmitter. If others dial the victim's number while the bug is in operation, they will get a busy signal. If the owner of the bugged phone wants to make a call, the eavesdropper can hang up and the line will be restored to normal. This arrangement can be used to bug a room through a telephone, but it cannot be used to eavesdrop on telephone conversations.

COUNTERMEASURES

Locating bugs is more art than science, even though certain technical means are available.

In general, locating bugs is more of an art than a science. As we saw earlier, the state of the art at present seems to favor the eavesdropper rather than the law-abiding citizen. When eavesdropping is strongly suspected in a business facility, the steps taken as countermeasures often assume "cloak and dagger" proportions. There is always some uncertainty about the situation, because even when all possible measures fail to locate a bug, there is still no absolute assurance that one is not present.

The first approach to providing a security area for discussion of proprietary information is a careful physical search. The suspected area should be inspected and every possible hiding place examined carefully. Particular attention should be paid to new additions in the area, such as pictures, plants, and lamps. These are favorite hiding places.

Probably one of the most successful ways of planting a bug in a business establishment is for a visitor to simply leave something behind. Typical items are briefcases, hats, raincoats, and catalogs. Any of these items might will conceal a miniature transmitter.

Traditional Search Methods

Wired microphones can often be located by first discovering the wires. A metal locator (see Chapter 16) is also helpful in locating concealed items.

In addition to conducting a physical search, most debugging experts believe in making rf field-strength measurements. These are usually made at the frequencies that are commonly used, but to be perfectly safe would require making measurements at all possible frequencies. This is usually considered impractical for normal business searches.

Many field-strength meters designed specifically as bug locators are commercially available. *Figure 19-11* shows the circuit diagram of a simple field-strength meter that will locate just about any hidden transmitter if it is brought close enough. It consists simply of a broad-band diode detector and a high-gain, integrated-circuit amplifier. The meter will deflect on very weak signals, and in some locations the sensitivity must be turned down to avoid indications caused by local broadcast stations. The signal causing the deflection may be identified by listening to the signal. A small speaker plugged into the phone jack will help in locating bugs. The gain of the amplifier is so high that when it is brought close to the microphone of the bug, feedback will occur and the device will howl. When trying to locate bugs with sound-operated relays, the searcher will usually talk continuously while conducting the search. If the searcher hears his or her own voice in the headphones, it is a positive indication that a bug is present and is being triggered by the voice.

**Figure 19-11.
High-Gain, Broad-Band,
Field-Strength Meter**

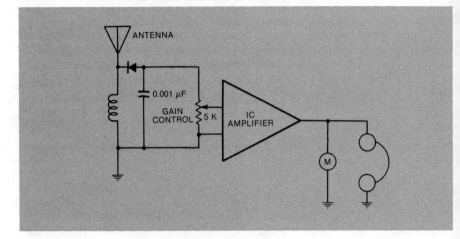

Other commercially available field-strength meters are tunable. These usually have a higher sensitivity but require much more time to operate.

Newer Search Methods and Preventive Care

A newer method of detecting bugs takes advantage of the fact that all bugs use transistors and that transistors are highly non-linear devices. The technique is shown in *Figure 19-12*. Here the search area is bombarded with a signal from a microwave transmitter. A microwave receiver is also beamed at the same area. If there are no non-linear devices in the area being searched, the signal from the transmitter will be reflected to the receiver without any change. If, on the other hand, there is a non-linear device, such as a transistor, in the field of the transmitter, it will generate harmonics of the transmitter signal. If there are two signals from the transmitter, the non-linear device will also generate sum and difference signals.

Most of the circuits of a bug are very small and respond well to microwave signals. This system has the interesting feature that a transistor doesn't even have to be energized in order to generate the spurious signals. Thus, it will not only detect the presence of active bugs, but it will also find dead bugs in which the batteries have run down.

**Figure 19-12.
Microwave Search
System**

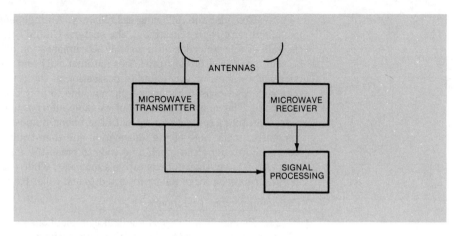

Protection of Business Secrets

No area should ever be casually assumed to be bug-free. Always be careful when discussing sensitive information.

Even though an area has been thoroughly searched and found to be clear of eavesdropping devices, it is still wise to treat business secrets at least as carefully as any other property of the same value would be treated. It is ironic that some firms will go to great lengths to provide proper protection for their material assets, but will freely discuss proprietary business secrets worth millions of dollars in completely insecure areas, such as restaurants, bars, and motel rooms. Whenever it is suspected that eavesdropping devices might be in use, conversations should be held in subdued tones and background noise (such as a radio playing) should be provided.

New Telephones

For the past several years it has been possible to buy telephones not produced by AT&T. These phones are a welcome blessing to those who would like a personalized instrument or service and functions not normally available through traditional sources of phone equipment. Some of these devices are sealed (i.e., disposable, unrepairable), so they are difficult to bug without leaving telltale marks on the case.

Telephone Answering Machines

Along with the variety of new telephones is an increase in the number of other telephone products. Telephone answering machines are as convenient for the phone owner as they are maddening for long-distance callers. Some of these products allow the owner to inject a touch-tone code into the line from a remote location to have messages played back over the telephone without returning to the home or office. These devices operate on codes, and they can be invaded by people who obtain the correct code either by the owner's carelessness or by experimentation or by other technical means. For this reason, it is not desirable to allow sensitive information to be left on an answering machine.

Consider the following case history. An independent manufacturer's representative in the eastern United States was working on the sale of a large order of industrial instrumentation devices. The products he sold monitored factory processes automatically and were in demand. An unethical competitor was found in possession of the representative's touch-tone code that caused his answering machine to play back over the telephone. The competitor received valuable information concerning the representative's contacts (along with the phone numbers they left). The competitor made note of the information and then transmitted to the answering machine the touch-tone code to erase the tape. As a result, the competitor knew the representative's business, while it looked to his clients like the representative never returned phone calls. He lost the sale.

Portable and Car Telephones

People who use portable and car telephones should be aware that others can easily eavesdrop on their conversations. Many businesses now own portable and car cellular telephones and consider them a real blessing. But many of those phones, built without scramblers, are easily intercepted by anyone with an inexpensive scanner receiver tuned to the cellular phone company's frequency.

Worse yet are the portable telephones used around the house. These instruments are extremely popular, found in almost every neighborhood. Unfortunately, there are limited numbers of operating frequencies for these products. You cannot only be overheard by people using scanner (and other forms of) receivers, but also by a considerable number of people who inadvertently (or intentionally) have an instrument with the same operating frequencies. Sensitive information should never be discussed over this type of telephone.

Telephone Inspection

Since telephones are frequently tapped and also used as hiding places for bugs, they should be thoroughly searched. Usually, this is best accomplished with the assistance of a representative of the telephone company. Being familiar with the equipment, they can quickly spot signs of tampering or the presence of alien equipment. Because of the many different places that a telephone line may be tapped, telephones should never be considered secure channels of communication for highly sensitive information unless some kind of speech scrambling device is used. These interesting and effective devices are described later in this chapter.

Discovered Bugs

After a bug has been discovered, it is not advisable to touch the bug until a course of action has been decided on. Touching or moving the bug will alert the eavesdropper to the fact that the device has been discovered. Several different plans of action are possible.

1. The bug can be left intact and false information can be given to the eavesdropper. Done properly, this may force the eavesdropper to reveal his or her identity.

2. The bug can be covered, impairing its effectiveness, and the area can be placed under surveillance. The eavesdropper, finding that the bug is not operating properly, may return to repair or replace it.
3. The bug simply may be removed. This is apt to create a false sense of security, however, because two bugs are often used in the expectation that one will be found and the victim will feel safe.
4. The most advisable course of action in most cases is to leave the bug intact and report the matter to the police and an attorney.

Illegal Jammers

Although transmitters that are designed to interfere with transmission of radio signals are forbidden by law, they are widely used and should be discussed. In fact, it seems that many business executives who have little electronic knowledge feel very secure when they know that any possible radio transmission from a conference room will be jammed.

Commercially available jammers vary considerably in their construction. The purpose of all these devices is to radiate broad-band noise that will mask the signal from a bug. While doing this, they usually do just as well at jamming radio and television signals in the area.

A schematic diagram of a buzzer-type jammer is shown in *Figure 19-13*. Some of these units are designed to fit into a fountain-pen case so that they can be carried about.

Figure 19-13. Illegal Buzzer-type Jammer

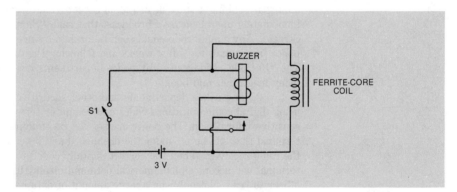

The buzzer shown is a crude form of jammer, even though often quite effective. Another form of jammer is the radio transmitter that is amplitude modulated with a square-wave generator. Both forms of jammer will wipe out a wide portion of the radio spectrum, which is the reason for their illegality.

SECURE COMMUNICATIONS

Scanner and other forms of radio receivers are used by hobbyists, but criminals also make use of the same receivers to monitor insecure communications.

One of the most serious eavesdropping problems today is the monitoring of police radio broadcasts by burglars hoping to avoid apprehension. More and more often, police answer a burglar alarm only to find that when they get there the burglar has already gone. Inexpensive portable pocket scanner receivers that will monitor police frequencies are available to anyone. Most of these receivers are used by law-abiding hobbyists who follow the police in their work and do no harm. But their availability makes it possible for burglars to carry receivers on burglaries and leave immediately if they hear a police cruiser being dispatched to the area. Some cities have passed ordinances forbidding the use of portable radios tuned to police frequencies, but these ordinances are usually ineffective.

Coded Police Messages

The most obvious approach to the problem is to use coded messages for dispatching police cars. This has been done for many years but has had almost no effect. First of all, the code must be very simple and easily remembered if all police officers are to use it and react to it instantly without recourse to a code book. It would be practically impossible to have a code name for each street in a city. Thus, even if the nature of the call were coded, the burglar could still profit from the broadcast. For example, a burglar robbing a store at 210 Main Street would leave the scene immediately upon hearing a broadcast that said, "Signal 50 at 210 Main Street." Any simple code could soon be broken by merely listening to the police frequencies for a few weeks and following the dispatched police cars. The "10 Code" widely used by police departments has been published in many magazines and books.

Many police departments and other security-conscious agencies are using digital communications codes and computer terminals for transmitting sensitive information. The police cruiser can be equipped with a computer terminal that sits on or under the dashboard and listens to the output of the radio receiver. When the correct digitally coded tones are received, the terminal will accept alphanumerical data and display it on a screen for the officer to read. Not only can a large amount of data be transmitted more accurately and in a shorter time than it could be hand copied, but it is more secure from casual eavesdroppers.

Military Messages

For years the military services have had very elaborate secure-communications systems for fixed locations, but even they have had trouble transmitting coded messages in the field where a quick response is required with no time for elaborate decoding. During World War II, the British forces used Irish troops who spoke the little known Gaelic language for secure communications. United States forces have employed native Americans in the same manner.

Speech Scramblers

The electronic answer to the problem of providing secure
communications is the use of speech scramblers. The scrambler is a small
device that is inserted between the microphone and the transmitter. It has
the effect of making the broadcast unintelligible unless a receiver
incorporating the proper descrambler is used.

Some very elaborate electronic coding systems are used by
military agencies, but these are usually classified as secret and are far too
elaborate for regular police or business use. The speech scramblers that are
in common use today operate on two basic principles—inversion and
splitting.

Inverters

Normal speech sounds consist of many different frequency
components, each having a different amplitude. A plot of amplitude versus
frequency of a typical speech sound is shown in *Figure 19-14*. In the
inversion scrambler, the order of these components is reversed. The result
is that when the signal is picked up on a regular receiver, the signal sounds
like monkey chatter—something like a single-sideband signal that is not
tuned in properly.

**Figure 19-14.
Frequency Spectrum of
Speech Sounds**

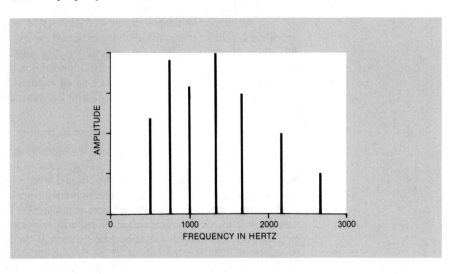

Figure 19-15 shows a block diagram of a simple inverter. The input
signal consists of speech sounds having components in the frequency range
of 250 to 2750 Hz. These signals are fed to a modulator where they are
heterodyned with a signal from a 3-kHz oscillator. Two different sets of
signals are produced in the modulator—the sum of the speech frequencies
and the 3-kHz signal and the difference between the 3-kHz signal and the
speech frequencies. A low-pass filter in the output lets only the difference
frequencies pass. Thus, the output frequencies are between 250 and 2750
Hz, but the spectrum is inverted. For example, an input component having

a frequency of 2750 Hz will beat with the 3-kHz signal to produce a component of 3000 − 2750, or 250 Hz. Similarly, a 250-Hz input signal will produce a 2750-Hz output signal.

**Figure 19-15.
Block Diagram of
Simple Speech Inverter**

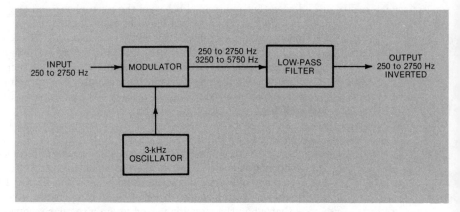

Note that if the input were an inverted spectrum, the output would be plain speech. This means that the same equipment can be used for both scrambling and descrambling.

Although the simple circuit of *Figure 19-15* is used in some scramblers, it has several disadvantages. Chief among these is that it is difficult to filter the 3-kHz signal and the original speech signal from the output. Adjustments are apt to be critical, and the unit is hard to keep properly adjusted in the field. If even a small amount of normal speech filters through, it will serve as a clue to the listener, allowing at least a guess at the message.

An Improved System

An arrangement that produces the same result but is much easier to adjust is shown in *Figure 19-16*. This system uses double modulation. In the first modulator, the speech is heterodyned with a high-frequency signal, for example, 13,000 Hz. Only the high-frequency components are passed on to the second modulator, which operates exactly 3000 Hz higher in frequency than the first modulator. Here, a filter selects the low-frequency, or difference, components. In this arrangement, if the input signal has a frequency of 2750 Hz, the output of the first modulator will be a frequency of 15,750 Hz. The output of the second modulator is then 16,000 − 15,750, or 250 Hz. Thus, the arrangement produces exactly the same result as the simpler circuit of *Figure 19-13*, but adjustment and maintenance are much more straightforward.

**Figure 19-16.
Double-Conversion
Speech Inverter**

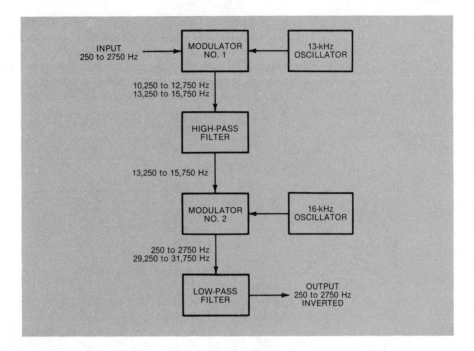

The chief disadvantage of the simple inverters just described is that their signal can be descrambled by using an ordinary signal generator, together with a regular receiver. If, using the frequencies in the previous examples, a signal generator is tuned exactly 3000 Hz below the carrier frequency and fed to an ordinary receiver, together with the inverted signal, the output will contain plain speech. There will be an annoying 3000-Hz beat present also, but the signal will be reasonably intelligible.

In spite of this limitation, a simple inverter can be quite effective. The first consideration in using a scrambler is to use it only where necessary. For example, ordinary police calls can be handled with plain speech, and scrambler speech can be used only for dispatching cars to an area where a crime is in progress. In this way, there will be less opportunity for anyone to record the scrambled signals and develop a descrambler.

Splitters

More elaborate scramblers use a principle called splitting, in addition to inversion. In these systems, the speech spectrum is broken into several separate bands by filters. Each of these bands may be transmitted plain or inverted, and the bands themselves may be interchanged. In transmission or transoceanic telephone conversations, the speech spectrum of 250 to 3000 Hz is split into five bands, each 550 Hz wide. The bands are interchanged and may be transmitted as either plain speech or inverted. The arrangement is changed once every twenty seconds.

Figure 19-17 shows a block diagram of a system that not only will invert speech, but will also split the speech spectrum into two halves that can be interchanged. Although the entire speech spectrum from 0 to 3000 Hz is applied to both channels, the filters in the system restrict the effect of channel A to those components from 0 to 1500 Hz and the effect of channel B to those components between 1500 and 3000 Hz.

**Figure 19-17.
Two-Channel Splitter
and Inverter**

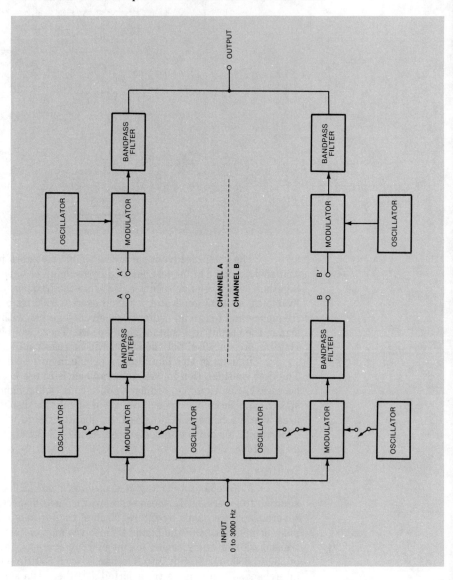

Consider how the system splits the speech spectrum without inverting it. In this case, the 10- and 8.5-kHz oscillators are used. The entire speech spectrum, 0 to 3000 Hz, is heterodyned with a 10-kHz signal in channel A. The output of the modulator contains both sum and difference components. It has components in the bands of 7 to 10 and 10 to 13 kHz. Only those components between 10 and 11.5 kHz can get through the bandpass filter. Thus, the output at point A is due only to those components of the input lying between 0 and 1500 Hz. Channel B operates in the same way; its output is in the same frequency range but is due to the components of the input lying between 1500 and 3000 Hz. Neither of the bands is inverted.

If in *Figure 19-17*, point A were connected to point A', and point B were connected to point B', the heterodyne process would be reversed in the second half of the system, and the output would be just like the input. If, on the other hand, point A were connected to B', and point B were connected to A', the two halves of the spectrum would be changed. That is, the output of channel A, due to the 0- to 1500-Hz portion of the input, would be shifted to lie between 1500 and 3000 Hz. Thus, the two halves of the speech spectrum would be interchanged. Such a signal would not be intelligible unless a similar process were repeated in the receiver.

In addition to being split, either of the channels in *Figure 19-17* may also be inverted. In this case, the 11.5- and 13-kHz oscillators are used. The output at point A would still lie between 10 and 11.5 kHz, and it would still be due only to that part of the input between 0 and 1500 Hz, but now the spectrum would be inverted.

Most of the more elaborate commercial scramblers on the market today operate on both the inversion and splitting principles. Although some are more elaborate and split the speech spectrum into four or more bands, the operating principle is the same as that of the system shown in *Figure 19-17*. These systems make it possible to use a great many different codes that can be changed frequently for additional security.

Speech scramblers are increasingly popular, both with police departments and with business organizations where secure communication is essential. Many scramblers are equipped for use with telephones to increase the security of telephone communications.

The scrambler, no matter how elaborate, does not guarantee permanent security of communications. It is always possible to tape the scrambled message and decode it by trial-and-error. The chief advantage of scrambling is that, with a good scrambler, it takes a great deal of time to break the code. This is long enough to protect emergency communications that require immediate action; by the time they are decoded, they will already have been acted upon and the need for secrecy will be past.

Digital Voice Communications

Many law enforcement agencies are using some form of digital modulation. This permits data to be transmitted over the regular channels and also gives a high degree of security to voice data. Digital modulation tends to provide a great deal of security for the following two reasons.

1. There are not many digital receivers available. Such a receiver would be difficult for an eavesdropper to find, whereas with ordinary fm any scanner can be used.
2. The digital signal sounds a great deal like ordinary noise. It is not easy to recognize that a signal is present when listening with an ordinary receiver.

Digital voice transmission has another advantage in that coding and decoding is reasonably easy. The digital signal will not be degraded by encoding it as a regular signal tends to be.

Electronic Cryptography

One way electronics can be used to increase the security of a computer system is with cryptography; that is, the encoding of the data into a secret code. The encoding of data is similar to encoding a message in English. It consists basically of substituting a code character for each character in the message.

The science of cryptography has been highly developed by military services for transmissions of vital national importance. Unfortunately, there are not many expert cryptanalysts in industry. There are more apt to be cryptanalysts with military experience attempting to break a code than to compile codes for security purposes.

Codebreaking is not nearly as difficult for the professional as it appears to the lay person.

To one unfamiliar with cryptography, most codes appear to be very secure, but this is deceiving. To the expert, breaking a code is not nearly as complicated as it seems.

Figure 19-18 shows a pseudorandom sequence generator that will generate a long series of binary 1's and 0's. It consists of a series of shift registers with feedback from two points along the string. This circuit can develop a series of almost a billion 1's and 0's that appear to be nearly random. In the system, this string of digits is added to the data at the transmitting end and subtracted at the receiving end. The device itself can be constructed on a printed-circuit card, or even on a monolithic integrated circuit. The operator need not have any idea of what is in the encoder or how it works.

**Figure 19-18.
Circuit to Develop
Pseudorandom Digital
Sequence**

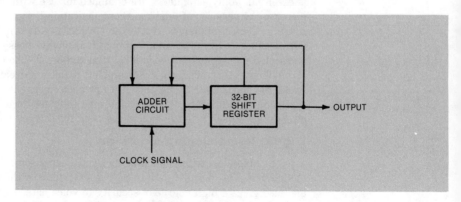

The U.S. National Bureau of Standards has issued a data encryption standard (DES). This standard covers the ways that a digital signal can have an encryption key added to it. There are over a dozen different integrated circuits available that will perform this function. The ICs can be used like black boxes. You don't have to know how they work to use them. They are fed plain data and an encryption key and what comes out is encrypted data. The reverse process takes place at the receiver. The coded message and the proper encryption key are fed into the IC and out comes plain text.

This system is effective because it has a very long encryption algorithm. It is 56 bits long and has 8 parity bits. This gives 72×10^{15} possible permutations. It has been estimated that it would take a modern supercomputer several years to break the code.

To the inexperienced, this encoding with a string of nearly a billion binary digits would appear to provide absolute security; it does not, however, for two reasons. First of all, anyone stealing data knows something about it. No one would go to the trouble of stealing anything that was of no value to him or her. This advance knowledge gives the thief some idea of what is in the data. It might not be much, but it is enough for an experienced cryptanalyst to decode a message with the aid of another computer. Second, breaking a code usually boils down to solving a number of linear equations. If not much advance information is available, the number of equations that must be solved is large, but if another computer is available, this is no problem.

More sophisticated encoding techniques are now available using non-linear circuit elements. These codes are much harder to break.

WHAT HAVE WE LEARNED?

1. Electronics plays a large role in eavesdropping. Examples of devices range from radio scanner receivers to overhear radio communications, to hardwired bugs, telephone taps, and miniature radio transmitters.
2. Hidden microphones can be a spike mike in an adjacent room, a parabolic or shotgun mike at a distance, a regular microphone (with or without radio transmitter) inside the room, or even the telephone transmitter element inside the room.
3. Modern technology makes it easy to build miniature radio transmitters. Because of antenna length restrictions, most transmitter bugs operate on VHF and UHF frequencies. Those frequencies in the 60- to 212-MHz region are most preferred, although frequencies up to 900 MHz are sometimes used.
4. Telephone tapping is relatively easy. It can consist of a resistance bridged across the on/off switch, a transmitter inside of the telephone housing, or a hardwire tap on the telephone junction box.
5. There are several countermeasures for use against radio transmitter bugs. A field strength meter or spectrum analyzer can reveal the transmitter's emissions, a radio receiver will howl with feedback when tuned to the bug's frequency, and a microwave system that excites semiconductor junctions inside of the transmitter is also available.

6. Speech scramblers make telephone and radio communications more secure. Two basic methods are used: (a) inverting and (b) splitting.

7. Digital electronics can help secure telecommunications. Digitization of voice signals renders them unreadable without a decoder. In addition, digital alphanumeric text can be sent, in either standard or encrypted coding, instead of voice communications.

Quiz for Chapter 19

1. The use of _____ has made possible microminiature radio transmitters and bugs.
   a. electronics
   b. spike mikes
   c. integrated circuits
   d. transistors

2. A shotgun microphone is highly:
   a. sensitive.
   b. directional.
   c. sensitive to interference.
   d. fragile.

3. The usual range of hidden radio transmitter bugs is about:
   a. 300 feet.
   b. 1 mile.
   c. 10,000 feet.
   d. 50 feet.

4. Radio frequencies used for bugging transmitters are usually between _____ MHz.
   a. 60–212
   b. 200–1000
   c. 1–10
   d. 10–50

5. Because of antenna length restrictions, the tendency for bug design is toward _____ frequencies.
   a. higher
   b. medium
   c. lower
   d. UHF

6. Find the length in feet of a quarter wavelength antenna for a frequency of 80 MHz.
   a. 4.5 feet.
   b. 8.2 feet.
   c. 6 feet.
   d. 3 feet.

7. Battery life of an unattended bug transmitter can be extended by using a(n) _____ on the bug.
   a. antenna
   b. sound-operated relay
   c. power amplifier
   d. crystal oscillator

8. The oldest form of electronic bugging is:
   a. remote microphone.
   b. miniature transmitters.
   c. telephone tapping.
   d. wired microphones.

9. A _____ sometimes can be hidden inside a victim's telephone to transmit sound to a distant location.
   a. radio transmitter
   b. microphone
   c. 500-Hz filter
   d. trigger circuit

10. A simple _____ can be used to locate transmitter bugs.
    a. searcher
    b. debugger
    c. field-strength meter
    d. seeker

11. A _____ search system works by exciting the pn semiconductor junctions within the bug.
    a. microwave
    b. spectrum analyzer
    c. field-strength meter
    d. hardwired

12. Both square-wave generators and buzzers are used as _____ to protect against radio transmitter bugs.
    a. searchers
    b. monitors
    c. roach killers
    d. jammers

13. The basic process used in speech inverters is:
    a. heterodyning.
    b. scrambling.
    c. inverting.
    d. tape recording.

14. One form of digital cryptography uses a(n):
    a. encoder.
    b. pseudorandom sequence generator.
    c. decoder.
    d. encrypter algorithm.

15. It is impossible to break digitally encrypted codes. True or false?

Personnel Identification and Verification

ABOUT THIS CHAPTER

In this chapter, you will learn the reasons for, and methods behind, various personnel identification devices. In addition, we will also address lie detectors and stress evaluators.

BACKGROUND OF PERSONNEL IDENTIFICATION

At one time, identification of personnel was considered to be strictly a human function. Security guards and bank tellers were charged with the responsibility of identifying the people they dealt with. The cost of using a person to recognize and identify other people is high and is not economically feasible in all situations. It has been estimated that over a year it takes 5.2 security guards to adequately cover one entrance twenty-four hours a day, allowing for a five-day week and the normal vacation and lost time.

Human guards make mistakes, so an automated system is needed to augment guards.

Human guards are not infallible. They get tired and can make mistakes. In some cases, they collaborate with an intruder. A system is needed that will automatically identify authorized persons, or at least assist the guards who are responsible for the identification.

Automatic equipment, such as the automatic tellers used by some banks, is efficient and inexpensive, but it lacks human judgment. The equipment will dispense cash to anyone who inserts the right card and punches the right code into a keyboard.

Special keys, encoded key cards, and electronic combination locks are all used to limit access...but there are problems if the user is careless.

We covered some of the more conventional methods of identification of personnel in the discussion of access control in Chapter 10. These include special keys, encoded cards, and electronic combination locks. All of these measures are good and are probably adequate where the risk isn't too great. For example, if an automatic bank teller was set to dispense not more than $200 to any one depositor over a twenty-four–hour period, the loss resulting from someone fooling the machine would not be severe. In highly sensitive situations, however, all of these means involve a certain amount of risk. Keys and cards may be lost or stolen, and people are notoriously loose lipped about such things as special code numbers.

Several electronic systems have been developed that will automatically identify a person on the basis of some physical characteristic that is not easily counterfeited.

ELECTRONIC FINGERPRINT IDENTIFICATION

It has long been recognized that the human fingerprint is a unique property of an individual. Fingerprints are used at all levels of law enforcement to recognize persons with criminal records. The reason that fingerprints have not been widely used to identify persons at security checkpoints or bank windows is that reading a fingerprint requires special training.

One way of using a fingerprint for identification is to compare a person's fingerprint with a photograph of the fingeprint of an authorized person. With regular photography, this is impractical, but with a comparatively new technique—holography—it can and is being done.

Older fingerprint identification systems used ordinary photos of prints. Modern systems use laser holograms.

Holographic Principle

Technically, holography is a technique for recording both the amplitude and the phase of an image and later reconstructing the image. *Figure 20-1* is a sketch of the method of making a holographic plate. The light source is a laser which produces coherent light. The light reaches the photographic plate through two paths. Through one path, it is merely reflected from the reference mirror onto the plate. In the other path, light is reflected from the object being photographed to the photographic plate. The result is that an interference pattern is recorded on the plate. The plate itself can respond only to the amplitude or amount of light and not its phase. The interference pattern, however, contains the phase information as well. It usually bears little resemblance to the object being photographed but appears to be an irregular pattern of fringes.

**Figure 20-1.
Making a Hologram**

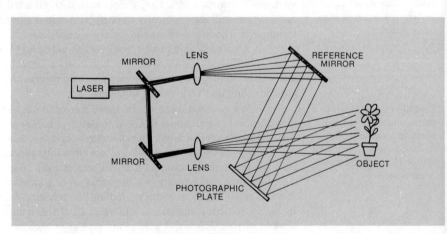

When the transparency is illuminated by a laser, the image of the photographed object will be seen as shown in *Figure 20-2*. There will be a virtual image that looks exactly like a three-dimensional image of the object. In fact, by moving slightly, the observer can actually see behind the object.

Figure 20-2.
Viewing a Hologram

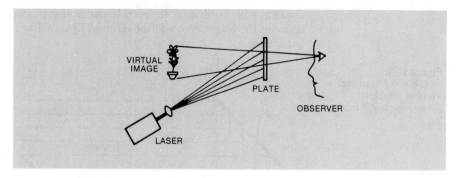

Automatic Personnel Verifier

Figure 20-3 shows an automatic personnel verifier based on the holographic principle. The person desiring to enter a facility carries a plastic card that has a holographic image of his or her fingerprint. The person inserts the card into a slot and then inserts a finger into an opening as shown in the figure. A fresh image of the fingerprint is made on a glass plate, and this is compared with the hologram on the card. If the two prints match, the person is allowed access. If not, or if the device is tampered with, an alarm is initiated.

Figure 20-3.
Automatic Personnel
Verifier *(Courtesy KMS*
Industries, Inc.)

Figure 20-4 shows the way the fingerprint is matched with its image. Light from a laser is focused through the fresh fingerprint onto a mirror, where it is then reflected onto the hologram of the fingerprint. If the fresh fingerprint matches the hologram, the light reflected from the hologram will focus to a bright spot. This is because the light, after it has passed through the fresh fingerprint and is reflected from the hologram, will actually be a reconstruction of the original beam of light from the laser used to make the hologram. If the fingerprint and hologram do not match,

the light will be diffused. A photoelectric sensor is used to distinguish between the bright spot and the diffused light and to trip an alarm in the latter case.

Figure 20-4.
Automatic Personnel
Verifier Principle
(Courtesy KMS Industries,
Inc.)

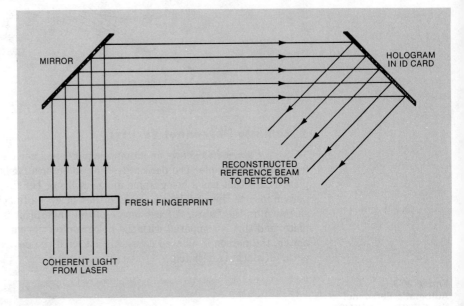

MIRROR

HOLOGRAM
IN ID CARD

RECONSTRUCTED
REFERENCE BEAM
TO DETECTOR

FRESH FINGERPRINT

COHERENT LIGHT
FROM LASER

HAND GEOMETRY

Certain properties of hands can be used in hand geometry identification systems.

Although it has been known for a long time that fingerprints are unique, it is also true that many other human characteristics are unique to the individual. An Air Force study of fitting high-altitude gloves to pilots some twenty-five years ago indicated that certain properties of the human hand such as the lengths of the fingers and palms were almost as unique as fingerprints.

This property has recently been used in a personnel identification system. In this system, certain characteristics of the hands of authorized persons are encoded on a card. The card is placed in a slot, and the hand is placed on a lighted surface where the corresponding characteristics are measured electronically. The two sets of measurements are then compared in a digital circuit. If the card belongs to the person whose hand is on the screen, access is permitted. Otherwise an alarm is sounded.

To allow for errors, the device is usually set to allow people a second try in case they placed hands on the screen incorrectly. This reduces the number of false alarms while ensuring that an unauthorized person is not allowed access.

RETINAGRAMS

A newer form of personnel identification device is the retinagram. This device uses a TV camera and a microscope to examine the pattern of blood vessels and other structures on the retinal surface at the rear interior of the subject's eye. Some anatomists are convinced that the details of blood vessel and structural patterns are almost unique to each individual.

In using the retinagram, the subject peers into the microscope eyepiece to permit a television camera to take a picture of the retina. The TV frame is digitized and stored in a computer where it is compared with a previously stored image. Retinagrams are still "frontier" devices, but their use can be expected to increase in the future.

VOICE PRINTS

Each human voice is sufficiently unique to be used for identification purposes.

No two people have exactly the same voice. To someone trained in voice recognition, the differences are great. In fact, the testimony of persons trained in voice recognition has been accepted as positive identification against persons accused of illegally operating a radio transmitter.

Although a human listener can recognize hundreds of different voices with little effort, recognizing voices automatically is not simple. It has been done successfully in the laboratory but has not been widely applied to identification equipment in the field. Voice printing is still somewhat experimental, but modern high-speed, high-capacity microcomputers have brought them a lot closer to general use. Still to solve are problems of foreign accents and changes in accent due to colds and sore throats. Under some present computer algorithms, an authorized person who has a sore throat could be classified as an unauthorized intruder.

One application of voice printing is the identification of anonymous telephone callers; a recording of the anonymous call is compared with recordings of the same statements by various persons suspected of making the call. At least one company is now offering this service to law enforcement agencies and security personnel.

PERSONAL IDENTIFICATION CARDS

The use of a personal identification card for various purposes is becoming quite common. *Figure 20-5* shows a card of this type that is used for gaining entry to a secure area. Usually, cards of this type are used with some kind of computer controlled system. The computer not only can recognize the number on the card, but it can also perform many related functions. It can check to see if the holder of the card is authorized for access to an area or a bank account. It can keep a record of just what times each card is used and for what purpose.

**Figure 20-5.
Personal Identification
Card**

Most people are familiar with the personal identification cards that are used by banks to permit transactions to be made through automatic unattended machines. The identification card, together with a secret code number, provides a great deal of security. Even if a card is stolen, the thief will not know the code number and, therefore, cannot use the card.

Most personal identification cards have a strip of magnetic material on the back of the card as shown in *Figure 20-6*. This strip is magnetized in a pattern that will record a number in binary form. Several different specifications for the encoding of such cards are in common use. The ABA (American Banking Association) code uses the binary number system shown in *Table 20-1*. Note that this is the ordinary binary code except for the digit at the extreme left. This is called a parity bit. A binary 1 is placed in this position when needed to make the total number of 1's in each character an odd number. The computer guards against mistakes or misreading of the card by checking each digital character to be sure that the total number of 1's is an odd number. This is called a parity check. If, for any reason, the number of 1's is an even number, it will be rechecked. If it is still even, the computer will recognize that something is wrong and will reject the card.

**Figure 20-6.
Magnetic Strip on
Personal Identification
Card**

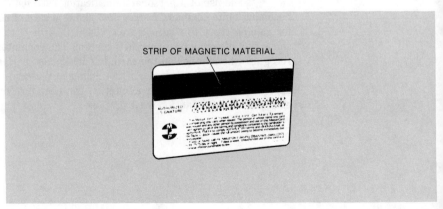

STRIP OF MAGNETIC MATERIAL

Table 20-1.
ABA Binary Code

Character	Code	Character	Code
1	00001	9	11001
2	00010	0	10000
3	10011	:	11010
4	00100	;	01011
5	10101	<	11100
6	10110	=	01101
7	00111	>	01110
8	01000	?	11111

VERIFICATION

One of the oldest security problems is determining the truth of testimony. Ancient methods for telling whether or not a witness was lying were far from adequate. In some of these testing procedures, both the innocent and the guilty perished from the procedure, thus eliminating the necessity of further investigation.

Many security investigations hinge on statements of witnesses and participants.

Much security and law enforcement work is based on information obtained from the testimony of various people. The selection of personnel for positions involving a high security risk is based to an amazing extent on statements made by them or on references provided by them. Much criminal investigation consists of following up clues that are contained in statements.

It is unfortunate that many people habitually treat the truth in a way that serves their personal interests. The exaggeration or the slanted statement is often more troublesome because it is only partially true, making an objective evaluation of the situation very difficult.

Many honest applicants have been denied employment because of a prejudicial character reference. An employee reporting on the circumstances of an intrusion may twist the facts not because he or she is guilty, but because honest testimony might direct attention to some other problem, such as neglect of his or her job. All of these compromises with truth only complicate the job of the security or law enforcement official.

No True Lie Detectors

Unfortunately, there is no electronic principle that can be utilized to tell the difference directly between true and false testimony. There are, however, many physiological characteristics that can be measured electronically to help a skilled operator distinguish between true and false statements.

The oldest device used to verify the truth of testimony is the polygraph, or lie detector. This device measures many physiological characteristics such as heart rate and skin resistance and plots them on a strip chart. Variations in these characteristics are then correlated with answers to questions. For example, the palms of some people will perspire when they feel tension, i.e., when they might be lying. This slight increase in perspiration will be accompanied by a change in the resistance measured at the skin.

The polygraph has many limitations. First of all, it has to be connected to the individual. This in itself produces tension and complicates the job of interpreting the measurement. Second, it is often considered an invasion of privacy and its use usually requires the consent of the person being questioned.

Psychological Stress Evaluator

The PSE may be used without the subject's knowledge...although such use might be illegal.

A development that has many advantages over the polygraph is the Psychological Stress Evaluator, or PSE. This device evaluates the psychological stress that a person experiences by making certain measurements from a tape recording of the person's voice. The PSE has the advantage of not requiring physical connection to the device. Therefore, the device can be used without the person's knowledge although it may not be legal to do so.

The operation of the PSE is based on the fact that there is normally a slight tremor—called a microtremor—in the muscles of the body, including the muscles that control the voice. Under psychological stress, this tremor is suppressed or completely eliminated. When the stress abates, the tremor returns.

The effect that the tremor has on the voice cannot be distinguished by the ear. When listening to a person speak, the listener cannot perceive the presence (or absence) of the tremor. The effect of the tremor is a small frequency modulation of about 10 Hz superimposed on the normal voice sounds.

This fm component on the voice can be measured by playing a tape recording of the voice through an analyzer similar to an fm discriminator and plotting the results on a strip chart as shown in *Figure 20-7*. For more detailed analysis, the tape speed of the playback can be changed.

**Figure 20-7.
PSE Components**

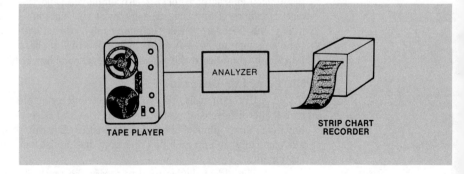

ANALYZER

TAPE PLAYER

STRIP CHART
RECORDER

Figure 20-8 shows two plots of the output of the analyzer. In *Figure 20-8a*, there is a constant, nearly uniform, motion superimposed on the trace. In *Figure 20-8b*, this tremor is missing at certain points on the trace. A skilled observer can readily detect the straight or diagonal lines that indicate psychological stress.

Figure 20-8.
Plots from PSE

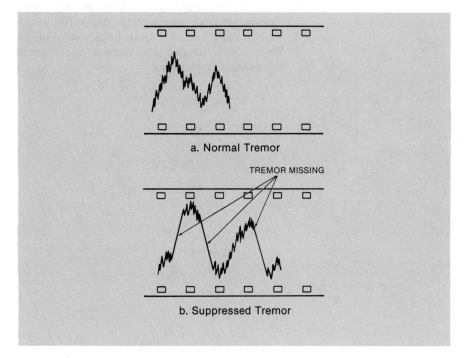

a. Normal Tremor

TREMOR MISSING

b. Suppressed Tremor

Skilled Operator Needed

In general, the PSE requires the services of a trained operator for effective use. The phrasing of the questions asked by the questioner is very important. It is possible for an unskilled questioner to induce stress in an innocent party. For example, if when questioning a suspect about an act, the questioner brings to mind another act of which the suspect was guilty in the past, stress may result.

The PSE is already used by many law enforcement agencies and security personnel. It has value not only in investigating a crime, but also in questioning applicants for sensitive positions before they are hired. Unfortunately, it also has possibilities for use in industrial espionage. The fact that tape recordings can be made of telephone conversations means that the technique can be used on people without their knowledge. False statements made to protect business statements may be detected, and slowly the secret that is supposed to be concealed is revealed.

WHAT HAVE WE LEARNED?

1. Human guards are not infallible, so some means of automatically identifying visitors is a useful adjunct.
2. Electronic account cards are secure only as long as the user keeps the code numbers secret.
3. Electronic fingerprint detectors use laser holography to compare a stored (authorized) fingerprint with the fingerprint presented by a visitor.
4. Modern identification methods include voice prints and retinagrams.
5. Voice print techniques allow some degree of prediction of stress, hence some indication of truth telling.

Quiz for Chapter 20

1. A laser hologram is used in:
   a. retinography ID.
   b. palm reading.
   c. fingerprint ID.
   d. magnetic card readers.

2. A laser produces:
   a. strong light.
   b. IR light.
   c. red light only.
   d. coherent light.

3. An air force study of high-altitude gloves revealed that _____ could be used for identification purposes.
   a. hand size
   b. hand coloration
   c. hand geometry
   d. fingerprints

4. A retinagram permits identification by examination of:
   a. eye.
   b. nose size.
   c. fingerprint.
   d. hand geometry.

5. Modern computers have made _____ more economical.
   a. fingerprinting
   b. hand geometry recording
   c. voice printing
   d. retinography

6. Personnel ID cards are much like:
   a. retinagrams.
   b. bugs.
   c. key cards.
   d. voice prints.

7. Electronic lie detection is an accurate science. True or false?

8. The psychological stress evaluator examines the subject's:
   a. fingerprints.
   b. hand geometry.
   c. retina.
   d. voice stress.

9. Both lie detectors and PSE devices require a _____ to be effective.
   a. willing subject
   b. stable power supply
   c. skilled operator
   d. digital recorder

10. A special transparency is used in:
    a. laser holography.
    b. fingerprint analyzers.
    c. PSE devices.
    d. voice printers.

Glossary

This list of terms and definitions was prepared by the Law Enforcement Standards Laboratory at the United States National Bureau of Standards.

Access Control: The control of pedestrian and vehicular traffic through entrances and exits of a protected area or premises.

Access Mode: The operation of an alarm system such that no alarm signal is given when the protected area is entered; however, a signal may be given if the sensor, annunciator, or control unit is tampered with or opened.

Access/Secure Control Unit: See "Control Unit."

Access Switch: See "Authorized Access Switch."

Accumulator: A circuit which accumulates a sum. For example, in an audio alarm control unit, the accumulator sums the amplitudes of a series of pulses, which are larger than some threshold level, subtracts from the sum at a predetermined rate to account for random background pulses, and initiates an alarm signal when the sum exceeds some predetermined level. This circuit is also called an integrator; in digital circuits it may be called a counter.

Active Intrusion Sensor: An active sensor which detects the presence of an intruder within the range of the sensor. Examples are an ultrasonic motion detector, a radio frequency motion detector, and a photoelectric alarm system. See also "Passive Intrusion Sensor."

Active Sensor: A sensor that detects the disturbance of a radiation field generated by the sensor. (See "Passive Sensor.")

Actuating Device: See "Actuator."

Actuator: A manual or automatic switch or sensor such as a holdup button, magnetic switch, or thermostat which causes a system to transmit an alarm signal when manually activated or when the device automatically senses an intruder or other unwanted condition.

Air Gap: The distance between two magnetic elements in a magnetic or electromagnetic circuit, such as between the core and the armature of a relay.

Alarm: An alarm device or an alarm signal.

Alarm Condition: A threatening condition, such as an intrusion, fire, or holdup, sensed by a detector.

Alarm Device: A device that signals a warning in response to an alarm condition, such as a bell, siren, or annunciator.

Alarm Discrimination: The ability of an alarm system to distinguish between those stimuli caused by an intrusion and those that are a part of the environment.

Alarm Line: A wired electrical circuit used for the transmission of alarm signals from the protected premises to a monitoring station.

Alarm Receiver: See "Annunciator."

Alarm Sensor: See "Sensor."

Alarm Signal: A signal produced by a control unit indicating the existence of an alarm condition.

Alarm State: The condition of a detector that causes a control unit in the secure mode to transmit an alarm signal.

Alarm Station: (1) A manually actuated device installed at a fixed location to transmit an alarm signal in response to an alarm condition (e.g., a concealed holdup button in a bank teller's cage). (2) A well-marked emergency control unit, installed in fixed locations usually accessible to the public, used to summon help in response to an alarm condition. The control unit contains either a manually actuated switch or telephone connected to fire or police headquarters or a telephone answering service. (See "Remote Station Alarm System.")

Alarm System: An assembly of equipment and devices designated and arranged to signal the presence of an alarm condition requiring urgent attention such as unauthorized entry, fire, temperature rise, etc. The system may be local, police connection, central station, or proprietary. (For individual alarm systems, see alphabetical listing by type, e.g., Intrusion Alarm System.)

Annunciator: An alarm monitoring device which consists of a number of visible signals such as "flags" or lamps, indicating the status of the detectors in an alarm system or systems. Each circuit in the device is usually labeled to identify the location and condition being monitored. In addition to the visible signal, an audible signal is usually associated with the device. When an alarm condition is reported, a signal is indicated visibly, audibly, or both. The visible signal is generally maintained until reset either manually or automatically.

Answering Service: A business that contracts with subscribers to answer incoming telephone calls after a specified delay or when scheduled to do so. It may also provide other services, such as relaying fire or intrusion alarm signals to proper authorities.

Area Protection: Protection of the inner space or volume of a secured area by means of a volumetric sensor.

Area Sensor: A sensor with a detection zone which approximates an area, such as a wall surface or the exterior of a safe.

Audible Alarm Device: (1) A noisemaking device, such as a siren, bell, or horn, used as part of a local alarm system to indicate an alarm condition. (2) A bell, buzzer, horn, or other noisemaking device used as part of an annunciator to indicate a change in the status or operating mode of an alarm system.

Audio Detection System: (See "Sound Sensing Detection System.")

Audio Frequency (Sonic): Sound frequencies within the range of human hearing, approximately 15 to 20,000 Hz.

Audio Monitor: An arrangement of amplifiers and speakers designed to monitor the sounds transmitted by microphones located in the protected area. Similar to an annunciator, except that supervisory personnel can monitor the protected area to interpret the sounds.

Authorized Access Switch: A device used to make an alarm system or some portion or zone of a system inoperative in order to permit authorized access through a protected port. A shunt is an example of such a device.

B.A.: Abbreviation for burglar alarm.

Beam Divergence: In a photoelectric alarm system, the angular spread of the light beam.

Break Alarm: (1) An alarm condition signaled by the opening or breaking of an electrical circuit. (2) The signal produced by a break alarm condition (sometimes referred to as an open circuit alarm or trouble signal, designed to indicate possible system failure).

Bug: (1) To plant a microphone or other sound sensor or to tap a communication line for the purpose of surreptitious listening or audio monitoring; loosely, to install a sensor in a specified location. (2) The microphone or other sensor used for the purpose of surreptitious listening.

Building Security Alarm System: The system of protective signaling devices installed at a premises.

Burglar Alarm (B.A.) Pad: A supporting frame laced with fine wire or a fragile panel located with foil or fine wire and installed so as to cover an exterior opening in a building, such as a door or skylight. Entrance through the opening breaks the wire or foil and initiates an alarm signal. (See "Grid.")

Burglar Alarm System: See "Intrusion Alarm System."

Burglary: The unlawful entering of a structure with the intent to commit a felony or theft therein.

Cabinet-for-Safe: A wooden enclosure having closely spaced electrical grids on all inner surfaces and contacts on the doors. The cabinet surrounds a safe and initiates an alarm signal if an attempt is made to open or penetrate it.

Capacitance: The property of two or more objects that enables them to store electrical energy in an electric field between them. The basic measurement unit is the farad. Capacitance varies inversely with the distance between the objects; hence the change of capacitance with relative motion is greater the nearer one object is to the other.

Capacitance Alarm System: An alarm system in which a protected object is electrically connected as a capacitance sensor. The approach of an intruder causes sufficient change in capacitance to upset the balance of the system and initiate an alarm signal. Also called "proximity alarm system."

Capacitance Detector: See "Capacitance Sensor."

Capacitance Sensor: A sensor that responds to a change in capacitance in a field containing a protected object or in a field within a protected area.

Carrier Current Transmitter: A device that transmits alarm signals from a sensor to a control unit via the standard ac power lines.

Central Station: A control center to which alarm systems in a subscriber's premises are connected, where circuits are supervised, and where personnel continuously record and investigate alarm or trouble signals. Facilities are provided for the reporting of alarms to police and fire departments or to other outside agencies.

Central Station Alarm System: An alarm system, or group of systems, the activities of which are transmitted to, recorded in, maintained by, and supervised from a central station. This differs from proprietary alarm systems in that the central station is owned and operated independently of the subscriber.

Circumvention: The defeat of an alarm system by the avoidance of its detection devices, such as by jumping over a pressure sensitive mat, by entering through a hole cut in an unprotected wall rather than through a protected door, or by keeping outside the range of an ultrasonic motion detector. Circumvention contrasts with spoofing.

Closed-Circuit Alarm: See "Cross Alarm."

Closed-Circuit System: A system in which the sensors of each zone are connected in series so that the same current exists in each sensor. When an activated sensor breaks the circuit or the connecting wire is cut, an alarm is transmitted for that zone.

Clutch Head Screw: A mounting screw with a uniquely designed head for which the installation and removal tool is not commonly available. They are used to install alarm system components so that removal is inhibited.

Coded-Alarm System: An alarm system in which the source of each signal is identifiable. This is usually accomplished by means of a series of current pulses that operate audible or visible annunciators or recorders, or both, to yield a recognizable signal. This is usually used to allow the transmission of multiple signals on a common circuit.

Coded Cable: A multiconductor cable in which the insulation on each conductor is distinguishable from all others by color or design. This assists in identification of the point of origin or financial destination of a wire.

Coded Transmitter: A device for transmitting a coded signal when manually or automatically operated by an actuator. The actuator may be housed with the transmitter or a number of actuators may operate a common transmitter.

Coding Siren: A siren that has an auxiliary mechanism to interrupt the flow of air through its principal mechanism, enabling it to produce a controllable series of sharp blasts.

Combination Sensor Alarm: An alarm system requiring the simultaneous activation of two more sensors to initiate an alarm signal.

Compromise: See "Defeat."

Constant Ringing Drop (CRD): A relay that, when activated even momentarily, will remain in an alarm condition until reset. A key is often required to reset the relay and turn off the alarm.

Constant Ringing Relay (CRR): See "Constant Ringing Drop."

Contact: (1) Each of the pair of metallic parts of a switch or relay which by touching or separating make or break the electrical current path. (2) A switch-type sensor.

Contact Device: A device that, when actuated, opens or closes a set of electrical contacts; a switch or relay.

Contact Microphone: A microphone designed for attachment directly to a surface of a protected area or object; usually used to detect surface vibrations.

Contact Vibration Sensor: See "Vibration Sensor."

Contactless Vibrating Bell: A vibrating bell whose continuous operation depends upon application of an alternating current, without circuit-interrupting contacts such as those used in vibrating bells operated by direct current.

Control Cabinet: See "Control Unit."

Control Unit: A device, usually electronic, that provides the interface between the alarm system and the human operator and produces an alarm signal when its programmed response indicates an alarm condition. Some or all of the following may be provided for: power for sensors, sensitivity adjustments, means to select and indicate access modes or secure mode, monitoring for line supervision and tamper devices, timing circuit for entrance and exit delays, transmission of an alarm signal, etc.

Covert: Hidden and protected.

CRD: See "Constant Ringing Drop."

Cross Alarm: (1) An alarm condition signaled by crossing or shorting an electrical circuit. (2) The signal produced due to a cross alarm condition.

Crossover: An insulated electrical path used to connect foil across window dividers, such as those found on multiple pane windows, to prevent grounding and to make a more durable connection.

CRR: Abbreviation for constant ringing relay. See "Constant Ringing Drop."

Dark Current: The current output of a photoelectric sensor when no light is entering the sensor.

Day Setting: See "Access Mode."

Defeat: The frustration, counteraction, or thwarting of an alarm device so that it fails to signal an alarm when a protected area is entered. Defeat includes both circumvention and spoofing.

Detection Range: The greatest distance at which a sensor will consistently detect an intruder under a standard set of conditions.

Detector: (1) A sensor such as those used to detect intrusion, equipment malfunctions or failure, rate of temperature rise, smoke, or fire. (2) A demodulator, a device for recovering the modulating function or signal from a modulated wave, such as that used in a modulated photoelectric alarm system. (See "Photoelectric Alarm System, Modulated.")

Dialer: See "Telephone Dialer, Automatic."

Differential Pressure Sensor: A sensor used for perimeter protection which responds to the difference between the hydraulic pressures in two liquid-filled tubes buried just below the surface of the earth around the exterior perimeter of the protected area. The pressure difference can indicate an intruder walking or driving over the buried tubes.

Digital Telephone Dialer: See "Telephone Dialer, Digital."

Direct Connect: See "Police Connection."

Direct Wire Burglar Alarm Circuit (DWBA): See "Alarm Line."

Door Cord: A short, insulated cable with an attaching block and terminals at each end. It is used to conduct current to a device, such as foil, mounted on the movable portion of a door or window.

Door Trip Switch: A mechanical switch mounted so that movement of the door will operate the switch.

Doppler Effect (Shift): The apparent change in frequency of sound or radio waves when reflected from or originating from a moving object. Utilized in some types of motion sensors.

Double-Circuit System: An alarm circuit in which two wires enter and two wires leave each sensor.

Double Drop: An alarm signaling method often used in central station alarm systems in which the line is first opened to produce a break alarm and then shorted to produce a cross alarm.

Drop: (1) See "Annunciator." (2) A light indicator on an annunciator.

Duress Alarm Device: A device that produces either a silent alarm or local alarm under a condition of personnel stress such as a holdup, fire, illness, or other emergency. The device is normally manually operated and may be fixed or portable.

Duress Alarm System: An alarm system employing a duress alarm device.

DWBA: Abbreviation for direct wire burglar alarm. See "Alarm Line."

E-Field Sensor: A passive sensor which detects changes in the earth's ambient electric field caused by the movement of an intruder. (See "H-Field Sensor.")

Electromagnetic: Pertaining to the relationship between current flow and magnetic field.

Electromagnetic Interference (EMI): Impairment of the reception of a wanted electromagnetic signal by an electromagnetic disturbance. This can be caused by lightning, radio transmitters, power line noise, and other electrical devices.

Electromechanical Bell: A bell with a prewound spring-driven striking mechanism, the operation of which is initiated by the activation of an electric tripping mechanism.

Electronic: Related to, or pertaining to, devices that utilize electrons moving through a vacuum, gas, or semiconductor, and to circuits or systems containing such devices.

EMI: See "Electromagnetic Interference."

End-of-Line Resistor: See "Terminal Resistor."

Entrance Delay: The time between actuating a sensor on an entrance door or gate and the sounding of a local alarm or transmission of an alarm signal by the control unit. This delay is used if the authorized access switch is located within the protected area, permitting a person with the control key to enter without causing an alarm. The delay is provided by a timer within the control unit.

E.O.L.: Abbreviation for end-of-line.

Exit Delay: The time between turning on a control unit and the sounding of a local alarm or transmission of an alarm signal upon actuation of a sensor on an exit door. This delay is used if the authorized access switch is located within the protected area, permitting a person with the control key to turn on the alarm system and leave through a protected door or gate without causing an alarm. The delay is provided by a timer within the control unit.

Fail Safe: A feature of a system or device that initiates an alarm or trouble signal when the system or device either malfunctions or loses power.

False Alarm: An alarm signal transmitted in the absence of an alarm condition. These may be classified according to causes: environmental (e.g., rain, fog, wind, hail, lightning, temperature, etc.), animals (e.g., rats, dogs, cats, insects, etc.), artificial disturbances (e.g., sonic booms, EMI, vehicles, etc.), equipment malfunction (e.g., transmission errors, component failure, etc.), operator error, and unknown.

False Alarm Rate, Monthly: The number of false alarms per installation per month.

False Alarm Ratio: The ratio of false alarms to total alarms; may be expressed as a percentage or as a simple ratio.

Fence Alarm: Any of several types of sensors used to detect the presence of an intruder near a fence or any attempt to climb over, go under, or cut through the fence.

Field: The space or area in which there exists a force such as that produced by an electrically charged object, a current, or a magnet.

Fire Detector (Sensor): See "Heat Sensor" and "Smoke Detector."

Floor Mat: See "Mat Switch."

Floor Trap: A trap installed to detect the movement of a person across a floor space, such as a tripwire switch or mat switch.

Foil: Thin metallic strips cemented to a protected surface (usually glass in a window or door) and connected to a closed electrical circuit. If the protected material is broken, breaking the foil, the circuit opens, initiating an alarm signal. Also called tape. A window, door, or other surface to which foil has been applied is said to be taped or foiled.

Foil Connector: An electrical terminal block used on the edge of a window to join interconnecting wire to window foil.

Foot Rail: A holdup alarm device, often used at bank cashiers' windows, in which a foot is placed under the rail, lifting it to initiate an alarm signal.

Frequency Division Multiplexing (FDM): See "Mutiplexing, Frequency Division."

Glassbreak Vibration Detector: A vibration detection system employing a contact microphone attached to a glass window to detect cutting or breaking of the glass.

Grid: (1) An arrangement of electrically conducting wire, screen, or tubing placed in front of doors or windows or both which is used as a part of a capacitance sensor. (2) A lattice of wooden dowels or slats concealing fine wires in a closed circuit which initiates an alarm signal when forcing or cutting the lattice breaks the wires. Used over accessible openings.

Sometimes called a protective screen. (See "Burglar Alarm Pad.") (3) A screen or metal plate, connected to earth ground, sometimes used to provide a stable ground reference for objects protected by a capacitance sensor. If placed against the walls near the protected area, it prevents the sensor sensitivity from extending through the walls into areas of activity.

Heat Detector: See "Heat Sensor."

Heat Sensor: (1) A sensor that responds either to a local temperature above a selected value, a local temperature increase which is at a rate of increase greater than a preselected rate (rate or rise), or both. (2) A sensor that responds to infrared radiation from a remote source.

H-Field Sensor: A passive sensor that detects changes in the earth's ambient magnetic field caused by the movement of an intruder. (See "E-Field Sensor.")

Holdup: A robbery involving the threat to use a weapon.

Holdup Alarm Device: A device that signals a holdup. The device is usually surreptitious, and it may be manually or automatically actuated, fixed or portable. (See "Duress Alarm Device.")

Holdup Alarm System, Automatic: An alarm system employing a holdup alarm device, in which the signal transmission is initiated solely by the action of the intruder.

Holdup Alarm System, Manual: An alarm system in which the signal transmission is initiated by the direct action of the person attacked or of an observer of the attack.

Holdup Button: A manually actuated mechanical switch used to initiate a duress alarm signal; usually constructed to minimize accidental activation.

Hood Contact: A switch used for the supervision of a closed safe or vault door. Usually installed on the outside surface of the protected door.

Impedance: The opposition to the flow of alternating current in a circuit. May be determined by the ratio of an input voltage to the resultant current.

Impedance Matching: Making the impedance of a terminating device equal to the impedance of the circuit to which it is connected in order to achieve optimum signal transfer.

Infrared (IR) Motion Detector: A sensor that detects changes in the infrared light radiation from parts of the protected area. Presence of an intruder in the area changes the infrared light intensity from his or her direction.

Infrared (IR) Motion Sensor: See "Infrared Motion Detector."

Infrared Sensor: See "Heat Sensor," "Infrared Motion Detector," and "Photoelectric Sensor."

Inking Register: See "Register, Inking."

Interior Perimeter Protection: A line of protection along the interior boundary of a protected area including all points through which entry can be made.

Intrusion: Unauthorized entry into the property of another.

Intrusion Alarm System: An alarm system for signaling the entry or attempted entry of a person or an object into the area or volume protected by the system.

Ionization Smoke Detector: A smoke detector in which a small amount of radioactive material ionizes the air in the sensing chamber, thus rendering it conductive and permitting a current to flow through the air between two charged electrodes. This effectively gives the sensing chamber an electrical conductance. When smoke particles enter the ionization area, they decrease the conductance of the air by attaching themselves to the ions causing a reduction in mobility. When the conductance is less than a predetermined level, the detector circuit responds.

IR: Abbreviation for infrared.

Jack: An electrical connector used for frequent connect and disconnect operations; for example, to connect an alarm circuit at an overhang door.

Lacing: A network of fine wire surrounding or covering an area to be protected, such as a safe, vault, or glass panel, and connected into a closed circuit system. The network of wire is concealed by a shield such as concrete or paneling in such a manner that an attempt to break through the shield breaks the wire and initiates an alarm.

Light Intensity Cutoff: In a photoelectric alarm system, the percent reduction of light that initiates an alarm signal at the photoelectric receiver unit.

Line Amplifier: An audio amplifier used to provide preamplification of an audio alarm signal before transmission of the signal over an alarm line. Use of an amplifier extends the range of signal transmissions.

Line Sensor (Detector): A sensor with a detection zone which approximates a line or series of lines, such as a photoelectric sensor which senses a direct or reflected light beam.

Line Supervision: Electronic protection of an alarm line accomplished by sending a continuous or coded signal through the circuit. A change in the circuit characteristics, such as a change in impedance due to the circuit's having been tampered with, will be detected by a monitor. The monitor initiates an alarm if the change exceeds a predetermined amount.

Local Alarm: An alarm that, when activated, makes a loud noise (see "Audible Alarm Device") at or near the protected area or floods the site with light, or both.

Local Alarm System: An alarm system that, when activated, produces an audible or visible signal in the immediate vicinity of the protected premises or object. The term usually applies to systems designed to provide only a local warning of intrusion and not to transmit to a remote monitoring station. However, local alarm systems are sometimes used in conjunction with a remote alarm.

Loop: An electric circuit consisting of several elements, usually switches, connected in series.

Magnetic Alarm System: An alarm system that initiates an alarm when it detects changes in the local magnetic field. The changes could be caused by motion of ferrous objects such as guns or tools near the magnetic sensor.

Magnetic Contact: See "Magnetic Switch."

Magnetic Sensor: A sensor that responds to changes in the magnetic field. (See "Magnetic Alarm System.")

Magnetic Switch: A switch consisting of two separate units: a magnetically actuated switch and a magnet. The switch is usually mounted in a fixed position (door jamb or window frame) opposing the magnet, which is fastened to a hinged or sliding door, window, etc. When the movable section is opened, the magnet moves with it, actuating the switch.

Magnetic Switch, Balanced: A magnetic switch that operates using a balanced magnetic field in such a manner as to resist defeat with an external magnet. It signals an alarm when it detects either an increase or decrease in magnetic field strength.

Matching Network: A circuit used to achieve impedance matching. It may also allow audio signals to be transmitted to an alarm line while blocking direct current used locally for line supervision.

Mat Switch: A flat area switch used on open floors or under carpeting. It may be sensitive over an area of a few square feet or several square yards.

McCulloch Circuit (Loop): A supervised single wire loop connecting a number of coded transmitters located in different protected areas to a central station receiver.

Mechanical Switch: A switch in which the contacts are opened and closed by means of a plunger or depressible button.

Mercury Fence Alarm: A type of mercury switch that is sensitive to the vibration caused by an intruder climbing on a fence.

Mercury Switch: A switch operated by tilting or vibrating which causes an enclosed pool of mercury to move, making or breaking physical and electrical contact with conductors. They are used on tilting doors and windows, and on fences.

Microwave Alarm System: An alarm system that employs radio frequency motion detectors operating in the microwave frequency region of the electromagnetic spectrum.

Microwave Frequency: Radio frequencies in the range of approximately 1.0 to 300 GHz.

Microwave Motion Detector: See "Radio Frequency Motion Detector."

Modulated Photoelectric Alarm System: See "Photoelectric Alarm System, Modulated."

Monitor Cabinet: An enclosure that houses the annunciator and associated equipment.

Monitor Panel: See "Annunciator."

Monitoring Station: The central station or other area at which guards, police, or commercial service personnel observe the annunciators and the registers reporting on the condition of alarm systems.

Motion Detection System: See "Motion Sensor."

Motion Detector: See "Motion Sensor."

Motion Sensor: A sensor that responds to the motion of an intruder. (See "Radio Frequency Motion Detector," "Sonic Motion Detector," "Ultrasonic Motion Detector," and "Infrared Motion Detector.")

Multiplexing: A technique for the concurrent transmission of two or more signals in either or both directions, over the same wire, carrier, or other communication channel. The two basic multiplexing techniques are time division multiplexing and frequency division multiplexing.

Multiplexing, Frequency Division (FDM): The multiplexing technique that assigns to each signal a specific set of frequencies (called a channel) within the larger block of frequencies available on the main transmission path in much the same way that many radio stations broadcast two programs at the same time that can be separately received.

Multiplexing, Time Division (TDM): The multiplexing technique that provides for the independent transmission of several pieces of information on a time-sharing basis by sampling, at frequent intervals, the data to be transmitted.

Neutralization: See "Defeat."

Nicad: (Acronym for "nickel cadmium.") A high performance, long-lasting rechargeable battery, with electrodes made of nickel and cadmium. Such batteries may be used as an emergency power supply for an alarm system.

Night Setting: See "Secure Mode."

Non-retractable (One-Way) Screw: A screw whose head is designed to permit installation with an ordinary flat bit screwdriver but which resists removal. They are used to install alarm system components so that removal is inhibited.

Normally Closed (NC) Switch: A switch in which the contacts are closed when no external forces act upon the switch.

Normally Open (NO) Switch: A switch in which the contacts are open (separated) when no external forces act upon the switch.

Nuisance Alarm: See "False Alarm."

Object Protection: See "Spot Protection."

Open-Circuit Alarm: See "Break Alarm."

Open-Circuit System: A system in which the sensors are connected in parallel. When a sensor is activated, the circuit is closed, permitting a current which activates an alarm signal.

Panic Alarm: See "Duress Alarm Device."

Panic Button: See "Duress Alarm Device."

Passive Intrusion Sensor: A passive sensor in an intrusion alarm system which detects an intruder within the range of the sensor. Examples are a sound sensing detection system, a vibration detection system, an infrared motion detector, and an E-field sensor.

Passive Sensor: A sensor that detects natural radiation or radiation disturbances, but does not itself emit the radiation on which its operation depends.

Passive Ultrasonic Alarm System: An alarm system that detects the sounds in the ultrasonic frequency range caused by an attempted forcible entry into a protected structure. The system consists of microphones, a control unit containing an amplifier, filters, an accumulator, and a power supply. The unit's sensitivity is adjustable so that ambient noises or normal sounds will not initiate an alarm signal; however, noise above the preset level or a sufficient accumulation of impulses will initiate an alarm.

Percentage Supervision: A method of line supervision in which the current in, or resistance of, a supervised line is monitored for changes. When the change exceeds a selected percentage of the normal operating current or resistance in the line, an alarm signal is produced.

Perimeter Alarm System: An alarm system providing perimeter protection.

Perimeter Protection: Protection of access to the outer limits of a protected area, by means of physical barriers, sensors on physical barriers, or exterior sensors not associated with a physical barrier.

Permanent Circuit: An alarm circuit that is capable of transmitting an alarm signal whether the alarm control is in access mode or secure mode. Used, for example, on foiled fixed windows, tamper switches, and superior lines. (See "Supervisory Alarm System," "Supervisory Circuit," and "Permanent Protection.")

Permanent Protection: A system of alarm devices such as foil, burglar alarm pads, or lacings connected in a permanent circuit to provide protection whether the control unit is in the access mode or secure mode.

Photoelectric Alarm System: An alarm system that employs a light beam and photoelectric sensor to provide a line of protection. Any interruption of the beam by an intruder is sensed by the sensor. Mirrors may be used to change the direction of the beam. The maximum beam length is limited by many factors, some of which are the light source intensity, number of mirror reflections, detector sensitivity, beam divergence, fog, and haze.

Photoelectric Alarm System, Modulated: A photoelectric alarm system in which the transmitted light beam is modulated in a predetermined manner and in which the receiving equipment will signal an alarm unless it receives the properly modulated light.

Photoelectric Beam-type Smoke Detector: A smoke detector with a light source that projects a light beam across the area to be protected onto a photoelectric cell. Smoke between the light source and the receiving cell reduces the light reaching the cell, causing actuation.

Photoelectric Detector: See "Photoelectric Sensor."

Photoelectric Sensor: A device that detects a visible or invisible beam of light and responds to its complete or nearly complete interruption. (See "Photoelectric Alarm System" and "Photoelectric Alarm System, Modulated.")

Photoelectric Spot-type Smoke Detector: A smoke detector containing a chamber with covers that prevent the entrance of light but allow the entrance of smoke. The chamber contains a light source and a photosensitive cell so placed that light is blocked from it. When smoke enters, the smoke particles scatter and reflect the light into the photosensitive cell, causing an alarm.

Point Protection: See "Spot Protection."

Police Connection: The direct link by which an alarm system is connected to an annunciator installed in a police station. Examples of a police connection are an alarm line and a radiocommunications channel.

Police Panel: See "Police Station Unit."

Police Station Unit: An annunciator that can be placed in operation in a police station.

Portable Duress Sensor: A device carried on a person that can be activated in an emergency to send an alarm signal to a monitoring station.

Portable Intrusion Sensor: A sensor which can be installed quickly and does not require dedicated wiring for the transmission of its alarm signal.

Positive Non-interfering (PNI) and Successive Alarm System: An alarm system employing multiple alarm transmitters on each alarm line (like a McCulloch loop). In the event of simultaneous operation of several transmitters, one of them takes control of the alarm line, transmits its full signal, then releases the alarm line for successive transmission by other transmitters, which are held inoperative until they gain control.

Pressure Alarm System: An alarm system that protects a vault or other enclosed space by maintaining and monitoring a predetermined air pressure differential between the inside and outside of the space. Equalization of pressure resulting from opening the vault or cutting through the enclosure will be sensed and will initiate an alarm signal.

Printing Recorder: An electromechanical device used at a monitoring station which accepts coded signals from alarm lines and converts them to an alphanumeric printed record of the signal received.

Proprietary Alarm System: An alarm system similar to a central station alarm system except that the annunciator is located in a constantly manned guard room maintained by the owner for internal security operations. The guards monitor the system and respond to all alarm signals or alert local law enforcement agencies or both.

Protected Area: An area monitored by an alarm system or guards or enclosed by a suitable barrier.

Protected Port: A point of entry such as a door, window, or corridor, which is monitored by sensors connected to an alarm system.

Protection Device: (1) A grid, foil, contact, or photoelectric sensor connected into an intrusion alarm system. (2) A barrier which inhibits intrusion, such as a grille, lock, fence, or wall.

Protection, Exterior Perimeter: A line of protection surrounding but somewhat removed from a facility. Examples are fences, barrier walls, or patrolled points of a perimeter.

Protection Off: See "Access Mode."

Protection On: See "Secure Mode."

Protective Screen: See "Grid."

Protective Signaling: The initiation, transmission, and reception of signals involved in the detection and prevention of property loss due to fire, burglary, or other destructive conditions. Also, the electronic supervision of persons and equipment concerned with this detection and prevention. (See "Line Supervision" and "Supervisory Alarm System.")

Proximity Alarm System: See "Capacitance Alarm System."

Punching Register: See "Register, Punch."

Radar Alarm System: An alarm system that employs radio frequency motion detectors.

Radar (Radio Detecting and Ranging): See "Radio Frequency Motion Detector."

Radio Frequency Interference (rfi): Electromagnetic interference in the radio frequency range.

Radio Frequency Motion Detector: A sensor that detects the motion of an intruder through the use of a radiated radio frequency electromagnetic field. The device operates by sensing a disturbance in the generated rf field caused by intruder motion. Typically a modulation of the field is referred to as a Doppler effect and is used to initiate an alarm signal. Most radio frequency motion detectors are certified by the FCC for operation as "field disturbance sensors" at one of the following frequencies: 0.915 GHz (L-Band), 2.45 GHz (S-Band), 5.8 GHz (X-Band), 10.525 GHz (X-Band), and 22.125 GHz (K-Band). Units operating in the microwave frequency range are usually called microwave motion detectors.

Reed Switch: A type of magnetic switch consisting of contacts formed by two thin movable magnetically actuated metal vanes or reeds, held in a normally open position within a sealed glass envelope.

Register: An electromechanical device that marks a paper tape in response to signal impulses received from transmitting circuits. A register may be driven by a prewound spring mechanism, an electric motor, or a combination of these.

Register, Inking: A register that marks the tape with ink.

Register, Punch: A register that marks the tape by cutting holes in it.

Register, Slashing: A register that marks the tape by cutting V-shaped slashes in it.

Remote Alarm: An alarm signal transmitted to a remote monitoring station. (See "Local Alarm.")

Remote Station Alarm System: An alarm system employing remote alarm stations usually located in building hallways or on city streets.

Reporting Line: See "Alarm Line."

Reset: To restore a device to its original (normal) condition after an alarm or trouble signal.

Resistance Bridge Smoke Detector: A smoke detector that responds to the particles and moisture present in smoke. These substances reduce the resistance of an electrical bridge grid and cause the detector to respond.

Retard Transmitter: A coded transmitter in which a delay period is introduced between the time of actuation and the time of signal transmission.

RFI: Abbreviation for Radio Frequency Interference.

Rf Motion Detector: See "Radio Frequency Motion Detector."

Robbery: The felonious or forcible taking of property by violence, threat, or other overt felonious act in the presence of the victim.

Secure Mode: The condition of an alarm system in which all sensors and control units are ready to respond to an intrusion.

Security Monitor: See "Annunciator."

Seismic Sensor: A sensor, generally buried under the surface of the ground for perimeter protection, which responds to minute vibrations of the earth generated as an intruder walks or drives within its detection range.

Sensor: A device designed to produce a signal or offer indication in response to an event or stimulus within its detection zone.

Sensor, Combustion: See "Ionization Smoke Detector," "Photoelectric Beam-type Smoke Detector," "Photoelectric Spot-type Smoke Detector," and "Resistance Bridge Smoke Detector."

Sensor, Smoke: See "Ionization Smoke Detector," "Photoelectric Beam-type Smoke Detector," "Photoelectric Spot-type Smoke Detector," and "Resistance Bridge Smoke Detector."

Shunt: (1) A deliberate shorting-out of a portion of an electric circuit. (2) A key-operated switch that removes some portion of an alarm system for operation, allowing entry into a protected area without initiating an alarm signal. A type of authorized access switch.

Shunt Switch: See "Shunt."

Signal Recorder: See "Register."

Silent Alarm: A remote alarm without an obvious local indication that an alarm has been transmitted.

Silent Alarm System: An alarm system which signals a remote station by means of a silent alarm.

Single Circuit System: An alarm circuit that routes only one side of the circuit through each sensor. The return may be through either ground or a separate wire.

Single-Stroke Bell: A bell that is struck once each time its mechanism is activated.

Slashing Register: See "Register, Slashing."

Smoke Detector: A device that detects visible or invisible products of combustion. (See "Ionization Smoke Detector," "Photoelectric Beam-type Smoke Detector," "Photoelectric Spot-type Smoke Detector," and "Resistance Bridge Smoke Detector.")

Solid-State: (1) An adjective used to describe a device such as a semiconductor transistor or diode. (2) A circuit or system that does not rely on vacuum or gas-filled tubes to control or modify voltages and currents.

Sonic Motion Detector: A sensor that detects the motion of an intruder by disturbance of an audible sound pattern generated within the protected area.

Sound Sensing Detector System: An alarm system that detects the audible sound caused by an attempted forcible entry into a protected structure. The system consists of microphones and a control unit containing an amplifier, accumulator, and a power supply. The unit's sensitivity is adjustable so that ambient noises or normal sounds will not initiate an alarm signal. However, noises above this preset level or a sufficient accumulation of impulses will initiate an alarm.

Sound Sensor: A sensor that responds to sound; a microphone.

Space Protection: See "Area Protection."

Spoofing: The defeat or compromise of an alarm system by "tricking" or "fooling" its detection devices, such as by short-circuiting part or all of a series circuit, cutting wires in a parallel circuit, reducing the sensitivity of a sensor, or entering false signals into the system. Spoofing contrasts with circumvention.

Spot Protection: Protection of objects, such as safes or art objects, which could be damaged or removed from the premises.

Spring Contact: A device employing a current-carrying cantilever spring that monitors the position of a door or window.

Standby Power Supply: Equipment that supplies power to a system in the event the primary power is lost. It may consist of batteries, charging circuits, auxiliary motor generators, or a combination of these devices.

Strain Gauge Alarm System: An alarm system that detects the stress caused by the weight of an intruder. Typical uses include placement of the strain gauge sensor under a floor joist or under a stairway tread.

Strain Gauge Sensor: A sensor which, when attached to an object, provides an electrical response to an applied stress upon the object, such as bending, stretching, or compressing.

Strain Sensitive Cable: An electrical cable designed to produce a signal whenever the cable is strained by a change in applied force. Typical uses include mounting it in a wall to detect an attempted forced entry through the wall, or fastening it to a fence to detect climbing on the fence, or burying it around a perimeter to detect walking or driving across the perimeter.

Subscriber's Equipment: That portion of a central station alarm system installed in the protected premises.

Subscriber's Unit: A control unit of a central station alarm system.

Supervised Lines: Interconnecting lines in an alarm system which are electrically supervised against tampering. (See "Line Supervision.")

Supervisory Alarm System: An alarm system that monitors conditions or persons or both and signals any deviation from an established norm or schedule. Examples are the monitoring of signals from guard patrol stations for irregularities in the progression along a prescribed patrol route and the monitoring of production or safety conditions such as sprinkler water pressure, temperature, or liquid level.

Supervisory Circuit: An electrical circuit or radio path which sends information on the status of a sensor or guard patrol to an annunciator. For intrusion alarm systems, this circuit provides line supervision and monitors tamper devices. (See "Supervisory Alarm System.")

Surreptitious: Covert, hidden, concealed, or disguised.

Surveillance: (1) Control of premises for security purposes through alarm systems, closed-circuit television, or other monitoring methods. (2) Supervision or inspection of industrial processes by monitoring those conditions that could cause damage if not corrected. (See "Supervisory Alarm System.")

Tamper Device: (1) Any device, usually a switch, used to detect an attempt to gain access to intrusion alarm circuitry, such as by removing a switch cover. (2) A monitor circuit to detect any attempt to modify the alarm circuitry, such as by cutting a wire.

Tamper Switch: A switch installed to detect attempts to remove the enclosure of some alarm system components such as control box doors, switch covers, junction box covers, or bell housings. The alarm component is then often described as being "tampered."

Tape: See "Foil."

Tapper Bell: A single-stroke bell designed to produce a sound of low intensity and relatively high pitch.

Telephone Dialer, Automatic: A device that, when activated, automatically dials one or more preprogrammed telephone numbers (e.g., police or fire department) and relays a recorded voice or coded message giving the location and the nature of the alarm.

Telephone Dialer, Digital: An automatic telephone dialer that sends its messages as a digital code.

Terminal Resistor: A resistor used as a terminating device.

Terminating Capacitor: A capacitor sometimes used as a terminating device for a capacitance sensor antenna. The capacitor allows the supervision of the sensor antenna, especially if a long wire is used as the sensor.

Terminating Device: A device used to terminate an electrically supervised circuit. It makes the electrical circuit continuous and provides a fixed impedance reference (end-of-line resistor) against which changes are measured to detect an alarm condition. The impedance changes may be caused by a sensor, tampering, or circuit trouble.

Time Delay: See "Entrance Delay" and "Exit Delay."

Time Division Multiplexing (TDM): See "Multiplexing, Time Division."

Timing Table: That portion of central station equipment that provides a means for checking incoming signals from McCulloch Circuits.

Touch Sensitivity: The sensitivity of a capacitance sensor at which the alarm device will be activated only if an intruder touches or comes in very close proximity (about 1 cm or ½ inch) to the protected object.

Trap: (1) A device, usually a switch, installed within a protected area, that serves as secondary protection in the event a perimeter alarm system is successfully penetrated. Examples are a tripwire switch placed across a likely path for an intruder, a match switch hidden under a rug, or a magnetic switch mounted on an inner door. (2) A volumetric sensor installed so as to detect an intruder in a lightly traveled corridor or pathway within a security area.

Trickle Charge: A continuous direct current, usually very low, applied to a battery to maintain it at peak charge or to recharge it after it has been partially or completely discharged. Usually applied to nickel cadmium (Nicad) or wet cell batteries.

Tripwire Switch: A switch that is actuated by breaking or moving a wire or cord installed across a floor space.

Trouble Signal: See "Break Alarm."

UL: See "Underwriters Laboratories, Inc."

UL Certificated: For certain types of products that have met UL requirements, for which it is impractical to apply the UL Listing Mark or Classification Marking to the individual product, a certificate is provided which the manufacturer may use to identify quantities of material for specific job sites or to identify field-installed systems.

UL Listed: Signifies that production samples of the product have been found to comply with established Underwriters Laboratories requirements and that the manufacturer is authorized to use the Laboratories' Listing Marks on the listed products that comply with the requirements, contingent upon the followup services as a check of compliance.

Ultrasonic: Pertaining to a sound wave having a frequency above that of audible sound (approximately 20,000 Hz). Ultrasonic sound is used in ultrasonic detection systems.

Ultrasonic Detection Systems: See "Ultrasonic Motion Detector" and "Passive Ultrasonic Alarm System."

Ultrasonic Frequency: Sound frequencies that are above the range of human hearing—approximately 20,000 Hz and higher.

Ultrasonic Motion Detector: A sensor that detects the motion of an intruder through the use of ultrasonic generating and receiving equipment. The device operates by filling a space with a pattern of ultrasonic waves; the modulation of these waves by a moving object is detected and initiates an alarm signal.

Underdome Bell: A bell, most of whose mechanism is concealed by its gong.

Underwriters Laboratories, Inc. (UL): A private independent research and testing laboratory that tests and lists various items meeting good practice and safety standards.

Vibrating Bell: A bell whose mechanism is designed to strike repeatedly and for as long as it is activated.

Vibrating Contact: See "Vibration Sensor."

Vibration Detection System: An alarm system employing one or more contact microphones or vibration sensors fastened to the surfaces of the area or object being protected to detect excessive levels of vibration. The contact microphone system consists of microphones, a control unit containing an amplifier and an accumulator, and a power supply. The sensitivity of the unit is adjustable so that ambient noises or normal vibrations will not initiate an alarm signal. In the vibration sensor system, the sensor responds to excessive vibration by opening a switch in a closed circuit system.

Vibration Detector: See "Vibration Sensor."

Vibration Sensor: A sensor that responds to vibrations of the surface on which it is mounted. It has a normally closed switch which will momentarily open when it is subjected to a vibration with sufficiently large amplitude. Its sensitivity is adjustable to allow for the different levels of normal vibration, to which the sensor should not respond, at different locations. (See "Vibration Detection System.")

Visual Signal Device: A pilot light, annunciator, or other device that provides a visual indication of the condition of the circuit or system being supervised.

Volumetric Detector: See "Volumetric Sensor."

Volumetric Sensor: A sensor with a detection zone which extends over a volume such as an entire room, part of a room, or a passageway. Ultrasonic motion detectors and sonic motion detectors are examples of volumetric sensors.

Walk-Test Light: A light on motion detectors that comes on when the detector senses motion in the area. It is used while setting the sensitivity of the detector and during routine checking and maintenance.

Watchman's Reporting System: A supervisory alarm system arranged for the transmission of a patrolling watchman's regularly recurrent report signals from stations along the patrol route to a central supervisory agency.

Zone Circuit: A circuit providing continual protection for parts or zones of the protected area while normally used doors and windows or zones may be released for access.

Zones: Smaller subdivisions into which large areas are divided to permit selective access to some zones while maintaining other zones secure and to permit pinpointing the specific location from which an alarm signal is transmitted.

Index

Answers to Quizzes

Chapter 1

1. a
2. false
3. a
4. c
5. a
6. d
7. b
8. false
9. a
10. d
11. c
12. b

Chapter 2

1. c
2. b
3. c
4. false
5. false
6. false
7. true
8. false
9. c
10. b
11. c

Chapter 3

1. d
2. a
3. b
4. c
5. c
6. d
7. d
8. a
9. a
10. b
11. a
12. c
13. d

14. detectors, signal processors, output devices.
15. c

Chapter 4

1. c
2. c
3. b
4. d
5. a
6. b
7. a
8. false
9. true
10. d

Chapter 5

1. b
2. c
3. d
4. c
5. a
6. a
7. b
8. d
9. b

Chapter 6

1. d
2. b
3. c
4. c
5. c
6. d
7. a
8. d
9. a
10. b

Chapter 7

1. d
2. b
3. a
4. c
5. b
6. c
7. true
8. b
9. d
10. b
11. a
12. c
13. c

Chapter 8

1. b
2. d
3. increases
4. b
5. d
6. b
7. d
8. a
9. c
10. a
11. b

Chapter 9

1. a
2. d
3. b
4. c
5. a
6. a
7. b
8. b
9. d
10. a

Chapter 10

1. d
2. a
3. c

4. d
5. normal secure, alarm, trouble, access
6. b
7. a
8. c
9. c
10. c

Chapter 11

1. c
2. punched card, bar code, magnetic strip
3. a
4. c
5. d
6. a
7. c

Chapter 12

1. d
2. true
3. a
4. b
5. c
6. d
7. b

Chapter 13

1. clock, unclocked (or direct)
2. a
3. a
4. a
5. c
6. c
7. a

8. **NOT, AND, OR**
9. **d**
10. **c**

Chapter 14

1. **true**
2. **multiplexed**
3. **c**
4. **a**
5. **c**
6. **b**
7. **a**
8. **true**

Chapter 15

1. **c**
2. **a**
3. **c**
4. **private company, central, autodialer or wire, local**

Chapter 16

1. **c**
2. **false**
3. **impedance, mutual inductance, induced voltage**
4. **b**
5. **c**
6. **d**
7. **a**
8. **a**
9. **b**
10. **c**

Chapter 17

1. **mechanical, electrical**
2. **time-consuming, unfamiliar**
3. **hot-fuse, electronic combination lock**

4. **c**
5. **hood lock, backup battery**
6. **special bolts**
7. **d**
8. **c**
9. **b**
10. **b**

Chapter 18

1. **d**
2. **a**
3. **c**
4. **a**
5. **a**
6. **b**
7. **d**

Chapter 19

1. **c**
2. **b**
3. **a**
4. **a**
5. **a**
6. **d**

7. **b**
8. **c**
9. **a**
10. **c**
11. **a**
12. **d**
13. **a**
14. **b**
15. **false**

Chapter 20

1. **c**
2. **d**
3. **c**
4. **a**
5. **c**
6. **c**
7. **false**
8. **d**
9. **c**
10. **a**

MORE
FROM
SAMS

☐ **John D. Lenk's Troubleshooting & Repair of Microprocessor-Based Equipment**
John D. Lenk
Here are general procedures, techniques, and tips for troubleshooting equipment containing microprocessors from one of the foremost authors on electronics and troubleshooting. In this general reference title, Lenk offers a basic approach to troubleshooting that is replete with concrete examples related to specific equipment, including VCRs and compact disc players. He highlights test equipment and pays special attention to common problems encountered when troubleshooting microprocessor-based equipment.
ISBN: 0-672-22476-3, $21.95

☐ **Basic Electricity & Electronics**
Training and Retraining, Inc.
A complete self-study course in electricity and electronics, this set of books provides constant student reinforcement through frequent quizzes. Concepts are broken into small units that require 20-30 minutes each to master. From basic principles to complex circuits, this five-volume set will teach you what you need to know to get started in the booming electronics field.
Volume 1: BASIC PRINCIPLES
ISBN: 0-672-21501-2, $11.95
Volume 2: AC/DC CIRCUITS
ISBN: 0-672-21502-0, $11.95

☐ **Design of Op-Amp Circuits with Experiments** *Howard M. Berlin*
An experimental approach to the understanding of op amp circuits. Thirty-five experiments illustrate the design and operation of linear amplifiers, differentiators and converters, voltage and current converters, and active filters.
ISBN: 0-672-21537-3, $12.95

☐ **Design of Phase-Locked Loop Circuits with Experiments** *Howard M. Berlin*
Learn more about TTL and CMOS devices. This book contains a wide range of lab-type experiments which reinforce the textual introduction to the theory, design, and implementation of phase-locked loop circuits using these technologies.
ISBN: 0-672-21545-4, $12.95

☐ **Electronic Prototype Construction**
Stephen D. Kasten
Breadboarding can be fun. Learn contemporary construction and design methods for building your working prototypes. Discusses IC-based and microcomputer-related schematics and ideas for evaluation and testing. Techniques include wirewrapping, designing, making, and using double-sided PC boards; fabricating enclosures, connectors, and wiring; and screen printing the panels, chassis, and PC boards.
ISBN: 0-672-21895-X, $17.95

☐ **RF Circuit Design** *Christopher J. Bowick*
Enjoy the benefits of two books in one. Use this in cookbook fashion as a catalog of useful circuits or as a reference manual. It clearly presents a user-oriented approach to design of RF amplifiers and impedance matching networks and filters.
ISBN: 0-672-21868-2, $22.95

☐ **Electronics: Circuits and Systems**
Swaminathan Madhu
Written specifically for engineers and scientists with non-electrical engineering degrees, this reference book promotes a basic understanding of electronic devices, circuits, and systems. The author highlights analog and digital systems, practical applications, signals, circuit devices, digital logic systems, and communications systems. In a concise, easy-to-understand style, he also provides completed examples, drill problems, and summary sheets containing formulas, graphics, and relationships. An invaluable self-study manual.
ISBN: 0-672-21984-0, $39.95

☐ **Reference Data for Engineers: Radio, Electronics, Computer, and Communications (7th Edition)**
Edward C. Jordan, Editor-in-Chief
Previously a limited private edition, now an internationally accepted handbook for engineers. Includes over 1300 pages of data compiled by more than 70 engineers, scientists, educators and other eminent specialists in a wide range of disciplines. Presents information essential to engineers, covering such topics as: digital, analog, and optical communications; lasers; logic design; computer organization and programming, and computer communications networks. An indispensable reference tool for all technical professionals.
ISBN: 0-672-21563-2, $69.95

☐ **Electronic Telephone Projects (2nd Edition)**   *Anthony J. Caristi*

Create a touch-tone dialer, conferencer, computer memory, electronic ringer, and 18 other creative projects that turn a telephone into a favorite household tool. This new edition contains seven completely new projects, clearly detailed with step-by-step construction details and procedures. Included for each project is a photo of the unit, schematic, printed-circuit board pattern, parts layout, and a list of all parts required. Introductory chapters outline telephone system operations and the general construction techniques you will need to build these projects.
ISBN: 0-672-22485-2, $10.95

☐ **Fiber Optics Communications, Experiments, and Projects**   *Waldo T. Boyd*

Another Blacksburg tutorial teaching new technology through experimentation. This book teaches light beam communication fundamentals, introduces the simple electronic devices used, and shows how to participate in transmitting and receiving voice and music by means of light traveling along slender glass fibers.
ISBN: 0-672-21834-8, $15.95

☐ **First Book of Modern Electronics Fun Projects**   *Art Salsberg*

Novice and seasoned electronics buffs will enjoy these 20 fun and practical projects. Electronics hobbyists are introduced to many project building areas including making circuit boards, audio/video projects, telephone electronics projects, security projects, building test instruments, computer projects, and home electronics projects. The necessary tools for each project accompany the step-by-step instructions, illustrations, photos, and circuit drawings.
ISBN: 0-672-22503-4, $12.95

☐ **Understanding Artificial Intelligence**
Henry C. Mishkoff

This book provides an introduction and basic understanding of this new technology. The book covers definitions, history, expert systems, natural language processing, and LISP machines.
ISBN: 0-672-27021-8, $17.95

☐ **Understanding Digital Logic Circuits**
Robert G. Middleton

Designed for the service technician engaged in radio, television, or audio troubleshooting and repair, this book painlessly expands the technician's expertise into digital electronics.
ISBN: 0-672-21867-4, $18.95

☐ **Understanding Automation Systems (2nd Edition)**
Robert F. Farwell and Neil M. Schmitt

For the newcomer, here is an in-depth look at the functions that make up automation systems—open loop, closed loop, continuous and semi-continuous process, and discrete parts. This book explains programmable systems and how to use micro-computers and programmable controllers.
ISBN: 0-672-27014-5, $17.95

☐ **Understanding Automotive Electronics (2nd Edition)**
William B. Ribbens and Norman P. Mansour

This book begins with automotive and electronic fundamentals—prior knowledge is not necessary. It explains how the basic electronic functions, including programmable microprocessors and microcomputers, are applied for drive train control, motion control and instrumentation. Illustrations clarify mechanical and electrical principles.
ISBN: 0-672-27017-X, $17.95

☐ **Understanding Communications Systems (2nd Edition)**
Don L. Cannon and Gerald Luecke

This book explores many of the systems that are used every day—AM/FM radio, telephone, TV, data communications by computer, facsimile, and satellite. It explains how information is converted into electrical signals, transmitted to distant locations, and converted back to the original information.
ISBN: 0-672-27016-1, $17.95

☐ **Understanding Computer Science Applications**   *Roger S. Walker*

This book discusses basic computer concepts and how computers communicate with their input/output units and with each other by using parallel communications, serial communications, and computer networking.
ISBN: 0-672-27020-X, $17.95

☐ **Understanding Computer Science (2nd Edition)**   *Roger S. Walker*

Here is an in-depth look at how people use computers to solve problems. This book covers the fundamentals of hardware and software, programs and languages, input and output, data structures and resource management.
ISBN: 0-672-27011-0, $17.95

☐ Understanding Data Communications
(2nd Edition)   *John L. Fike et al.*
Understand the codes used for data communications, the types of messages, and the transmissions channels—including fiber optics and satellites. Learn how asynchronous modems work and how they interface to the terminal equipment. Find out about protocols, error control, local area and packet networks.
ISBN: 0-672-27019-6, $17.95

☐ Understanding Digital Electronics
(2nd Edition)   *Gene W. McWhorter*
Learn why digital circuits are used. Discover how AND, OR, and NOT digital circuits make decisions, store information, and convert information into electronic language. Find out how digital integrated circuits are made and how they are used in microwave ovens, gasoline pumps, video games, and cash registers.
ISBN: 0-672-27013-7, $17.95

☐ Understanding Digital Troubleshooting
(2nd Edition)   *Don L. Cannon*
This book presents the basic principles and troubleshooting techniques required to begin digital equipment repair and maintenance. The book begins with overviews of digital system fundamentals, digital system functions, and troubleshooting fundamentals. It continues with detecting problems in combinational logic, sequential logic, memory, and I/O.
ISBN: 0-672-27015-3, $17.95

☐ Understanding Microprocessors
(2nd Edition)   *Don L. Cannon and Gerald Luecke*
This book provides insight into basic concepts and fundamentals. It explains actual applications of 4-bit, 8-bit and 16-bit microcomputers, software, programs, programming concepts, and assembly language. The book provides an individualized learning format for the newcomer who wants to know what microprocessors are, what they do, and how they work.
ISBN: 0-672-27010-2, $17.95

☐ Understanding Solid State Electronics
(4th Edition)
William E. Hafford and Gene W. McWhorter
This book explains complex concepts such as electricity, semiconductor theory, how electronic circuits make decisions, and how integrated circuits are made. It helps you develop a basic knowledge of semiconductors and solid-state electronics. A glossary simplifies technical terms.
ISBN: 0-672-27012-9, $17.95

☐ Understanding Telephone Electronics
(2nd Edition)   *John L. Fike and George E. Friend*
This book explains how the conventional telephone system works and how parts of the system are gradually being replaced by state-of-the-art electronics. Subjects include speech circuits, dialing, ringing, central office electronics, microcomputers, digital transmission, network transmission, modems, and new cellular phones.
ISBN: 0-672-27018-8, $17.95

Look for these Sams Books at your local bookstore.

To order direct, call 800-428-SAMS or fill out the form below.

- -

Please send me the books whose titles and numbers I have listed below.

_____

_____

_____

_____

_____

Enclosed is a check or money order for $ _____
Include $2.50 postage and handling.
All states add local sales tax.

Charge my: ☐ VISA ☐ MC ☐ AE
Account No. _____ Expiration Date _____

☐☐☐☐☐ ☐☐☐☐☐ ☐☐☐☐☐ ☐☐☐☐☐

Name *(please print)* _____

Address _____

City _____

State/Zip _____

Signature _____
(required for credit card purchases)

Mail to: Howard W. Sams & Co.
          Dept. DM
          4300 West 62nd Street
          Indianapolis, IN 46268